REPARENTING SCHIZOPHRENICS

THE CATHEXIS EXPERIENCE

REPARENTING SCHIZOPHRENICS

THE CATHEXIS EXPERIENCE

Schizophrenics in Treatment: An Ethnographic
Study of Ritual Healing and Symbolic Action

By

ELAINE CHILDS-GOWELL, R.N., Ph.D.

AN AUTHORS GUILD BACKINPRINT.COM EDITION

AN AUTHORS GUILD BACKINPRINT.COM EDITION

Published by iUniverse.com, Inc.

For information address:
iUniverse.com, Inc.
620 North 48th Street, Suite 201
Lincoln, NE 68504-3467
www.iuniverse.com

Originally published by Christopher House

ISBN: 0-595-13191-3

Printed in the United States of America

Dedicated to
Dick, Tim, Karen,
Gladwyn
The Two Margarets
&
Gene

ACKNOWLEDGMENTS

I wish to acknowledge the assistance and direction of all the members of my committee without whose encouragement and inspiration this dissertation would not have been written. Especial thanks to Eugene Humm, Ph.D., whose attention to detail is most valued. Thanks also to Jacqui Schiff and all the members of the Cathexis Community who assisted me in this research. My family deserves special recognition for their patience and understanding throughout the period of my studies.

This dissertation and the four years of study prior to it were made possible through a Special Nurse Doctorate Research Fellowship awarded by the Research Training Section, Nursing Research Branch Division of Nursing, Department of Health, Education and Welfare, Grant #5F04-NU-27,253-04.

PREFACE

We call ourselves a community which espouses a commitment to break down the barriers developed as a result of a society with too many walls. Out of a fabric of human contact, interpersonal relatedness and honest communication, we have devised an island within our culture which for some of us is gratifying, and for others is health-giving.

Elaine Childs-Gowell describes us as a cultural system, like a tribe, with a structure, rituals, a language, expectations and goals. For some of us the goals are intrinsic to survival—for others Cathexis provides a refuge from the lack of contact which permeates our culture. This study describes who and what we are, and what we do in a language which is strange to us. However, we recognize ourselves in this different frame of reference. We appreciate the new self-awareness the study has brought to us.

Mental health concerns all of us. As new alternatives to the problems of mental illness are sought, we hope that sharing our experiences with the leaders, healers, philosophers and scientists who take the time to know us and understand us, will facilitate the development of meaningful programs elsewhere.

Jacqui Lee Schiff, M.S.S.W.

CONTENTS

Preface ix

Introduction—Overview 11

    Urban Anthropology
    Culture and Personality: Medical
      Anthropology (Ethnopsychiatry)
      Schizophrenia—Psychopathology
      Double-Bind
    The Community
    International Implications
    Chapter Resume

1. Theoretical Issues 21

    Evolutionary Structuralism
    Ritual and Ritual Process
    Symbols and Symbolic Language
    Adaptation
    Psychopathology
    Cognition
    Transformation
    Language and Experience
    Ritual Healing
    Culture and Madness
    Curanderismo
    Psychiatry
    Rites-of-Passage
    The Human Potential Movement
    Schools of Psychotherapy
    Transactional Analysis
      Definition
      Historical Background
      Membership
      Transactional Analysis Theory

1

Basic framework
Script theory
  Degree of damage
  Decisions
Contracts
Structural analysis
The development of ego states
Treatment process
General Systems Theory
  Closed and Open
  Feedback Control Networks
  Rites-of-Passage
  Models
2. Methods   61
Introduction
Hypothesis Testing
Experimental Versus Experiential Data
  Gathering
  Psychological Data Collection Techniques
  Diagnosis
    Lattice of criteria
    The Diagnostic and Statistical Manual II
    Transactional Analysis definition and diagnosis of
      schizophrenia
      T.A. definition of schizophrenia
      Problems of the definition of schizophrenia
      Summary of diagnostic and definitional issues
    The Minnesota Multiphasic Personality Inventory
    Semantic Differential Test
    Life History Information and World View
  Experiental Sources of Data
  Participant-Observation
  Culture Shock and Cognitive Dissonance
  Recording, Taping, and Confidentiality
  Personal Involvement
Summary
3. Cathexis: The Dialectic Between "Real" and "Not Real" . . .   82
California Mystique
History of Cathexis Community
Contexts
  The Cathexis Social Structure (Staff and Participants)

Philosophy of Cathexis
Physical Contexts
Theoretical Basis (The Transactional Analysis Model
   as Applied at Cathexis)
Temporal Contexts
   Entering
   Experiencing
      "Healing and Dealing"
      Responsibility—learning the "Deal"
   Leaving the program
Transactional Contexts
   Healing rituals
   Thinking rituals
      Think about feelings
   Feeling rituals
   Doing and Being rituals
      Acting out
   The Drop-In Center
      Reparenting
      Nurturing
   Group therapy
      House group
      Marathon groups
         Separation and isolation
         Leveling and status stripping
         The liminal phase
         Peak experiences
         Reintegration
Summary
4. Madness: In the Beginning and at the End 141
Interview Techniques
Schizophrenia as Psychopathology
The Cathexis Sample: Life Script Questionnaire
   and Interview Data
   Cultural and Family Data
Relationships in the Family
   Family World View
      Mother
      Fathers
      Punishment
World View and Self Concept

Self System: The Scare
Self System: Life, Death, and Suicide
Self System: Dreams and Future
Self System: Body and Bodily Sensations
Views on Child-Rearing or "Crazy-Making"
Family Secrets
Real Versus Not Real
  The Special Case of Hebephrenics
  Expectations of Treatment at Cathexis
"I Am Less Crazy Now Than When I Started":
  A Year Later
Experiential Data
  Process
  A Personal Example of How Cathexis Reculturation
    Affects Self Concepts, Etc.
  The Cultural Interpretation in Cathexis Society
  Differentiating Feelings
    Seeing vs looking
The Minnesota Multiphasic Personality Inventory
  and the Semantic Differential Results
  Minnesota Multiphasic Inventory
    Clinical evaluations of MMPI
Minnesota Multiphasic Inventory Statistical Analysis
  Semantic Differential Test Results
    Evaluation
    Potency
Summary
5. The Paradox of Magic and Science 203
  Process
    Metaphors
    Ritual Process
    Language
      Altered states of consciousness
      Metalanguage
      Ethnopsychiatry
    Cathexis
  Social Control and Power
    Survival
    Conflict
    Conformity

Contents

    Reciprocity
    Symbiosis
    Logic
    Ritual
    Developmental Factors
    Hungers (Drives or Needs)
    Systems
    Energy
    Entropy
    Synergy
  Implications for Further Study
    Natural Symbols
    Natural Character
    A New Profession in Western Urban Settings
      "Ritual Guides or Masters"
  Conclusions
Epilogue 227
Glossary 231
Bibliography 239
Index 259

LIST OF FIGURES

1-1. The Process of Cognition 29
1-2. The Ego States................................. 48
1-3. Ego States 50
1-4. Ego States 50
1-5. Maturation of Ego States 51
1-6. Contaminations 52
1-7. Transactions 53
2-1. Rectangular Solid of Data 71
2-2. Semantic Space 72
3-1. Relationships Between Types and Modes of Discounting . 95
3-2. Discounting Stimuli by Area and Mode 97
3-3. Discounting Problems by Area and Mode 98
3-4. Discounting Options by Area and Mode 99
3-5. Karpman's Drama Triangle 108
3-6. Redefining Hexagon 110
4-1. Ethnic Origin of Subjects in Study 144
4-2. Religious Background of Subjects 145
4-3. Age Breakdown of Subjects 146
4-4. Typical Script Matrix for Subjects of Cathexis 148
4-5. Minnesota Multiphasic Inventory Scores 192
4-6. Diagnostic Categories Before and After 194
4-7. Point Changes in Scores on MMPI Scales 196
4-8. Individual's Change in Semantic Differential for Self
     Concept 197
4-9. Change in Semantic Differential for All Subjects, All
     Concepts 197
4-10. Comparison of Self and Therapist With Significant Others 198
5-1. Model of Ritual Process 205
5-2. Model of Process of Psychopathology 220

REPARENTING SCHIZOPHRENICS

THE CATHEXIS EXPERIENCE

INTRODUCTION—OVERVIEW

The other does not exist: this is rational faith, the incurable belief of human reason. Identity = reality, as if in the end, everything must necessarily and absolutely be one and the same. But the other refuses to disappear; it subsists, it persists; it is the hard bone on which reason breaks its teeth. —Antonia Machado

A primary process does not develop from the cumulative experience of whole peoples whose deepest material and spiritual needs and wants have for long been denied any legitimate expression. — Victor Turner

Archetypal myths are themselves generative of patterns of and for the individual and the corporate process. Myth often makes life bearable for many peoples. Powerless feelings are mitigated because people believe that somewhere, sometime, by some magic, the discomfort of their present circumstances will be alleviated by the supernatural, the fairy godmother, the handsome prince. Such belief systems allow the individual to feel safe again for a time. People devise systems for themselves which provide answers and comfort in the face of what appear to them to be insurmountable odds against their survival.

Survival is probably always the key issue — even in our own affluent, comfortable society. Survival with a warm, loving, but violent father may provoke a child to invoke some magic from the mythology to help him deal with the violent and unpredictable moments in his life. Believing in the magic and in the myths gives people power to transcend present difficulties. Believing in magic keeps people hopeful. Hope for a better situation, better times, someday. For these and other reasons, people ascribe to the Shaman, to the witch doctor, to the psychotherapist a certain magical power.

Some people keep from feeling crazy by believing in magic. For others, believing in magic may keep them crazy. Not knowing how to solve problems, and using magical thinking, relying on myth,

11

instead of logical problem-solving is a way in which many people deal with their world. But the devotion of energy to magic and to wishful thinking keeps many people in anomic frames of reference.

Anthropologists have always been interested in why and how people use magic. Many miles of typescript have passed in the service of describing the rituals and symbols people use to keep their own particular kinds of myths going. The magic of the *churinga* and of the *ocimbanda* have aroused the curiosity of ethnographers who want to know how magic works in the lives of primitive and exotic peoples. The myths and magic in the lives of modern western man has begun to arouse attention recently (Berne, 1972; Harris, 1974). Lately, there is a developing interest in western urban life (Foster, 1974). Psychotherapy and its parallels in curandismo, Naven, and Ndembu ritual, magic and witchcraft is coming more into focus. Do peoples in western rationalist societies believe in fairies, in the supernatural? How do they use these beliefs? What kinds of adaptations are necessary to get along in urban industrial environments? How are rituals, adaptation and modern psychiatric treatment intersecting to create change in individuals and groups? This is a major thesis here. The field of anthropology offers an extensive literature and a longstanding interest in ritual, symbols and allied topics. Modern psychotherapy offers a systematic approach to psychopathology and to social interaction among which is Transactional Analysis (Berne, 1961). The key issues we will be addressing are ritual and psychotherapy.

People have frames of reference which are idiosyncratic, but in some manner they manage to survive in their particular environments. People adapt, overadapt and cognize their worlds in vastly individual ways. Sometimes people find that the adaptations that they have so carefully worked out in their families of origin do not serve them in the larger world beyond that family. Their maladaptation is sometimes seen as psychopathology. Often the maladaptation may serve them well, but they experience continual and acute discomfort in their efforts to function in what they perceive as a hostile and uncaring world. What happens to people who have learned the adaptive strategies labeled as schizophrenia? There is a lot of information about what happens to these people when they meet the established framework of traditional psychotherapy (Szasz, 1961). This thesis describes what happens to schizophrenics who meet and involve themselves in the ritual healing, symbolic language experiences of a Transactional Analysis community named Cathexis.

This book will consider how "magic" serves to bring people into the treatment setting. How magic keeps them there for awhile will be addressed. How the magic is turned around to assist in an alteration of cognitive systems will be looked at. How magic serves in assisting persons to become functional in an urban society is explicated. Sometimes mythology and magic are useful. Though the ritual process may seem to be successful due to some kind of wizardry or witchcraft, it is actually a carefully planned series of cognitive and affective experiences, it has a form and a structure.

Psychic opening (heightened awareness and receptivity to learning) does occur as a part of ritualized events. In healing rituals, this is often the case. When psychic opening is used as a means for causing behavioral change and personality transformation in individuals, the process becomes a type of rite-of-passage. Ritual manipulation of behavior and of emotional responses can result in a state of mind in which the individual's usual defenses are challenged and are no longer viable for him. In this opened state, the individual is more receptive to new information, and major changes in behavior, perceptions, personality and cognition are the result (Holloman, 1974: 265).

The transformations which occur as the result of ritual manipulation of behavior are the major focus of this study. The process through which the person experiences the healing community often at first seems to be some form of magic to him. Depending upon his cognitive framework, he will see the ritual experience as a type of witchcraft. As his cognitive skills improve he will begin to structure the environment for himself in order to supply himself with the necessary experiences for bringing about his own transformation. The rituals, healing strategies and psychic openings experienced by the individuals at Cathexis will be described.

Definitions will be clarified in the chapter on the Conceptual Framework. The major concepts will be ritual, adaptation, cognition, transformation and psychopathology. The description of the intersection of these with a modern treatment modality will follow. The psychiatric treatment community is in a major western urban setting where the "reparenting" mode of Transactional Analysis (Schiff, 1971:71) is the central treatment approach. It is "reparenting" which is at the root of the healing rituals structured for the patients in their interactions with the persons in the community.

All words which are specific to the model will be capitalized and will be described in a glossary.

Inasmuch as Cathexis is in an urban setting, the place of Anthropology in urban areas will be clarified. This is to expiate the notion that the exotic and far-off still are more valid scenes for the ethnographic researcher.

URBAN ANTHROPOLOGY

The field of ethnography encompasses the study of the ordering of social experience in everyday life. Can anthropology be used in urban settings? This is now a controversial issue among ethnographers. According to Foster (1974:1) urban anthropology now constitutes a major revolution in the definition of subject matter inside anthropology. Urban anthropology is in its infancy and has yet to define its boundaries and settle on the most appropriate research strategies. How a community is defined, and how the urban ethnographer settles on his research strategy is still open to debate. In the urban setting there is a "lack of sharp spacial and temporal boundaries and culture, language, society and biology do not intersect as well in the city as they do in the tribe or village" (Agar, 1974: 130; Barth, 1969). The approach to culture used by Liebow (1967) to define the streetcorner; or Gans (1962), the "urban village"; or Agar (1974) the culture of the "street junkie," provides one solution to the problem of setting boundaries. Gumperz (1964) has suggested "speech community," meaning any group whose communicative modes have to be learned by the outsider in order to know the community. According to Goodenough, by gaining the knowledge necessary to understand the symbol system in a community the ethnographer thus gains a knowledge of that culture.

It is becoming more and more possible for the ethnographer to use the participant-observation techniques on communities bounded by their ritual processes, as well in complex societies as in the simpler societies. Urban anthropology is a field recognized as such by some of the leading authorities in the area. Foster says, the interest is part of an evolutionary process and a natural outcome of the interest of anthropology in the chain of events leading peoples from tribal through peasant societies and culminating in the transformation of the peasant societies through their mass exodus to the city (Foster, 1974:1-13). The limitations set by studying people in urban environments are exemplified by studies such as those of Byrie, whose retirement population was bounded by a fence, and Kemper, who had to seek out all the migrants from a single village. Just as boundaries are sought after to define fields, so do boundaries set the limits on empires. In the search for boundaries and empires, another field in Anthropology has arisen—Medical Anthropology. This field is often within the bounds of Urban Anthropology, but not always.

CULTURE AND PERSONALITY: MEDICAL ANTHROPOLOGY (ETHNOPSYCHIATRY)

Since this field is a new one, and not entirely crystalized in the experience of anthropology, it is experiencing the same kind of inquisition that urban anthropology is undergoing. It is a field which has yet to define its boundaries and, perhaps, even its name. Evidently it is because anthropologists do not know exclusively just what medical anthropology is, that it is difficult to define the limits of the newer fields within its bounds. The editorial in *Medical Anthropology Newsletter* (August 1975: vol. 6 [4], 1-1) states:

> ... it is clear to me that the qualities that make anthropology indispensable to medicine are exactly the qualities I have just mentioned—namely, that nobody (and least of all an anthropologist) knows conclusively what anthropology is, except that it is the serious study of Man. ... Anthropology is an anti-creed—it is distilled self-consciousness—and as such it must and can live with the perpetual fever of suspended judgment.

Presumably then, any of the processes which may be seen as healing rites, or any of the attempts by peoples to find ease from physical and emotional burdens, may be defined as being within the province of medical anthropology.

As so often happens in the process of defining fields, the question arises as to "What's in a name anyway?" Hence it is not my purpose to enter into the argument which has been ongoing to date: is psychological anthropology a part of medical anthropology, or is it the other way around? And what of "culture and personality?" Since this book bridges several fields which touch on the old mind-body issue, it is by way of acknowledging that all of these areas overlap in some way that I bring this up. The main focus of this book is the behavior of persons with psychopathology before and after treatment for schizophrenia. This next process also involves boundaries. There are as many opinions about the etiology of schizophrenia as there are authorities on the subject. I have chosen to view schizo-phrenia as an adaptational strategy developed by the individual as a response to the double-bind (Bateson, et al., 1972).

SCHIZOPHRENIA – PSYCHOPATHOLOGY

Synonymous to or of related meaning to Goffman's (1956) view of "presentation of self" are such terms as "self system," "role defin-ition," "ego boundaries," and "schizophrenic." These definitions encompass the cognitive framework of people and the particular way in which certain persons view their worlds.

In the current framework, the schizophrenic is seen as having learned to express a set of adaptations to Western society which are considered maladaptive to the criteria for success in a work-oriented culture. Marcuse, in his theory of the "performance principle," has pointed up work-orientation as a source of madness (1955). Szasz has long derided the medical model as the cause of mental illness (1961). Jules Henry, in books *Culture Against Man* and *Pathways to Madness*, points up that society and the family structures within Western society are responsible for the adaptations which are seen as psychopathology. Others such as Laing, Devereaux, Frank and Wallace have suggested that the environment has something to do with the way in which the mad person reacts. In the West, it is evident that the schizophrenic seems to have rejected the "perform-ance principle" in his alienation from the principles of work-orienta-tion. Haley (1969:145) describes them as having a good grasp of "the art of being schizophrenic." They present themselves as a bur-den to the nuclear family in lost creativity and lost income. Schizo-phrenia continues to represent a high cost to communities as its victims seem to end up as frequent residents of mental hospitals.

DOUBLE-BIND

The double-bind parenting of the schizophrenic is described by Bateson, et al. (1954). This theory assumes a general systems theory framework. Transactional Analysis and Script Theory supply the systems of Ego States, and the Parenting Models which are presumed to cause schizophrenic modes of adapting. As described by Bateson, et al., the "double-bind" is a situation in which no matter what a person does, he "can't win." It is hypothesized that a person caught in a repeated double-bind ends up with psychopathology often labeled as schizophrenia. Bateson and his associates based their theory partly on the communications theory which Russell called the Theory of Logical Types (1910). In double-bind, a break occurs in the communication between the power figures and the child. The authors of the double-bind have pointed out that a series of ingredients are necessary for a double-bind to occur. They are:

1. two or more persons, one of whom is a "victim"
2. repeated experiences, i.e., a recurrent theme
3. primary negative injunction, e.g., "do so and so or you are no good" or the withdrawal of love resulting in a kind of abandonment of the child
4. a secondary injunction which conflicts with the first at a more abstract level
5. a tertiary negative injunction prohibiting the victim from escaping the field by capricious promises
6. finally, the set of ingredients is no longer necessary when the victim has learned to perceive his universe in double-bind patterns, i.e., incorporated the double-bind

Following in this same vein is the Transactional Analysis Script Theory as developed first by Berne (1961) and further by Steiner (1971; 1975). "A script is a complex set of transactions, by nature recurrent" (Berne, 1961). Steiner developed the Script Matrix and a coherent method for analyzing scripts. The substantive work with schizophrenia as pathology, using Transactional Analysis and Script Theory, has been done by Schiff and associates (1971; 1975). Script Theory is a method for outlining the way in which people are in double-bind with their parents, or how they double-bind themselves. It ascribes how they use mythology and magical thinking as one of the processes in this pattern. Further definition of schizophrenia as psychopathology will occur in Chapter II: Conceptual Framework.

THE COMMUNITY

The community in this study follows Firth's traditional definition of the theme: "a body of people sharing in common activities and bound by multiple relations in such a way that the aims of any individual can be achieved only by the participation in action with others" (1951:41). Further, they are a community in another sense, in that they are diagnosed as schizophrenics. The diagnosis is made both by clinical appraisal and by means of the MMPI, a standardized personality test specifically devised for the diagnosis of schizophrenia (Butcher, 1969). The social field (and network) of the community study is concerned with the individuals who participate in the face-to-face interactions which revolve around Cathexis School and the activities which it comprises. Though it is true that the individuals in this community are part of a larger network which encompasses their families and the larger society, the social field of this study is limited or bounded by a small set of social positions and is presented in a small number of "multiplex" social relationships (Gluckman, 1955:18-19) which center in the Cathexis School and its components. The interactions and rituals described occur in the Drop-In setting, the Group Therapy, the Marathon Experiences, the Residences and the "Schiff Family Structure." The other aspects are included in the tangential manner in which they impinge on the ritual processes to be described.

INTERNATIONAL IMPLICATIONS

Epidemiology: No doubt some of the difficulty in determining the incidence of schizophrenia in a cross-cultural perspective is due to diagnostic criteria. However, despite methodological obstacles, there are data to indicate that although schizophrenia does occur in developing countries, the rates are lower than in developed countries (Kiev, 1972:140-163). This question will be considered in more detail later in this book.

Despite difficulty in diagnostic agreement, there are crosscultural aspects which demand attention. The diagnosis of schizophrenia has been demonstrated to share the same characteristics in a number of western and nonwestern societies. The incidence of schizophrenia in nonwestern countries rises where exposure to western ideologies are currently increasing (Kiev, 1964; 1972:141). Diagnostic tests are being standardized in several nonwestern countries, the MMPI being one of them. The MMPI is being developed in Japan and in India, for example.

The Transactional Analysis treatment models are experiencing a rapid assimilation by professionals and laymen across the world. There are now treatment communities in Argentina, Mexico, Holland, Italy, India, Australia and altogether too many places to name here. The International membership of the Transactional Analysis Association has increased geometrically since 1970 when the first International Conference was held in San Francisco. In 1975, the first European Conference was held in Geneva, Switzerland. There is now a British T.A. Association with its own journal. The first Pan-American T.A. Conference was held in 1976. Possibilities for studying communities bounded by their investment in the T.A. model now exist in many regions of the world. The opportunity to study the double-bind theory through a general systems approach, such as T.A. in cross-cultural perspective, is more of a possibility.

CHAPTER RESUME

The study outline follows: Chapter I will address itself to the conceptual framework of the study. The theoretical aspects of this study provide a discussion of the issues upon which the research is based. The concepts are of significance to ethnography, psychotherapy and the general systems theory. This chapter addresses itself to the major concepts of ritual, symbolic action and communication as they interrelate with the theories of adaptation and Transactional Analysis. The issues of cognition and transformation will be explicated. Ritual healing as it relates to psychiatry, to learning theory and to linguistics will be considered. The recent works of Turner, Firth, Douglas and others will be the seminal material for the descriptive and expressive components of the book. The chapter also places the Transactional Analysis paradigm in historical perspective with the "Revolution in Psychiatry" (Becker, 1964:1-7) and with the "Human Potential Movement" (Maslow, 1968; Otto, 1966).

Chapter II outlines a description of the methods used in the study. The methods used are chosen to discover answers to the hypothetical issues as to whether a community approach such as that of Cathexis really does work in changing the Schizophrenic World View. The participant-observation method is described and the pros and cons of the experiential data-gathering techniques are discussed. Anecdotal records of the investigator's own ritual defense dropping (psychic opening), backed by those of patients in the setting are supplied in Chapter IV. Further sources of data include pencil and paper tests, self-reports, interviews with the Life Script Questionnaire and tape recordings.

Chapter III depicts the setting in which the study was conducted. The history, organization and structure of the Cathexis community are outlined. The philosophy, the staff, the participants and the healing model employed at Cathexis are described. Included in this chapter is a discussion of the ritual processes experienced by the participants and staff. This chapter includes a discussion of the special argot which comes from Transactional Analysis. The ritual process and its language imply a transformation from old symbolic frames and old metaphors to a different set of symbols and metaphors with differing affect and thought processes. The chapter concludes with a description of the personal experiences I had in participating in the various contexts, physical, transactional and theory building parts of the healing process.

The description of the persons who participated in the study comprises the fourth chapter. This chapter will describe the participants at the beginning and the end of the twelve months of the study. The behavior, lifestyles and world view of these people and what they were like before and after the major healing experiences, comprise the bulk of this chapter. It describes the transformational nature of the experiences in Cathexis. The symbols and metaphors which condense the individuals' World Views, and changes in their self-concepts after one year of living in and experiencing T.A. as applied at Cathexis are described.

The fifth chapter encompasses a discussion of the reasons that Cathexis Community seems to work. There is a discussion of the dialectic between Magic and Science. Magic is defined and the issues of Social Control and Power are explicated. Included in this chapter are implications for ethnography and for psychiatry of the experience of this study. The meaningful regularities in the experiences of the participants in the ritual cycles depicted in the study are summarized. The future of this type of study is considered.

Chapter I

THEORETICAL ISSUES

The core of Culture and Personality in Anthropology is the socialization process, i.e., how babies are enculturated—how the process works to produce emic phenomena, i.e., the plans, rules, values and how this is evidenced in behavioral terms— i.e., how emics causes the etics.
—*Marvin Harris*

Adaptation of the subject to the objects of its knowledge does exist and is merely an example of the organism's adaptation to its environment. In both cases the criterion for adaptation is success of this adaptation, whether it be a matter of survival or comprehension. —*Jean Piaget*

The dialectical process which occurs between the individual and his environment can have one of two usual outcomes. One outcome is that the individual is personally comfortable and powerful in his ecological niche. He and his associates experience him as "adjusted" and he is seen as having adapted successfully to his society. Another outcome finds the individual personally uncomfortable and powerless in his ecological niche. He and his associates experience him as maladapting and his behavior is seen as psychopathological in his society.

In order to understand the theory of psychopathology proposed here, it is necessary to see the development of several fields to this end. First, Anthropology which offers the study of (1) ritual, (2) ritual symbols, (3) linguistics, and (4) ethnomethodology. Further, within these fields we find Cognitive Anthropology which has close ties with the field of Educational Psychology and the learning theories as explicated by Jean Piaget (1971). Subsuming these fields is the General Systems Theory (Von Bertalanffy, 1968) which phrases adaptation as a system of the interaction of the individual and his environment. The link between these is the notion of ritual as a cybernetic feedback system. Linguistically, ritual is seen as metaphor. Metaphor is metalanguage. This implies a hierarchy of meaning and a logical sequence or process, which process ties it into communication theory and Bateson's (1969) notion of metalanguage as double-bind. Bateson's work is based on Russell's (1910) Theory of Logical Types.

EVOLUTIONARY STRUCTURALISM

Definition, in general, poses problems for many reasons. For our purposes, we will turn to the details of the major concepts used here to Piaget (1969; 1971), Bateson (1972), Langer (1962), Count (1973), Berne (1961; 1964; 1971a; 1971b; 1972; 1975), Kohlberg (1969), Holloman (1974), Reynolds (1974), Rappaport (1968) and Turner (1967; 1969a; 1969b; 1974; 1975). This is necessary because of the specific and definite direction this book will take.

There is a polarization between the ideals of the evolutionary structuralists and the semiotic structuralists. The former are those structural theorists who are concerned with the developmental and evolutionary structural processes such as described by Piaget (1971) and Count (1973). The structural theorists represented by Levi-Strauss (1967; 1969a, 1969b; 1973) are not interested in process, evolution or the developmental issues, but about structure. Essentially, the focus of this essay will follow the framework offered by the evolutionary structuralists. This point of view takes the stand that there is a physiological reality underlying structure. The structures referred to herein are built on the fact of the nervous system of man, and that in itself represents a structure. This view posits that behavior, that is of interest to anthropologists, is the result of the work of the nervous system. The nervous system itself results from an interaction between the person's genetic predispositions, and the ecological niche in which the organism finds itself. That is, there is a transactional experience between the brain and the environment. Among the situations in human life that provides for transactional experiences between brain and environment, and subsequent changes are those dramas provided for by ritual and ritual process. This is also seen as the generative approach.

RITUAL AND RITUAL PROCESS

Lewinian Field Theory (1935) and General Systems Theory (Von Bertalanffy, 1968) provide two major foundations for the definition of ritual. From Von Gennep's *Rites de Passage* (1976), ritual is defined as a period of transition marked by three phrases: Separation, Margin (or Limen—Latin for threshold) and Aggregation. Turner (1969) and Rappaport (1968) provide detailed descriptions of these phases.

Separation: The first phase (separation) provides symbolic behavior which signifies the individual's or group's detachment from their usual community or mode of behaving. Characteristically the individual is symbolically killed or, in some similar manner, separated from ordinary or profane relationships. The person moves out of the realm of the usual or ordinary and prepares for the next phase.

Margin (Limen): The ensuing or in-between phase which Turner names "liminal" is an intervening state. It comes between the ordinary phases of life and the status of the actor or performer is ambiguous. He is in a realm which has none of the attributes of the past or of the future status. It is a nonordinary state.[1] In this state, given the proper ingredients, the individual experiences a *communitas* within himself and with the ritual participants and/or objects. More will be said about this state of communitas later.

Aggregation: The third phase completes the Rite of Passage. The ritual subject (or group) is reincorporated with the ordinary or usual community. This phase symbolically allows a rebirth of the individual to his usual life experience and he is taken back into the midst of his usual life and associates.

Briefly, then, ritual is a "patterned process in time" which is both diachronic and synchronic (Turner, 1969). Ritual performances are phases in broad social processes. Rituals are like cybernetic feedback loops in systems. They serve to anticipate deviations in the system or to correct deviations in the system. Rappaport (1971:23) offers the following definition of ritual process as "a standardized system of stereotyped behaviors and communications which manipulate human emotion toward a preset end result." Rappaport, Turner and Douglas (1972) point out that an important part of ritual process is the recurrent relationship of phenomena from nature and from bodily functions. Such phenomena as birth, death and developmental crises are reenacted over and over again. The middle phase, margin or

limen, is the pivotal phase in ritual process. It is around the phenomenon which Turner calls *communitas* that the basic dynamic
nature of ritual processes occur.

Associated with the process are symbolic objects and specific
behaviors, each of which has a specific meaning. These meanings
may be different depending upon the context or field in which the
ritual is a phase. The major focus in the study of ritual is the *behavior*
directed at the *symbol* and the *situation* in which the specific ritual
and/or ritual symbol are being experienced. The sharing of the
meanings of these symbolic objects and/or behaviors is often the root
for the experience of communitas.

Communitas: Before going on to discuss symbols and their nature,
it is essential to amplify the central meaning of the marginal or
liminal phase mentioned above. The margin, or limen, is characteristically where the individual or group participants experience the
sense of communitas. Communitas is a "bond uniting ... people
over and above any social bonds (Znaniecki in Turner, 1969:45). It
is often a sacred condition. It is linked with spontaneity and freedom
as opposed to structure which is linked to obligation, jurality, law,
constraint, etc."

> In liminality, communitas tends to characterize relationships between
> those jointly undergoing ritual transition. The bonds of communitas are
> anti-structural in the sense that they are undifferentiated, equalitarian,
> direct, extant, non-rational, existential, I-Thou (in Feuerbach's and Buber's
> sense) relationships. Communitas is spontaneous, immediate, concrete—it
> is not shaped by norms, it is not institutionalized, it is not abstract. Com-
> munitas differs from the camaraderie found often in everyday life, which
> though informal and egalitarian, still falls within the general domain of
> structure, which may include interaction rituals. (Turner, 1974:174)

The coherence of a completed social drama is itself a function of
communitas. An incomplete or unresolved drama would then manifest the absence of communitas. Consensus on values is not the basic
issue. Consensus, being spontaneous, rests on communitas not on
structure. The components of the liminal phase and of communitas
are the conditions for the production of root metaphors, conceptual
archetypes and paradigms, models for and the rest.

In conclusion, ethologists have little difficulty in defining ritualized behavior as producing "signals which release appropriate action
with a minimum of delay" (Huxley, 1966: 257). Ritual communication gives rise to two functions in the ethologist's view: (1) the

canalization of aggression in a manner permitting its discharge without damaging fellow members of the species and (2) formation of a bond which keeps together two or more individuals as described in K. Z. Lorentz's (1966) books and articles. In terms of phylogeny, ritual behavior is a rapid process, easily recognized and defined with facility. On the other hand, anthropologists have difficulty defining ritual, perhaps because of their own position of being betwixt and between the sciences and humanities. This essay will be taking the phylogenetic view of ritual as (1) canalization of energy, and (2) formation of a bond through communitas. The bonding vehicles in ritual process are the symbols and symbolic language and ensuing action. Further discussion of these concepts follows.

SYMBOLS AND SYMBOLIC LANGUAGE

> The tragedy and grandeur of symbolic man is that his sense of worth is irrevocably inseparable from his symbolic constructions. (Becker, 1964:41)

Turner, who arranged the New Orleans symposium on *Forms of Symbolic Action* (1969) has produced one of the more lucid discussions of the nature of symbols. Briefly he states that "the smallest portion to which a ritual sequence or dynamic total can be reduced by subdivision without losing its semantic structural identity is the ritual symbol" (Turner, 1969b:8). He has tried to simplify the various controversies on the definitions of symbol by offering the following schema: primarily there are multivocal and univocal symbols.

A multivocal symbol is a thing (work, object behavior, person, place, time, etc.) accepted by persons of the same culture as "naturally typifying or representing something by possession of analogous qualities or by association in fact or thought" (*Oxford Concise Dictionary*). Multivocal means that the symbol condenses many meanings or references. The references or significations are united in a single cognitive and affective field.

Univocal (having only one meaning) symbols result from the dissolution of multivocal symbols. Turner (1969b:9) sees ritual symbols as having a bipolar quality. The multivocal symbol may be composed of (1) an iconic symbol vehicle, that is, sensorily perceptible characteristics which have associations easily related denotatively, (2) a set of denotations or primary meanings, and (3) a set of connotations implied in addition to the primary meaning.

Further, multivocal ritual symbols tend to polarize their references, clustering more closely at a physiological pole or at an ideological pole. He has called these two poles orectic (affective and bodily process oriented) and normative (related to ideas, moral or ethical systems). Douglas' polarization of "flesh" and "spirit," Schneider's qualities of "blood" and "marriage" and the Huxley-Lorentz "Phylogenetic" and "psychosocial" are similar bipolar designations.

Multivocality and polarity are not the only structural properties of ritual symbols. Turner goes on to suggest that there are three dimensions of significance for symbols: (1) the exegetic which are the explanations given by the native for ritual symbol, (2) the operational significance which is what the participants in the ritual say and do with the symbol, and (3) the positional dimension which is the gestalt of the symbol, that is, its relationship to other symbols in the system. A symbol may be meaningful only in the way in which it complements or opposes its polar opposite.

Finally, in terms of the symbol's exegesis (how the participant defines the symbol) there are three semantic considerations: (1) nominal, meaning the name that the symbol is assigned in the ritual context, (2) substantial, meaning the culturally selected material and natural properties, and (3) artifactual basis which represents the symbol after it has been shaped into a cultural form by human activity.

The biological referents, meaning the physiological meanings may be the reinforcers of the will. These symbols and associated rituals may be the source of energy required by individuals to keep up obligations and avoid illicit behaviors in societies.

Finally, ritualization and the symbolic systems associated with it provide the tools for the individual's adaptation to the environment. It is through symbols that people cognize themselves and their place in their world. Symbols are the means by which energy is exchanged or joined by individuals in the recognition of their existential condition. Symbols provide the vehicle for the experience of *anomia* or *communitas*, for *entropy* or *synergy*. Symbolic systems are at the root of the successful adaptation or of the psychopathology of human beings. Rituals—Healing Rituals—provide the medium for the symbolic channelizing of energy in a manner which permits discharge without damage and for the formation of a bond between and among the persons engaged in the ritual. Healing rituals provide for the mobilization of energy and its efficient use through symbolic action. Through symbolic action the internal integrity of the patient is restored.

Where ritual does work, the exchange of qualities between the semantic poles of the symbols seems to achieve genuine carthartic effects. There is often, as results in some cases a real transformation of character and of social relationships. Turner (1974:56) suggests that anomia (and psychopathology) is prevented where there is a high level of communitas in the society. The experience of psychopathology comes out of the lack of communitas in the socialization of the individual.

ADAPTATION

Consideration of man's use of ritual and ritual symbols must include, ultimately, man's fit with his environment. The dialectic between man's behavior and his econiche involves the concept of adaptation. According to Lewin (1935) adaptation is behavior developed by an individual organism with respect to its environment. Adaptation is seen as a degree of correspondence between an organism and its environment. Alland has reviewed fully the current state of the theory of adaptation (1975:59-73) and he describes the views of the major theorists in anthropology as ranging from the ecological viewpoint to the structuralist viewpoint. He points out that these lines of development can be reconciled in a unified approach to human adaptation.

Adaptation is a major concept in biology, psychology and anthropology. Structural ecology takes the premise that human behavioral systems are the outcome of an adaptational process and that human brain hardware shapes response patterns according to internal rules. It is at the intersection of these fields that the definition arises. Alland offers a General Systems Theory approach to adaptation by stating that:

> ... it can be seen as a temporal process of positive feedback in which transgenerational changes are directed by selective forces in the environment .... Adaptation also refers to response processes which occur within individual organisms as they adjust through negative feedback to environmental changes during their own lifetimes. (1967:119)

When an individual does not behave in a manner which is culturally consonant, or consensually validated, the behavior is regarded as maladaptive. Adaptation is an individual's or group's structure for survival in a particular environment. The person whose behavior is dissonant or who is anomic, is seen as not adapting (maladapting). Psychopathology is defined as behaviors which are maladaptive for the individual's own society. The concept of psychopathology is seen in biogenetic structuralism as being conceptually a part of the adaptational strategies of the individual and hence within the conceptual boundaries of adaptation theory.

PSYCHOPATHOLOGY

Psychopathology may be defined as a system of maladaptive behaviors (Laughlin and d'Aquili, 1974; McManus, 1975). Psychopathology is (1) a system of self-presentation, cognition and behavior which keeps the organism from successfully adapting, (2) it is an adaptation of some kind which does not meet the consensus, (3) it is behavior which is recognized in some way as different from the expected sets of behaviors of others of the same age or sex in the culture, and (4) further, it is a framework of misrepresentations of cognitive data on the part of the individual. The psychopathological organism does not cognize the environment in a way which would make it possible for it to behave in a manner which meets the consensus. The person is not willfully nonconformist. Usually they are uncomfortable with their own behavior. Persons who are termed maladaptive in Western society can be seen as not having developed an emotionally satisfying, or socially acceptable pattern of expression and action (and are in frequent discomfort). In order to master the ability to exercise a rational hold on the world, the individual must have grasped a symbol system which is viable for his society. Symbols express the social order. If the person is unable to function in the elementary process of transacting with others with symbols which are consensually valid, then he is for that moment, experiencing psychopathology.

COGNITION

Cognition as defined by Piaget (1971) is expressed as knowledge of the environment and of the self. Piaget claims that knowledge is a process rather than a state. The process appears in three forms: (1) instinct, a sort of neuronal mode of knowing, (2) knowledge of the structure and function of experience, and (3) developmental

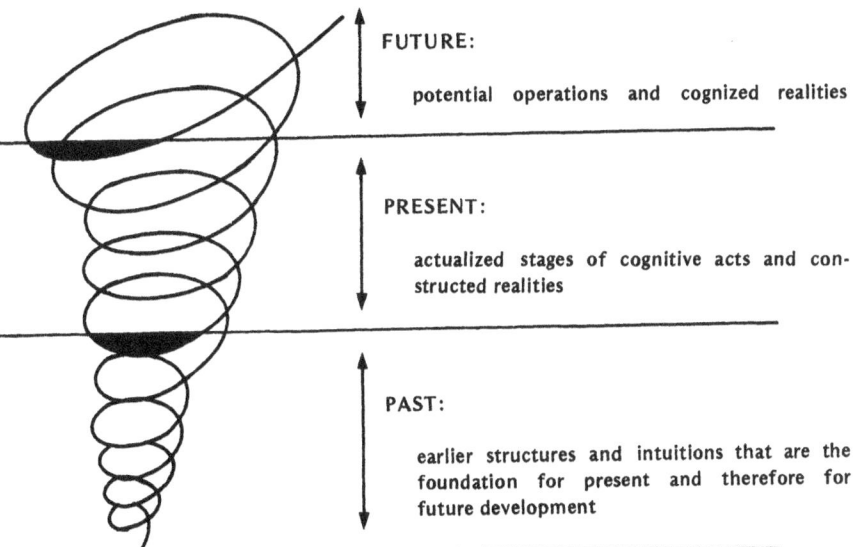

FUTURE:

potential   operations   and   cognized   realities

PRESENT:

actualized   stages   of   cognitive   acts   and   constructed realities

PAST:

earlier   structures   and   intuitions   that   are   the
foundation   for   present   and   therefore   for
future development

Figure 1-1. THE PROCESS OF COGNITION (McManus, 1975).
Spiral development: the constructive assumptions of spiral development.

aspects of knowledge.   The process of experiencing the environment and the self is then termed cognition, and it is the end result
of the developmental progression of the individual. Affect, emotion,
and motivation are a joint function of cognition and the physio-
chemical system.

Cognition is a process governed by neurophysical and biological
imperatives influenced by environmental, cultural and family factors.
Piaget's findings indicate that there are specific kinds of knowledge
which occur as a natural outgrowth of intellectual activity.   He
suggests that specific kinds of learning are a function of the interaction with significant adults. He states that: (1) children's thought
processes and language are different from adults, they perceive the
world from a different perspective, (2) children must manipulate
their environments in order to gain knowledge of it—they learn
best from acting *on* their environment and from interesting and
moderately novel experiences, (3) there are stages of thought processes through which children pass and often the child is the best

judge of his own interests, limits and motivations, (4) interaction, consensual validation and relevant physical experiences among and between children and sensitive adults are essential for appropriate growth of the cognitive processes (Ginsburg and Opper, 1969: 230-231). The process by which the child gains knowledge is an example of symbolic transformation.

Bruner (1962; 1966), following Piaget, offers three major phases or stages in the cognitive maturation of the individual: (1) enactive, in which the individual acts upon the environment and experiences the environment as an extension of self, (2) iconic, in which the individual begins to see the environment in symbolic (containing many references) terms, perceives, and stores information on several levels as separate from self, and (3) conceptual in which the individual self and the environment are incorporated and defined in terms of language as a system of symbols. The phases are overlapping and intertwined as in a spiral of ever widening scope. Each loop of the spiral represents Time in development. (See Figure 1-2)

The end result of the cognitive developmental process is the "frame of reference," "world view" or "cultural map" as viewed by the individual. These latter can be seen as the person's internal organization of his environment, which is only the inner half of the picture. The other half is seen in terms of the individual's behavior in and towards that environment. The final product of a systematic and carefully programmed process which results in the internal frame of reference by which the individual construes his environment and hence his way of behaving in that environment. Adaptation is one of two cognitive and biological constants (Piaget, 1970b; 1971); the other function is the ability of the system to organize the internal environment.

Adaptation is the process through which the person using his internal frame of reference deals with, and constructs the external frame of reference. It is the resultant behavior between the organism and the environment. Transformation is the process by which the individual deals with the sensory data taken into his internal frame of reference and the subsequent organization of the data.

TRANSFORMATION

As described previously, cognition is a developmental process. Each succeeding stage being dependent upon completion of the previous stage for maximum operational efficiency. Therefore, the more complex the cognitive frame of the person, the more pieces of information the person will be able to synthesize, absorb and use. The process of taking bits of information and changing them to fit the inner frame of reference is a transformative process (see Redefining ff.). Where an individual's inner frame of reference cannot be validated by the external reality, the transformative process is seen as noncongruent with verifiable reality. This state of affairs is defined in a previous section as maladaptation, or even psychopathology. For example: consider three persons listening to a popular song called "Evil Woman." One interprets the song personally, perceives it to mean that the singer is referring to her. She responds with fear and threatens to kill herself reasoning "they know about me now, and are even broadcasting it over the radio!" The other listeners perceive the song as the lament of a jilted lover with no personal context. One may see the song as a folk comment on lovers, feels "sorry" for the singer, the other may see the song as "sexist" and become indignant about this type of song. Each person has an idiosyncratic transformational process. The first person's process will be seen as pathological.

Transformation is a process of data intake, data retrieval, data organization, data synthesis and, finally, data use. There are different degrees, types and levels of transformation. These are dependent on time primarily. If the transformative process is occurring in a given moment, in the now, it can be considered synchronically. If the process is historical, and occurs over a period of time, it is considered diachronically. Other considerations are, what the person does with the sensory input internally, how does he behave in relation to that input, what is his adaptive capacity? All of these are dependent upon his idiosyncratic transformative process. The individual's adaptive capacity is dependent upon how adequate this process is at coordinating the outside world with the internal model of the world. The transformative process may be occurring in relation to symbols within ritual, outside of ritual, and within his own thought processes. At a total level, transformation occurs when there is a behavioral or personality change.

The whole developmental process of the individual is an example of the capacity of the individual in terms of the transformation of structure. As the child grows through each developmental period, he experiences a transformation of structure. At any point where conditions and interactions with adults in his environment are not optimal, there may occur a fixing of the process in relation to that particular event. These stoppages cause distortions in the cognitive system. The person may become protective of the distortion in his internal organization around that event. These protective stances (defense mechanisms, Redefinitions) are maintained by the person because they may be viewed as necessary to the person to avoid overstimulation or understimulation from the environment. According to Transactional Analysis and other theories of personality, the person makes decisions (Decision Theory) about his environment which are of importance to him in terms of his survival at that moment in time. Given the organization of the person's internal frame of reference, the flexibility of that organization; its complexity; and the need as he sees it for adaptation to the external environment, the person will either transform his inner frame of reference to fit the verifiable reality, or he will try to make the external reality fit his internal frame of reference. The degree to which the individual attempts to transform his environment to fit a nonverifiable internal frame of reference is seen as pathology.

As noted in the section on symbols and symbolic language, Becker's statement (1964:41) "the tragedy and grandeur of symbolic man is that his sense of worth is irrevocably inseparable from his symbolic constructions." It is by the process of symbolic transformation (Langer, 1964: Chapter 2) that the individual defines his *self* and his *notself*. Symbols express the social order. The way in which the individual transforms the perceptual field into his symbolic structure defines the self.

Metaphors are seen by both Turner and Langer as part of the transformation process. Turner suggests that when ritual works, there is an exchange of qualities between the semantic poles, a cathartic effect is achieved which causes transformations of character (Turner, 1974:56). He notes that there has been an increasing interest in the roles of symbols in social and cultural practices. Abraham Kaplan notes that scientific models are actually "scientific metaphors" (1964:265) and that "a metaphor like an aphorism condenses in a phrase, a significant similarity." He points out that the scientist recognized similarities that have previously escaped us and systematizes them. This view is supported by Kelly (1955: 32-34) who indicates that the hypotheses and sources of these are the basis by which the individual checks out and tests his environment. This happens whether the individual is scientific model-building, or whether in daily practice of personal life.

Reusch (1973:Chapter 22), Bateson (1972) and Lilly (1967) talk about such totalities as "metacommunication," "metalanguage" and "metaprogramming." Metaphor is metacommunication; there are many meanings condensed therein. Metacommunicative processes are statements about statements that condense or shape the general meaning of words so that information is condensed into a transaction of significant meaningfulness. Ruesch points out that the majority of persons with psychopathology have trouble with metacommunication. Rules of metacommunication are learned only through consistent contact with one and the same expressive group. Interrupted, discontinuous, insensitive or nonexistent human relations during development prevent the mastery of metacommunication (1973: 424). Thus, inadequate understanding of metacommunicative patterns leads to maladaptation and psychopathology. The individual's social processes which connect him with his surroundings are thus impaired. The development of language through experience is a vital process in normal growth and development.

LANGUAGE AND EXPERIENCE

> If ritual is the cradle of language, metaphor is the law of life. It is the force that makes it essentially relational, intellectual, forever showing up in new, abstractable forms in reality, forever laying down a deposit of old, abstracted concepts in an increasing treasure of general words. (Langer, 1956:141)

Langer goes on to say that language in its literal capacity, is a stiff and conventional medium, poorly adapted to the expression of genuinely new ideas which usually have to break in on the mind in some blinding flash or bewildering metaphor. But she points out that *"bare denotative language* is a most excellent instrument of exact reason, it is in fact the *only general precision instrument* [emphasis mine] the human brain has ever evolved." It is the lack of a literal bare, denotative language and the experience to go with it that differentiates the schizophrenic from others. That is, schizophrenics lack the capacity to distinguish the literal from the metaphorical, the denotative from the connotative, due to inadequate metalinguistic competence.

To continue this line of thinking, if a person's early years have been characterized by extremes of overprotection and/or over-rejection, he is apt to develop a set of stereotyped symbols which may be highly idiosyncratic, viable only in the extremes of the world of his family. Such a narrow set of symbols will limit the individual's capacity to transact in a complex and demanding urban society. This person becomes alienated and anomic, then experiences further oppression and rejection of the Self. The person's manner of presenting himself will appear inflexible, "flat," and often inappropriate for the milieu in which he is interacting, i.e., lacking the metacommunicative texture of usual language. According to Goffman (1959:7ff) the self is presented to each situation in congruence with what the individual *perceives* is the appropriate manner.

Since everything that makes a person is contained in his symbolic self, then his whole human existence depends on symbolic satisfactions (Sullivan, 1956). A person who sees objects in only one dimension, cannot possibly construct a self in relation to three dimensional people and objects. He cannot ever solve even the first of basic human problems as stated by Kluckholn (1950: 193-393): "what kind of reactions can one expect from volatile human objects."[2] The symbolically impoverished individual is then trapped in a situation where there are few behavioral options in his repertoire.

A number of writers discuss what Becker calls "the puzzling phenomenon of schizophrenic language" (1964: 51). When words no longer refer to "potential organismic action, or to any felt organismic involvement, they lose their quality as true language." In the schizophrenic, the connections between feeling and movement, feeling and body, thinking and body seem to be "short-circuited" (i.e., no connection of denotation, connotation and of action). Thence, as Becker points out, there is no tie up between emotion and experience. He calls schizophrenic flatness "eerie, because symbolic dexterity is divorced from a lived experience of the sense of the words" (Becker, 1964: 52).

Maher (1968: 60) finds that schizophrenic utterances are the end result of two factors: (1) the vulnerability of sentence structure (metalanguage) to attentional lapses, and (2) the inability of patients to inhibit associational intrusions, particularly at these lapse points. They cannot seem to be able to handle complex ideas, metaphors and condensed meanings. This inability to sort out or screen meaning, feeling and symbol, to focus conceptually, puts the individual in a situation where the environment is bombarding him with sensation. He is not able to cope and reverts to his defense systems.

Langer points out that speech is the readiest active termination of that basic process in the human brain which she terms the "symbolic transformation of experiences," and that ritual is a symbolic transformation of experiences that no other medium can express (1956). Healing rituals in some settings provide the milieu in which the person begins to deal with metaphor and metalanguage effectively.

RITUAL HEALING

The western psychotherapeutic paradigm is characterized by a vast array of conflicting, interchangeable and interlocking methods and theories. Although there is a great diversity among them, they are all attempts to heal by persuasion. This means to induce changes in the psychiatric patients' or the believers' attitudes and behaviors (world views) which seem to cause the life style of suffering of the individual. These methods share features with all forms of persuasion and healing (Frank, 1961:x). All types of persuasion entail some form of trance state or altered-state of consciousness. Frank identifies the following features common to healing ritual processes: (1) they are conducted by a trained, socially sanctioned healer whose powers are accepted by the sufferer and by his social group and are an important segment of the process; (2) the sufferer seeks relief of the suffering from the healer; (3) by means of a circumscribed, more or less structured series of contacts between the healer and the sufferer through which the healer with the aid of the group proceeds to produce changes in the sufferer's emotional state, attitudes and behavior; (4) all involved believe that these changes will be helpful; (5) the healing influence is primarily exercised by words, acts and rituals in which the healer, the sufferer and the group participate (although in some settings, physical and chemical adjuncts are used).

CULTURE AND MADNESS

Kiev (1968: 175) asserts that culture creates characteristic types of conflicts that are handled in both healthy and unhealthy ways depending on the individual's personal history, constitution and life experience. Another hypothesis is offered by Hsu (1961: 400) wherein he maintains that the particular family dyad is a basis for certain kinds of cultural functioning or disfunctioning. A carefully detailed exposition of how five western urban American families went about setting the stage for madness in one or more of their children is given by Henry (1965). He proposes his type of study as a means for defining the cultural, parenting, family and social factors which contribute to "mad" behavior. He describes the family attitudes towards thinking, feeling, and problem-solving which seem to nurture the destructive and aberrent tendencies of the person who is "mad." Others proposing political, cultural and family factors in madness are Laing (1960; 1967; 1969; 1970), Szasz (1957a; 1961; 1970), Bateson (1956) and Marcuse (1962). All agree that when these same factors are integrated in consistent, conflictual, protected ritual settings, they become a part of the healing process. It is the conflicted manner in which thinking, feeling and problem-solving are taught that causes the confusion and psychopathological behavior.

CURANDERISMO

In a study of *curanderos*, Kiev (1968) identifies some of the factors in the healing process. Special effort was made to determine how the patients viewed their illness in relation to the concepts of healing presented by the *curandero*. He points out that: (1) the patient's favorable expectations are reinforced by the treatment setting and techniques and by the faith conveyed by the healer that the patient will respond to treatment; (2) the healer's initial pessimism heightens ambiguity and creates increased anxiety in the patient promoting his desire to please the healer; (3) there is a connection of the treatment with the dominant values by enlisting the support of the community, this further reinforces faith in the healer; (4) suggestibility is increased by participation in emotion-arousing group dances and songs, further inclining the patient to expect help. Community support, participation in the ritual, direct commands, reassurance and environmental manipulation are supportive and anxiety-reducing; (5) possession experiences and group involvement lead to attainment of high status in the ritual roles which lead to the opportunity to act out aggressive and sexual behavior, to role reversal and temporary license for the actors; (6) the use of influence to arouse emotion and promote cathartic and acting out experiences has therapeutic value; (7) the beliefs and values of the group are used as a fulcrum to influence successful treatment and lead to the reintegration of the patient into the community. These elements are found in a wide range of psychotherapeutic systems. Certain emotional states are activated by the person's expectations interacting with the group forces and may contribute either to healing or to the reinforcement of pathology. Wallace (1962; 1966) has written in similar terms of revitalization movements, and Geertz (1968) and others support this thesis. It should be noted that this material from Kiev, Frank and others is relevant to and amplifies the information discussed in the sections on Ritual Process and Symbols.

PSYCHIATRY

Modern western dynamic psychiatry has as its goal change of the behaviors which are disruptive to the individual and to society. The patient experiences the growth of insight into the nature of his difficulties. The therapist assists the patient to see the influence of his early life decisions, attitudes and behaviors on the patterns of his daily life and his transactions. As a result of the "transference phenomenon,"[3] and through the incorporation of new information, the patient gains a different world view. Bandura states unequivocally that "psychotherapy is learning" (Bandura, 1961: 143-154). The establishment of an intense dependency relationship and the manipulation of the dependency encourage the patient to change. The giving up of accustomed ways of doing things is the key feature of dynamic psychiatry. Chapple (1970: 303) includes the psychoanalytic approaches among the transformational modes when he says that "the various new approaches developing at various points in contemporary society to ease status/interactional transitions should be looked at in terms of their ritual significance to the individual." That is, the actual experiences of Rites-of-Passage in Psychiatry should be studied.

RITES - OF - PASSAGE

Healing rituals mobilize powerful emotional forces that then shape the process of the individual's or the group's life. Rituals involve a preparatory period that represents a break from the person's usual routines. The participants in the ritual help the individual by performing parts of the ritual. Some rituals elicit confessions of a specific type of personal transgressions, and the sharing of these. Some ceremonies are highly charged emotionally. Emotional excitement is often intensified by specific forms of repetition (such as dancing, chanting, etc.). Sometimes these are enhanced by a strong emotional or physical shock. Most rituals have some form of symbolic trappings of an aesthetic or evocative nature. The individuals who undergo an encounter group or confrontation experience a transformation of key mental processes. Following the ritual process they are often changed in their perception of self, and in their world views in specific parts. Frequently the nature of the transformation is in terms of the specific ways in which they view themselves in relation to their environments and the persons around them. Holloman describes her own personal experiences at Esalen as being a change of this nature (1974). Esalen is one of the many Growth Centers which are the places where the Human Potential Movement is seen in practice.

THE HUMAN POTENTIAL MOVEMENT

It has been estimated that hundreds of thousands of persons have shared encounter and group therapy experiences at such places as Esalen. There are now Growth Centers in most major cities. Each patterned on a different school of psychotherapy, or combining several schools. There is also extensive cultural borrowing from Eastern modes such as T'ai Ch'i and Shiatsu massage to Sufism and varying forms of Yoga. The Esalen Catalog is an example of the eclecticism now available to the average middle-class urbanite. Symbolic transformation of self, and in some cases major changes in world view are experiences occurring in these centers. The source of the changes in western society according to Leonard (1974), Thompson (1971) and Goodman (1969), is the Human Potential Movement.

There is believed to be a healing or reworking of old psychic wounds as a result of the "psychic opening," and altered states of consciousness, experienced in such Growth Center groups. *"Psychic opening"* is defined by Holloman (1974) as a "state in which all or most (or some) of the individual's defenses are lowered simultaneously ... this creates a vulnerability and a high suggestibility." The emotional peaking allows the individual to accept new thoughts and new material about his self system which may result in a change in the symbols and metaphors the individual holds about himself. Psychic opening can be brought about ritually by a variety of methods such as: (1) drugs, (2) specific cultural techniques such as teachings, meditations, etc., (3) manipulation of emotions through role plays, psychodramas, gestalt methods, (4) brain washing techniques. Any and all of these methods involve requiring a change of perception on the part of the participant, and are followed by a change in thought patterns and in feeling modes.

SCHOOLS OF PSYCHOTHERAPY

Research on the Human Potential Movement includes such varied studies as those on Communication by Bateson and Ruesch and by Ruesch (1975: 228; 1961: 20) to the studies coming out of the National Training Laboratories influenced by Kurt Lewin and his associates (Golumbiewski, 1970). The history of the Human Potential Movement, Humanistic Psychology and more recently Transpersonal Psychology movements are outlined by Bach (1972), Yaloms, Lieberman and associates (1974). The latter outlines ten "schools"[4] or approaches to psychiatric ritual healing. In the 1968 and 1974 studies carried out by Yaloms et. al., also in the *Annual Review of Psychology* (1976), Yaloms offers the following "schools" or approaches: (1) National Training Laboratories traditional approach developed on the East Coast; (2) National Training Laboratories "Western"; (3) Gestalt, developed by Fritz Perls and followers; (4) Esalen eclectic, based on work by Otto, Schutz and others; (5) Transactional Analysis developed by Eric Berne; (6) Synanon, involving hard ("rip-off") confrontation of behavior; (7) Psychodrama (modified Moreno); (8) Time-extended or Marathon meeting approach written about initially by George Bach; (9) Psychoanalytic encounter; and (10) Leaderless Encounter-group experiences. To this list may now be added the Body Technique schools arising out of the work of Wilhelm Reich, Ida Rolf and Moshe Feldenkreis. The research on small group process, the successes and the failures has covered nearly every possible arrangement with almost every possible end, and close to every kind of person involved in the goal of personal change or healing. There is no single technique, type of group or theoretical orientation which works for all of the people involved. Lieberman (1976: 213-250) points out research inducing change in small groups covers the range from group psychotherapy to experiential groups, consciousness-raising activities (rap groups) and self-help groups. He points out that the processes are the same, or sufficiently related, the goals often identical and the client populations overlapping. He notes that "boundaries often reflect professional narrowness and language systems more than substantive differences" (Lieberman, 1976: 218). This is an important factor to keep in mind because of the religious fervor with which individuals embrace any one of the "schools" which has been effective for them personally. The research has focused on leadership style, schools of therapy, types of clients and outcomes. The indications are that change occurs in some people and not in others. The outcomes vary depending upon the factors (variables are many) in each situation. Controls are difficult to achieve because of strict laboratory conditions, and control of variables nearly impossible. Further research may eventually produce an empirically-based theory of group process and group change.[5] Essentially, the final data on success or failure of technique is not complete as of this date.

Transactional Analysis is the "school" of therapy used by the Cathexis Community which is the focus of this study. A major criterion for understanding the conceptual framework upon which this study is based will be the need for an understanding of the major issues in T.A., its theory and practice. The following section is devoted to its explication.

TRANSACTIONAL ANALYSIS

Definition

Transactional Analysis is the name given by Eric Berne (1958) to what he terms "a new and effective method of group therapy." It is an approach to interactional psychotherapy. The concepts and techniques have been oriented toward achieving the optimal outcomes from group settings. It is a contractural form of therapy by which the subject enters into treatment. The key process is Structural Analysis. The purpose of this approach is to increase awareness of the persons in treatment, with the ultimate goal of making new Decisions about their future behavior and life course.

Historical Background

Eric Berne was a psychoanalyst practicing in the San Francisco Bay area between the 1950s and 1960s until the time of his death in

1970. He belonged to the Psychoanalytic Institute until he resigned due to the concern of his fellow analysts that he was not "practicing psychoanalysis anymore." Berne was psychoanalytically trained; he studied under Federn. He underwent analysis with Erik Erikson. He was firmly grounded in the psychoanalytic movement at a time when it was experiencing a number of schisms into different schools. His writings show the influence of his teachers and contemporaries. The psychiatric literature contains a number of articles delineating Berne's theories. They are influenced by the theories of Freud, Adler and Jung among others. Berne was also well grounded in the traditional classical literature. Mythology and Biblical tradition show up in his writings. For instance, the universal concepts of the multiplicity of man's view of himself, fate, mythical heroes in drama, are apparent in the concepts of Ego States, Script, and drama ("all the world's a stage"). Berne has always been conscious of the debt he owes to the people in his background and the people with whom he associated. He acknowledges the fact that beyond his conceptualization of Ego States and Structural Analysis, much of the theory of T.A. was developed in the seminars by the joint efforts of the patients and the professional people who attended. "The Seminar" is a key process in the formation and development of T.A. Theory. The original seminar occurred spontaneously and consisted of Berne, David Kupfer and a social work supervisee, Joe Concannon. It met in Carmel, California, and was gradually attended by more and more people interested in Berne's approach. Finally the seminars became the place where all the subsequent materials on T.A. were worked over. Many of the people involved in the early seminars later published their own articles and books on the additions to the theory of T.A. as they were constructed. Among these people are John Dusay (Egograms), Claude Steiner (Script Matrix), Stephen Karpman (Drama Triangle), Robert and Mary Goulding (Decisions) and Jacqui Schiff (Passivity and T.A. treatment of psychotics).

By Berne's own account he developed the notions of "Ego States" and "Structural Analysis" in his years of practice as an Army psychiatrist in the late 1940s. In the Army he began experimenting with group treatment. By 1957 he had developed enough of his theory to present a paper at the Western regional meeting of the American Group Psychotherapy Association in Los Angeles. The title of this paper was "Transactional Analysis: A New and Effective Method of Group Treatment." The same year he published an article in the *American Journal of Psychotherapy*, called "Ego States in Psychotherapy." Each one of his theories were tested out in "The Seminar."

Through the seminars, Berne's various professional positions, the *Transactional Analysis Bulletins*, and other professional contacts, his ideas began to reach a larger professional and lay audience. Some of the books by Berne, and others, have been picked up by the public and have become bestsellers. This last fact has forced professionals all over the country and the world to take notice of the theories and to develop their own professional expertise to meet the queries and demands of their clients.

By 1976, there were Seminars in most of the major cities of the United States, in some of the Latin American and European countries and in Canada. By the time the twelfth International Transactional Analysis Association meeting was held in San Francisco in 1976, the membership of the Association had grown to over 10,000 members. A growing membership is occurring in other countries outside the United States. Aside from the annual summer meeting of the ITAA, there is now a Winter Congress of Advanced Members, a European Conference, and a Pan-American Conference. The meetings are for the purpose of examining advanced members, presenting papers, and conducting workshops in the field of Transactional Analysis. All of the meetings and seminars are open to all persons who express an interest in T.A. and who desire to learn about it (or contribute to it).

Membership

Membership in the ITAA is represented by three classes or levels. The first level is that of Regular Member. This membership level implies that the person has taken the T.A. 101 course. Clinical membership involves a minimum of two years training in a T.A. Institute under the supervision of a Teaching Member. It requires that the candidate take a written examination and present himself to a Board of Examiners for an Oral Examination based upon the presentation of tape recordings of his work, a thorough review of his knowledge and a defense of his style of work. The Teaching Member level of membership involves three or more years of supervised work wherein the person is himself training Clinical Members and teaching in the community. The examination involves presenting himself before several boards of Advanced Teaching Members of the ITAA. Each of these levels of membership is defined in terms of the numbers of hours of experience and numbers and kinds of experiences. There are a number of Institutes throughout the world where these training experiences may be acquired. A large part of the technique of treatment is carried out via demonstrations, practicum courses, workshops, marathons and personal therapy.

The T.A. literature continues to develop and grow. In addition to the *Transactional Analysis Journal*, which is published four times a year, there is a *Script*: Newsletter, a *British T.A. Journal* and a large number of books and pamphlets. Articles in other publications and journals are rapidly appearing. Much of the literature in T.A. is designed to interest the lay person.

Transactional Analysis Theory

(Basic framework)

Human motivation is viewed differently in T.A. than in most other approaches to psychotherapy. Besides stressing the biogenetic drives related to survival, T.A. also stresses the basic human needs which are directly related to the everyday behavior of the individuals. It is postulated that time is structured by each individual in terms of basic hungers: Stroke hunger, Structure hunger, Excitement hunger, Recognition hunger, and Leadership hunger. Stroke hunger is an outgrowth of the original contact hunger (see Bowlby) of the child. The child's need to be physically close, held, rocked and breathed upon by empathic persons is pivotal. Physical contact and the exchange of heat, the warmth of another living body are considered to be a most valued source of Strokes. A Stroke is defined as "a unit of recognition, such as 'Hello!'" (Berne, 1964: 15). Basically, all of the "hungers" listed, come under the rubric of "Strokes."

Structure hunger defines the dilemma of what to do with 24 hours a day, 7 days a week, 52 weeks a year. Most people in most societies have surplus time which has to be filled in some way. T.A. postulates that the most stimulating or exciting ways of filling time are usually the most valued by human beings. Most of the theory in T.A. is based on the understanding that much of human behavior (at least in modern society) is aimed at the structuring of time in interesting and exciting ways. Eric Berne defines the structuring of time in six ways: he places them in a hierarchy of importance for weight or value of Strokes (Berne, 1975: 22). These are Withdrawal, Rituals,[6] Pastimes, Activities, Games (interpersonal), and Intimacy or Authenticity (*Communitas* as in Turner, *I-Thou* as in Buber). Among the most common ways for exchanging Strokes are Games, and among the most exciting and rewarding are interpersonal intimacy or communitas. Basic in T.A. is the thesis that the need for excitement is so great in humans that a drama underlies every human interaction. This claim was explicated by Stephen Karpman (1968) in his theory of fairy tales and the Drama Triangle. Much of T.A. treatment is directed at delineating the individual motivation underlying Game Playing and the Drama Triangle. This is achieved through a process known as Script Analysis.

(Script theory)

Most dependency behavior and lack of autonomous functioning is seen as the result of each person's investment in a life Script, or its alternative Counterscript. The Script is an implicit plan for one's life established at an early age by each person as a way of getting his needs met in the world of his childhood. It is seen from the point of view of the life position in which he finds himself. The life position is based on early decisions about oneself and others involving the view of OK-ness and NOT OK-ness. It takes the form of "I am (or am not) OK," "you are (or are not) OK." The life position sets out the options the young person sees in his world, and sets the limits of his general *world view* (see Frames of Reference ff.). It sets the plan he will make an effort to fulfill throughout his own life. The Counterscript is based on instructions from parental figures about how to be OK or not OK with the parental figures and thus get Stroked. The life plan demanded by a person's Script may include anything from "dropping dead" or "going crazy" to "almost *always* succeeding (and failing)" or "growing old alone," or "*always* winning at any cost." (Most Scripts involve absolutes like "never," "always.") Each Script provides means of fulfilling time with the drama that avoids boredom and gives the person's life a direction, however painful the plot may prove to be.

Instead of uncovering repressed traumas in the person's history, the treatment *is aimed at identifying the illusions governing the person's present actions.* The decisions based on the illusions shape a person's life course as though he were playing out a drama on a stage. Script action or drama is closely associated with the playing of Games which are a series of Duplex Transactions. The Transactions occur at two different levels of communication simultaneously: the social level, and the psychological level. Each Game has a Switch or unexpected twist which leads to a Payoff. The Payoff is a particular state such as guilt, depression or anger. These states of being, or "feelings" are referred to as Stamps because they are collected in the same way as the trading stamps were collected for trading-off on items. The kind of feeling Payoff the person collects, i.e., the brand of Stamps, define his Racket. It is thought that a person will collect his particular brand of Stamps, in order to get the intermediate Payoff (depression, guilt, anger, despair, etc.) which if repeated over and over again, over time will bring about the long-term Payoff or Script Payoff of "going crazy," "killing myself," "getting in jail" or other less Tissue-damaging Payoffs.

(Degree of damage)

Both Games and Scripts are seen as occurring in individuals in a matter of degree. Some person's Games and Scripts will be First Degree, others Second Degree, and others Third Degree. The Third Degree usually involves bodily harm of some nature. Third Degree Games and Scripts are seen as eventually leading to untimely death, and range from frankly suicidal or homicidal goals, to more covert self-destructive goals such as psychosomatic illnesses, imprisonment, drugs, alcohol, smoking, etc. The aim of Script Analysis is to make the person aware of his Life Plan and how he is living it out. Processes involve sharing freely with the person all of the tools and information which is secured through the Script Analysis and Game Theory. As a result of this strategy, T.A. is a highly confrontive treatment mode.

(Decisions)

Once a person is aware of his Life Plan, the Games and Rackets and Payoffs which constitute his Script, he is faced with deciding what he wishes to do with this information. The Theory of Decisions and Redecisions (Goulding, 1972:62) is another aspect of T.A.

theory. This involves clarifying early Decisions made on the basis of faulty or child level data and illusions about the world. It requires that the individual make a new decision around this material. It is the prerogative of the patient to decide the need for these kinds of life changes.

Transactional Analysis is a Contractual form of treatment in which the patient specifies that which he wishes to change, and the therapist indicates his acceptance of the Contract to bring about the change, and the conditions under which he will work with the patient. The treatment relationship comes to an end when the Contract is fulfilled, unless the Contract is amended, a new Contract made, or the relationship is reopened on the initiative of the client.

(Contracts)

Contracts in Transactional Analysis Treatment are patterned on legal instruments (Steiner, 1971; 1975: 244). A Contract involves an explicit agreement between a patient and a therapist which states the goal of the treatment during each phase of the process. They can be Hard or Soft in nature. The former are contracts which are explicitly measurable in terms of outcome: such as increasing one's income, changing living arrangements, effecting a divorce. The latter involves less measurable entities such as "liking myself better," "differentiating between mad and scared," "learning to be less rigid." Steiner points out that there are four aspects to contracts: Mutual Consent, Valid Consideration, Competency and Lawful Object. The basic transactions of the first are: (1) a request for treatment, (2) an offer of treatment and (3) acceptance of treatment. The Valid Consideration refers to benefits conferred upon the client by the therapist, and vice versa, which may be bargained for and eventually agreed upon. Competency implies that the mental faculties of both parties are not impaired or impoverished by age, brain damage, or drugs, i.e., not coming to a session inebriated on the part of either. Lawful Object infers that the contract is not in violation of the law, not against public policy or morals. A more complete discussion of the contract in therapy can be found in Steiner's *Games Alcoholics Play* (1971: 106-112). Rogers (1969) addresses himself to the issues of contractual therapy and education. Contracts are a pivotal issue in Transactional Analysis Treatment.

One of the major implications of the contractual nature of T.A.

treatment is the philosophy of equality in the treatment process. The therapist is OK and so is the client. This means that a great deal of time in the treatment is devoted to the two individuals sharing a common Frame of Reference, a common understanding of what constitutes "psychopathology," and what must be done in order to "cure it." Therefore a great deal of information-sharing occurs as part of the process. Persons involved in T.A. become well grounded in the principals of the theory, and become well aware of their own problems within that Frame of Reference. The philosophy assumes that the patient, given enough time and the appropriate environment, is capable of learning the theory, and of changing his world view in those areas in which he sees he needs to change. They are apt to have "homework" and "assignments" of new ways of behaving to experiment with so they can compare their old ways with their new ways. This is part of a therapeutic operation which is called gaining Permission. Permission is effective in proportion to the amount of Protection offered by the therapeutic environment and the effectiveness or Potency of the therapist. A major goal of most persons involved in T.A., either as patients or as therapists, is to be more effective, i.e., more Potent in their functioning. *Potency* then is a highly valued quality in this frame of reference. Potency is related to the ability of the individual to recognize his own motivations, and to control the Cathexis of energy in his operations. This implies the will to focus or concentrate psychic energy in a part of one's personality or on a given object (Berne, 1963b: 146).

(Structural analysis)

Based on a General Systems theory approach to psychotherapy (Von Bertalanffy, 1968), the early foundations of T.A. found its form in Structural Analysis. This is a process devised by Berne (1963b:241) of identifying Ego States in each person. Berne defined an Ego State as "a coherent system of feelings with its related set of behavior patterns." In this systematic approach of looking at persons, he identified three such Ego States: the *Parent*, the *Adult*, and the *Child*. Typically, they are drawn with the Parent on top, the Adult in the middle, and the Child on the bottom (Figure 2). The Parent represents exactly the values, prejudices, prescriptions, advice and instructions on how these should appear in behavior, and what will happen if they do not. The Adult is the part of the personality

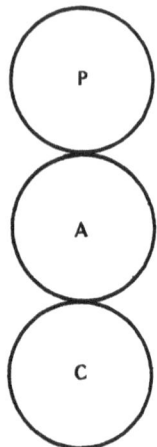

Figure 1-2. THE EGO STATES

which is the data recording, data retrieval and decision-making part of the personality. It acts as a computer, recording data and using it for computing future events. The Child constitutes that part of the individual which expresses the feelings, attitudes and behaviors which actually existed in that person up to the age of six or seven years. Though similar conceptually to the notions of Ego, Superego and Id, they differ in that each Ego State is an actual living and breathing personality.

The Cathexis of energy in a particular Ego State is manifest in the way in which a person feels, thinks or acts in a given situation. The Cathecting of an Ego State means that the Ego State is activated in that particular instant. When a person activates Parent, it is from that operational center that the person functions just then. One of the goals of T.A. is to learn the potential of one's Ego States, and to change the manner in which a person activates these Ego States. It is a basic assumption in T.A. that many of the behavioral difficulties in which people find themselves result from inappropriate Cathexis of a particular Ego State for a particular situation, e.g., telling a "dirty joke" at a formal occasion, or laughing aloud in a prayer service.

(The development of ego states)

The Ego States are seen as further subdivided in terms of the developmental stages or phases through which an individual passes in the first six years of his life. This aspect of the theory has its roots in the Freudian model and parallels the Pigetian model of child development. The Ego States are seen both structurally and functionally. Structurally there will be first, second, and third order Structural Analysis. This follows the development of the child (see Figure 1-3). Functional Analysis (see Figure 1-4) follows the kinds of behaviors one is apt to observe operationally in looking at or in hearing a person. (Third order will not be discussed here.) Developmentally these Ego States are seen to emerge in the child in approximately the following sequence. At birth the child is only C_1 (Natural Child). The A_1 (Adult in the Child, also known as the Little Professor) begins to develop sometime in the later half of the first year of life. The P_1 (Parent in the Child or Adapted Child) starts formation sometime around age three and continues through to age six. Overlapping this and beginning development between two and three years of age is the A_2 (Adult) and the P_2 (Parent) takes shape and starts development around four or five years. It can be represented schematically in the following manner after Gedo and Goldberg (1973) and Haykin (1976). (See Figure 1-5)

(Treatment process)

It is a major premise of T.A. that structurally and functionally, everyone has the same Ego States and is capable of applying the theory of Transactional Analysis to his problems. It is only motivation or inclination which limits the willingness of the individual to change his life patterns. For this reason, most T.A. therapists do not separate people in terms of categories (women's groups, older persons, schizophrenics, etc.). People are usually put into treatment groups in a random manner. The process of therapy is much the same for all persons following somewhat the same format: first persons learn the language of Transactional Analysis so that the therapist and all members of the group share the same group culture and language. Secondly, Structural Analysis is focused on and the issues of defining Ego States proceeds. This is done by a process

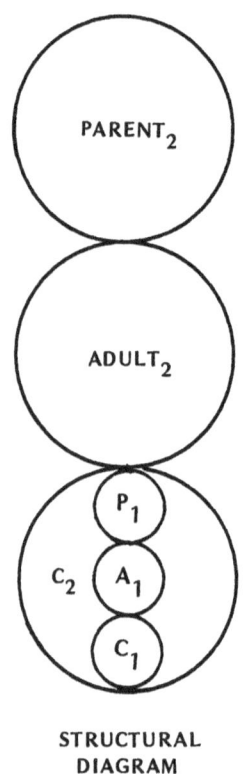

STRUCTURAL
DIAGRAM

Figure 1-3. EGO STATES.

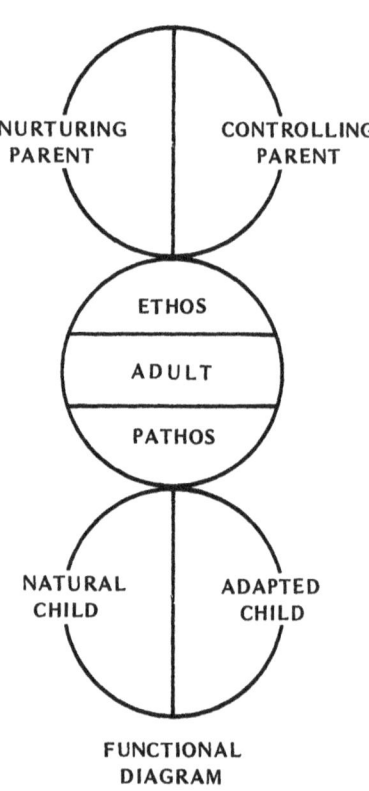

FUNCTIONAL
DIAGRAM

Figure 1-4. EGO STATES.

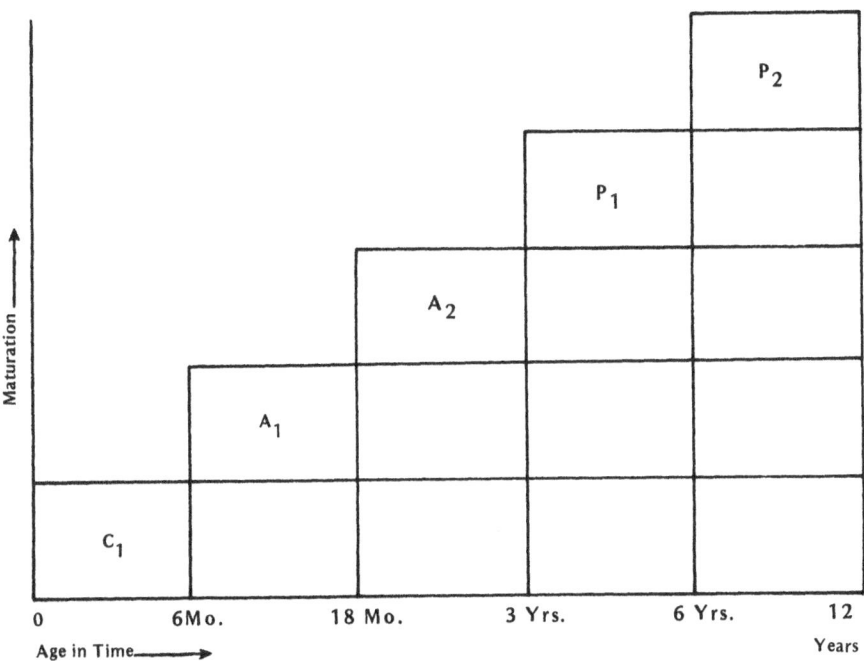

Figure 1-5. MATURATION OF EGO STATES.

called Decontamination and Reinclusion. Contamination between Ego States exists when the boundaries between them overlap (see Figure 1-6) or, when at the behavioral level, the subject misidentifies the content or actions of one Ego State as belonging to another Ego State. Exclusion implies that a person is not aware of the existence of an Ego State and never Cathects it (Figure 1-6). Structural Analysis is followed by Transactional Analysis. This process involves an analysis of the Ego States *from* which the Transactions occur and of the Ego States *to* which these Transactions are directed (Figure 1-7). This is the communication theory part of the process. Following this, or consonant with these first two operations, will be the processes of Script Analysis and recapitulation of old Decisions. The completion of a Contract constitutes a Cure. Therefore, in the course of T.A. treatment there will be a series of "cures" based on the completion of a series of Contracts. In the final analysis, the person eventually achieves what may constitute a major change in his Basic Script and hence in his *world view*.

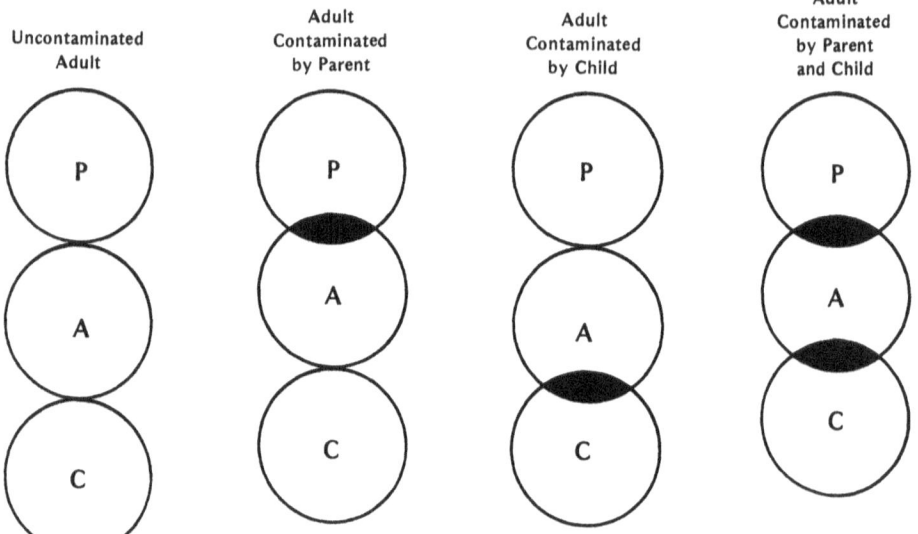

Figure 1-6. CONTAMINATIONS.

The implications of T.A. for the individual are that there is *no* vast and unbridgeable gap of status and understanding between the therapist and the client. There is a body of knowledge and a *common language* which can be used by both in the process of the person's treatment. This does not mean that the patient gains a professional education in this process, what it does mean is that professional concepts have been expressed in a vocabulary which is readily understandable by the layman. For Berne:

> . . . there was no such thing as a weak or defective Adult ego state, but only Adult ego states which had inadequate or inaccurate data about the world, or Adult ego states which were not sufficiently cathected ("Plugged in"). Since everyone has an Adult everyone is entitled to certain kinds of consideration. (Holland, 1974: 364)

GENERAL SYSTEMS THEORY

As proposed, Transactional Analysis is a General Systems Theory approach to the study of human personality and human interactions. What is General Systems Theory? Within the past fifteen to twenty years, considerable interest has arisen around the possibility of formulating a methodological approach to all of the sciences (hard and soft), that would supply the researcher with a *common language* and a set of *common tools* with which other researchers in these fields could communicate (T. A. fits this criterion). It is hoped that the development of a general systems theory will provide a basis for the integration of scientific knowledge across a broad spectrum of disciplines (Buckley, 1968; Kast and Rosenzweig, 1970; Lederer, 1968; Von Bertalanffy, 1968; Burton, 1957; and others). The general systems theory may act as a means for the transfer of principles from one field to another.

A system is described as an "organized or complex whole: an assemblage or combination of the things or parts forming a complex or unitary whole" (Kast and Rosenzweig, 1970: 110). It is also defined as "sets of elements standing in interaction" (Von Bertalanffy, 1968: 37). A system is more than the sum of its parts, it indicates the way the parts operate in relation to one another (Lederer, 1968: 88), for example, Ego States. Von Bertalanffy who coined the phrase "general systems theory," says that it can serve as a regulatory device to distinguish analogies and homologies, that is, meaningless similarities and meaningful transfer of models from one system to another (Lederer, 1968: 80). He follows this by saying that the theory allows for a new model of man as an active personality system with emphasis on creativity and individual differences, and further, that life is not a comfortable setting down in preordained grooves of being. At best life is an *elan vital* where man is inexorably driven to higher forms of existence. "Man is not a passive receiver of stimuli coming from an external world, but in a very concrete sense creates his world" (Lederer, 1968: 192-194). Along these same lines, Levi-Strauss suggests that man's intellect is such that he proposes a Parkinson's law, i.e., the human mind expands and elaborates cultural detail to fill whatever "space" is available (Strauss, 1971: 225).

Closed and Open

Systems are either Open or Closed. Some systems are closed in terms of their surrounding environment, allowing no interaction between the system and the environment beyond its boundaries. Biological and social systems are open and are in constant interaction

FRIEND I   FRIEND II

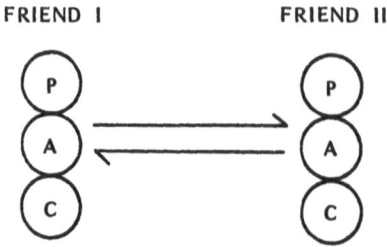

I: Did you go to the
   store today?

II: Yes, three times.

COMPLEMENTARY

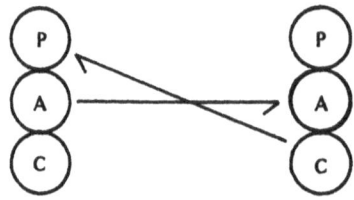

I: Did you go to the
   store today?

II: Why do you always
    bug me about where
    I've been?

CROSSED

Social level:
   I: It's time to fix
      dinner
   II: Yes it is

Psychological level:
   I: I don't want to
      cook today

   II: Why do I always
       end up doing it?

ULTERIOR

Figure 1-7. TRANSACTIONS.

with their environments (see note 6, Boulding's Hierarchy). There are a number of principles which hold for both. Von Bertalanffy holds to the notion that the various fields of science have evolved parallel ideas. He sees this parallelism as providing an opportunity to formulate and develop principles which hold for systems in general. One of these ideas is that of feedback control networks or cybernetic systems.

Feedback Control Networks

Cultural and subcultural groups are examples of open systems which are characterized by an exchange of *energy* in the form of *information* with the environment (Hall, 1956: 81-92). Exchange of information is by *feedback control mechanisms* whereby part of the output of the system is fed back to the input in order to affect future outputs. Negative feedback systems such as systems of punishment, praise or sanctions in societal groups (deviation counteracting feedback networks). Positive feedback systems (deviation amplifying feedback networks) such as praise, punishment, rewards, etc., present the other type of feedback. All systems that are self-regulating and goal-directed (teleological) have both positive and negative feedback control mechanisms (Maruyama, 1963: 304ff).

Other aspects of general systems theory are "networks" and "information." These concepts are useful in the study of societies because networks are self-modifying through the input of information. Learning and purpose are seen in terms of internal rearrangement which are relevant to goal-seeking. Complex feedback networks deal with "messages" and "symbols." A network is described as:

> . . . a system of physical objects (people, ego states, items) interacting with each other in such a manner that a change in the state of some of the elements is followed by a determinate pattern of changes in other related elements. (Deutch, 1948: 392)

An example of this is the internal dialog between Ego States resulting in a transaction with another person, resulting in learning occurring.

Rites-of-Passage

Values, consciousness, will, autonomy, freedom and coherence are all concepts which can be looked at through the cybernetic (feedback) model (Deutch, 1948: 399). Societies, communities, healing rites, are all complex learning networks. Systems tend to maintain a "steady state" (equilibrium) and have internal mechanisms to assure that the steady state is maintained, or restored when overloaded or assaulted. Examples of rituals used for returning a system (society) to its steady state would be the *Naven* (Bateson, 1958: 175). The *Naven* ritual and the *Gahuku Gama* (Kenneth Read in lecture notes, 1972), and *Pigs for the Ancestors* (Rappaport), and *Healing Rituals at Cathexis* (see Chapter IIIff.) are systematic and stereotyped activities engaged in by persons in these societies. The standard expressions and exchanges experienced in these rituals allow for the participants to release tension (energy) and to say things that they would not otherwise be allowed to say. The result of the release of tension (energy) and the ritual expressions restore the groups to equilibrium. Ritual process is systematic and logical.

The logic of systems analysis is to (1) supply the tool for disclosing the process of disorganization (entropy) inside the system; (2) supply tools for returning the system to a steady state (Raymond, 1950: 157); and (3) supply a knowledge of the constraints in the system whereby alternatives for decision-making are limited. Constraints (see options ff.) are those activities and relationships which reduce alternatives and thence the possible outcomes of the interactions. Nadel gives several examples of self-regulation (constraints) in societies he has studied (Nadel, 1953: 405). The more people involved, and the more complex the conditions surrounding the goals, the more difficult the decision process, and the more complicated the constraint systems. The more paradoxical the situation, the less logical it is.

Several other general systems theories involve *game theory* which is a branch of *decision theory* and *model building* (Buckley, 1968: 490-513), (Rappaport and Horvath, 1959: 75). In game theory, the study is made of the decision-making which must be made not only in the face of uncertainty, but also must take into account the presence of other decision makers in the system. Some or all of these decision makers' interests may be opposed to those of the initiator, thus giving rise to *conflict*. (For instance, the internal dialog between the Parent and the child inside an individual, or other types of communication.) In the mathematical framework, the competition is rational between two or more antagonists for maximum gain and minimum loss. In human game theory often the stakes are higher, and not quantifiable (Berne, 1964).

Models

Models are abstractions of the real world; a model makes possible the identification and manipulation of variables, thus revealing the problem areas in the organization being studied. It is then possible with the use of a model to compare the actual system with the simulated system. The structural analysis model and transactional analysis models of Transactional Analysis are examples of general systems theory. Model building involves a knowledge of *boundaries*. A boundary is that line which delineates what is inside and what is outside the system. Tangible boundaries are, for example, the skin, the outside of a bottle, the number of people in a group. The definition of an Ego State is an intangible boundary, the multiple roles of a person and various status positions are such examples. The operational definition of *boundary* is "the line forming a closed circle around selected variables where there is less energy across the boundary as within the boundary" (Chin, 1969: 300) (cf. Ego States, Contamination, Exclusion).

Energy: The identification and analysis of how energy operates in a system is a major focus of a systems analysis. Tensions, conflict, stress and strain lead to two kinds of activity: those which directly alter the structure itself and bring about change, and those which do not alter the structure. *Change* is a derived consequence of how well the parts of the system fit together or how well the system fits in with the other surrounding and interacting systems. The source of change lies primarily in the structural stress or strain (energy) internally created or externally induced. The process of change is itself a process of energy reduction, or energy increment. The goals and directions of the system are emergent from the structures in the system or from the imposed sources of stress. Goals are often analyzed as set by vested interests of one part of the system (Chin, 1969: 309) (such as Parent values vs. Child needs). The cybernetic model shows the place of tension-reduction, response-to-stimulation, motivation and energy allocation within a larger unit of relationships of the components. It emphasizes time, feedback and information (communication) (Shibutani, 1968: 330).

In conclusion, this chapter addressed itself to the concepts underlying this study. They include the theory of Transactional Analysis in summary, the concepts of cognition, adaptation, psychopathology, transformation, ritual and symbolic expression. Also included is a brief discussion of the Human Potential Movement and theory about Healing Rituals. A general discussion of the General Systems Theory completes the framework of this section. The following chapter addresses itself to a discussion of the methodology which was followed in this study.

NOTES AND REFERENCES

1. The concept of *Altered States of Consciousness* covers a wide array of human experiences. They may be divided into drug-induced states and nondrug-induced states. They range from comments of peak excitement described by such words as "ineffable," "unbelievable," "incredible," through light trances to dream states. The list includes drug-induced experiences with Lysergic Acid diethylamide 25, Peyote, tobacco, Methamphetamine and other chemical agents. The "Aha" phenomenon of the Gestalt Therapy experience may be included too. Meditational experiences, and flashes of intuitive knowing such as described by some of the scientists who have made new and exciting intellectual connections are also included. In essence, any human experience which is nonordinary, nonlinear, nonanalytical and reportedly not explicable with "ordinary language" may appear under the rubric of "Altered States of Consciousness" (Tart, 1969; Lilly, 1972; Smith, 1975).

2. Each culture must provide answers for what can be called "The Four Common Human Problems": Only when one has answers to them can the human animal function with predictability in an otherwise chaotic world (Becker, 1964: 12). The problems are: (1) what kind of reaction is one to expect from volatile human objects? (2) what are the supports and limitations of my powers? (3) in what sequential schema is my action to be embedded? (4) how can I best orient my action to safety and to maximum satisfaction? (cf. Kluckhohn, 1950).

3. Transference and Countertransference. These have historically been the bugaboos of traditional therapists. This phenomenon refers to the exchange of power which occurs in therapeutic relationships. Patients often wish to invest therapists with authority and responsibility which they are unwilling to accept, and reenact early childhood scenes with the therapist taking the role of the person in authority. In T.A. treatment it is often the policy to accept the patient's investment of power (transference) to the extent that it is possible to use the power for change. This may involve the therapist in entering the Game and playing it out consciously in order for the patient to see what happens when they initiate a Game.

4. References useful as introductions to the theory behind each of the schools of therapy and encounter methods are: Gibb (1970) (general review), Perls, Hefferline and Goodman (1951) (Gestalt); Schutz (1967) (Esalen Encounter); Lowen (1970:ff) (Bioenergetics); Adam Smith (1975) (general overview).

5. Berne (1972: 22) defines Ritual as a "safe form of social action." He says "These are highly stylized interchanges which may be informal or may be formalized into ceremonies which are completely predictable. The transactions which make up Ritual convey little information but are more in the nature of signs of mutual recognition. The units of a Ritual are called Strokes, by analogy with the way in which infants are given recognition by their mothers. Rituals are programmed from outside by tradition and social custom. Ritual, as a form of structuring time, is intended in a very limited sense by Berne and does not convey the depth or breadth that is conveyed by the definition in anthropology, as noted earlier in the chapter.

6. Kenneth Boulding has provided a taxonomy of systems (1956: 197-208): they are: (1) Static Structures—at the level of frameworks, e.g., the Universe; (2) Clockworks—simple dynamic systems with predetermined motions, unaffected by outside conditions; (3) control mechanism systems, e.g., thermostats, self-regulating and dependent upon their own feedback systems—these are open systems, and are seen as at the level of the cell; (5) genetic societal level—which may be like the level of the plant; (6) the animal system—is characterized by increased mobility and interaction with the environment; (7) the human level—this is also a system with self-awareness, goal-directed behavior and the ability to utilize language and symbols in interaction with the system outside its own boundaries; (8) the social system or systems of human organization— here is a consideration for the content and meaning of messages, the nature and dimensions of value systems, the transcription of images into historical record, the areas of art, music and poetry, and the complete gamut of human emotions; (9) the transcendental systems—which complete the classification of levels. These are the ultimates, the absolutes, the inescapable unknowables and they also exhibit systematic structure and relationships and are in open interaction with other systems.

Chapter II

METHODS

I will say no more about it. Words do not express thoughts very well. They always become a little different immediately they are expressed, a little distorted, a little foolish. And yet it also pleases me and seems right that what is of value and wisdom to one man seems nonsense to another.

—Herman Hesse

INTRODUCTION

Knowledge, its nature and how it is acquired, is a central issue in all academic endeavors. This section discusses how the knowledge about the Cathexis community was acquired. It includes a discussion of what techniques were used, and how they were used. Included also is a discussion of the process of diagnosis.

There are many methods for gathering data. The range of choice is limited only by the creativity and investment of the researcher. There is no such thing as *the* scientific method (Naroll, 1970: 25). There are many models for eliciting information, none of which is adequate if used by itself. The subculture of Anthropology has long stressed close, intimate relationships with the informants and their social scene. This has raised conflicts around the issue of whether traditional field work methodology is adequately *scientific*. Whether large quantities of data make up for carefully designed sampling techniques is another aspect of this conflict. To bring about a meeting of both ends in this conflict it is now acceptable to include quantitative data-collecting in the traditional participant-observation approach.

HYPOTHESIS TESTING

The basic reason for gaining knowledge is to test hypotheses. The focus lies in finding out if a theoretical framework about a specific issue is correct. The methods used in this study were chosen to assist in the discovery of information about psychiatric healing rituals and the experiences of the persons involved in the Cathexis community. The hypothesis being tested is addressed to the following questions. Does the Transactional Analysis model of psychotherapy affect a change from a psychopathological world view to a "normal" world view?

> Persons involved in Transactional Analysis Treatment will show changes in (1) personality profiles, (2) World View, and (3) personal constructs about Self and Significant others.

The close participant observation of a western psychiatric setting will reveal specific parallels in ritual and symbolic action with others across cultures.

EXPERIMENTAL VERSUS EXPERIENTIAL
DATA GATHERING

Experiments, if well done, are persuasive and are suited to rigorous hypothesis testing. The obstacles to elegant experimental research design in the field are large. The control of variables is often of stupendous proportions. Samples and appropriate control devices frequently do not fit the field. Sometimes the carefully devised experimental plan falls through once the investigator has reached the field. The essence of the experimental approach is the control group. This study utilizes a blend of quantitative data collection methods with experiential methods. It is not an experimental study.

Psychological Data Collection Techniques

The disagreement about the validity of psychological data gathering methods as against systematic field work observation techniques continues. There are risks involved in either choice. On one hand, the projective and other psychological instruments are being touted as good ethnoscientific tools. On the other hand, it is argued that the test materials do not measure up to even minimal common sense criteria of adequacy in data collection. Whatever the disagreements, the ethnographer is also faced with having to deal with the issues of personal bias and desire to "prove" the hypothesis. To minimize this issue, I have settled on a blending of field observation techniques with psychological test methods. The field work data was obtained through the means of participant-observation methods, personal experience, taped and written interviews, verbal accounts, pencil and paper responses to a standard questionnaire (the Life Script Questionnaire) and two psychological tests, the Minnesota Multiphasic Inventory and the Semantic Differential.

Diagnosis

Diagnosis is a method for classifying phenomena related to the health-illness continuum. It establishes a lattice of criteria whereby correlated sets of characteristics (i.e., syndromes) can be lumped together under a standard rubric. Classifying is an essential process in science. The recognition·of natural groups of phenomena is prerequisite to explaining phenomenological processes.

Diagnosis allows the scientist to see certain groups of behaviors in any category. Categorizing symptoms, behaviors, etc., make possible the application of specific treatment strategies. It gives the scientist more specific information about the kinds of situations which will be used to bring about change. It is a type of classifying system which relates the type of psychopathology to the type of treatment required. In the diagnosis of psychopathology there are sociological, biological and psychological parameters. This makes the description in unitary terms impossible. Numerous criteria are involved.

(Lattice of Criteria)

A set of criteria for diagnosis of psychopathology, established by the International Congress of Psychiatry in 1957, appears in the *Diagnostic and Statistical Manual II*. It provides a symptom complex by which most Western Psychiatrists classify schizophrenia. These criteria are supported by various test materials, among which is the MMPI. This test was designed originally for the diagnosis of schizophrenia (see description of the test ff). The MMPI supplies some of the hard data by which developmental correlates and subtypes of schizophrenia can be identified. It has been a diagnostic tool for over 20 years and is still used as an adjunct to clinical diagnosis. Another set of diagnostic criteria, supplied by the Transactional Analysis approach, views personality as a system of Ego States in disequilibrium with each other or with other Ego States.

(The Diagnostic and Statistical Manual II)

The criteria in this manual for schizophrenia are as follows. A person with schizophrenia as a diagnosis will have: (1) *Delusions—* defined as a belief at variance with the beliefs or sentiments accepted in the cultural system to which the individual belongs (Leighton, 1965: 39) [as can be seen, the concept "delusion" is already subject to personal interpretation] (2) *Schizophrenic thinking—*the thought processes are dependent on inner fantasies of the individual and subject to wish-fulfillment. The concrete and symbolic are characteristically confused. Frequent misunderstanding of metaphor occurs with this type of thought process; (3) *Hallucinations—*the experiencing of sensory perceptions which are not validatable consensually by others present; (4) *Schizophrenic actions—*although schizophrenia is primarily a "thinking disorder," there are certain actions which are characteristic of some schizophrenics such as gesturing, posturing, autistic behaviors, physical and mental incapacitation and unexpected emotional explosions; (5) *Inappropriate affect—*manifested by either no show of emotion when such is expected by the milieu, or showing emotion not consonant with the context, e.g., laughing at a funeral; (6) *History—*age of onset of the symptoms, mode of onset, timing of onset, and family history.

(Transactional Analysis Definition and Diagnosis of Schizophrenia)

> Diagnosis is important. It is used to define the therapeutic problem and enables us to relate information about successful interventions from one patient to another. It provides therapists with a Frame-of-Reference to make it possible for them to communicate successfully with the patient. (Schiff, 1975: 72)

In some institutions and communities, diagnosis is used as a label for the persons in treatment. This is not the case at Cathexis. The diagnosis is used to deal with the problem which presents itself in the current interaction. That is, whatever the person is saying or doing at the moment is the source of the diagnosis for that moment. Since most of the clients in this setting carry the label of schizophrenic, it is important to understand what this means in this context. It is important to note that there is a difference in *what* is classified: people, or characterological states (which is relatively fixed) versus adaptational position, strategy, acts (recurring but situational and fluid). Diagnostic method can have deep theoretical, and even political implications. Diagnosis also includes some type of method for knowing what is happening to the person at the beginning of treatment as against what is going on at the end of treatment.

(T.A. Definition of Schizophrenia)

This is a General Systems Theory approach to personality and assumes that personality consists of three main parts: Parent, Adult and Child. Each of these parts of the personality presents a consistent pattern of feelings and experiences directly related to a corresponding consistent pattern of behavior. (For a complete discussion of the elements of the system see the preceding chapter section on T.A. and the glossary at the end of this thesis.) At Cathexis, schizophrenia is defined as characterized by:

> . . . a locked system of messages in the Parent, corresponding adaptations in the Child, and an Adult which is misinformed. . . . The adaptations are the result of reinforcement of adaptive response-patterns around survival issues such as strokes and feelings, which are maladaptive to the society generally or the needs of the individual. With a Child who perceives the pathology as necessary for survival, a Parent who confirms this, and an Adult unable to contradict it, the person has no exit from the system without external intervention. (Schiff, 1975: 75)

With a thorough understanding of this definition, diagnosis continues throughout any and all transactions and does not assume a concrete form or label. Behaviors are constantly and consistently diagnosed. Each time a person uses an Ego State inappropriately, or manifests some part of their thinking disorder, the behavior is fed back to him immediately. This process gives him a constant source of diagnostic information on his behavior. The T.A. diagnostic method then is processual. The participants are presented with frequent input on what is validatable (real) and what is not validatable (not real) as the process occurs. Any retreat to the old Frame of Reference which relates only to his internal experiences is confronted. Any response from an overadapted position, which excludes an Ego State in the transaction then becomes part of the diagnostic process and the treatment intervention. Schizophrenics have not had an adequate experiential validation of their own Frame of Reference and that of the external world to develop the mechanisms which "normals" use to adjust to discomfort in ways which relate to external reality. As noted, they have few criteria for judging what is concrete (real) and what is symbolic (not real).

(Problems of the Definition of
Schizophrenia)

There are a number of problems inherent in the definition of schizophrenia. Chief problems are the following issues: (1) many schizophrenics are highly intelligent people, research indicates that they are usually above the average population—this means they are often more intelligent and clever than most clinicians (personal communication, Dr. Doerr, Department of Psychology, U. W. Hospital); (2) they have a highly developed sense of intuition (Berne, 1971) and consequently overadapt to the personality of the clinician, quickly giving him what they intuit he wants from the interview— sometimes the diagnosis ends up being the projection of the clinician's personality on the patient; (3) diagnosis and definition of behaviors are often dependent on the clinician's response and attitudes towards the patient (Leighton, 1965: 60-62); (4) even bizarre behavior has its human qualities and can be overlooked depending on the context, or on the energy the clinician is investing in the process; (5) language, symbols and metaphors have special meanings, even for the clinician, and semantic difficulties arise in the diagnostic process; (6) a diagnosis is the result of a relationship between the clinician and the patient. If the clinician has ideosyncratic criteria for differentiating the concrete from the symbolic, then diagnosis is further complicated by the power issue. It can then have serious political and civil rights ramifications.

Summary of Diagnostic and
Definitional Issues

There are theoretically motivated types of classification which ought to be useful in supplying treatment strategies. There are arbitrary types of classification which are not likely to prove useful for treatment. Diagnostic and treatment strategies which focus only on classification of symptoms or characterological states are apt to miss the underlying dynamic structures. It is important throughout treatment that the person involved gain knowledge of the behaviors which are inherent in his psychopathology.

The Minnesota Multiphasic Personality Inventory

The MMPI has come to occupy a unique place among objective measurements of personality characteristics. Because of its popularity among clinicians, it has been used on a larger number of studies than any similar tool. It has been used as both a clinical instrument for classifying the individual patient and as a research tool for testing hypotheses. The general approach it represents, eliciting information by forced choice on the basis of sampling of verbal responses, has never won unanimous endorsement among behavioral scientists. However, it continues to occupy a prominent place in the literature.

Among the MMPI uses is the categorizing of responses. Items for each scale of the MMPI were selected by contrasting the responses of nonpsychiatric subjects with those of people who fit the particular clinically diagnosed category. In these analyses, more than 1,500 nonpsychiatric subjects were used; 774 visitors to the University of Minnesota hospitals, 265 "normal" clients from the University of Minnesota Testing Bureau, 265 WPA workers and 254 medical patients from the general wards of the University of Minnesota hospitals. More than 800 psychiatric patients constituted the clinical pool. Their responses constitute the various scales of the MMPI. Such categories as schizophrenia, hypochondriasis, depression, etc. were thus delineated. Through a testing and retesting process, a basic pool of items was assembled. These items showed a percentage frequency difference between the "normal" group and the criterion group (two or two and one half times the standard error). Further, a good many items in the basic pool were eliminated because they showed overlap in validity with some other clinical syndrome (Dahlstrom and Welsh, 1960).

As a part of the MMPI, effort was made to obtain detailed information from subjects. Selected persons were asked to respond in writing to four questions from Scale 8 (Sc) of the MMPI and to react to each question selected in terms of the *meaning* of the question. They were told to state what they *think* and *feel* about the question and why they answered it true or false. The purpose of this was to obtain further information on the presentation of the self at the beginning and at the end of a year's exposure to the treatment model. The questions selected for this purpose were #33, #196, #322, #359. These questions were selected on the basis of the research of item content for the scale done by Rorer (1963) and Lewis (1961). Scale 8 of the MMPI contains 78 items dealing with social alienation, isolation, complaints of family alienation, bizarre feelings, influence of external agents, peculiar bodily dysfunction and general dissatisfaction with self and life. This scale was developed on schizophrenic individuals and is used in the categorizing of the schizophrenic type. Persons who score high on this scale are seen by clinicians as misunderstood, alienated, anomic and peculiarly not a part of their social environment. They have been found to have basic questions about their own worth, and hold their identity in question. They are confused about how one goes about the business of being a socialized human being. They are frequently lacking in the fundamentals which are the key to successful relations with other human beings. Persons who score high on Scale 8 are usually withdrawn people, have few friends if any, and seem to spend much of their time alone. There are disturbances in thinking and communication skills. According to Butcher (1969: 294) typically, such a person "has problems which stem from the early establishment of an attitude of distrust toward the world. These are people who, as children, acquired a set to perceive other people as hostile, rejecting, and dangerous." They frequently have a pattern of unexpectedly striking out in anger. This pattern, when continued into adulthood, reinforces their general alienation from others. Further, according to Butcher (1969: 294), "these people are very difficult to work with psychotherapeutically because they cannot permit a focalization of issues, they never settle on anything long enough to allow a real coming to grips."

The semantic analysis was done to secure further information about the cognitive orientations of the informants and to find out if and why they answered the questions differently before and after a year of treatment. This portion of the tool was not completed by the subjects due to scheduling and other difficulties. The material which was obtained is included in the descriptive data in Chapter III.

Among the questions one might ask are, why use the MMPI? What is the psychologist trying to prove by the use of this type of analytical tool? What is the subject showing by making particular responses to certain questions? The MMPI is organized around a framework common in trait psychology. Its organization is thought to describe a structured approach to the subject's presentation of self. The MMPI reflects the individual's responses to the sets of questions which are arranged to represent certain ways of viewing the world. Added to the component of clinical judgment, the MMPI separates the category of schizophrenic from nonschizophrenic. It provides a set of categories by which persons who deviate from "normal" can be sorted out.

Given that schizophrenia is a way of perceiving the world, and dealing with it, the MMPI may be a tool for categorizing persons who fit this world view. It may be helpful though, to note that the MMPI typologies were developed on the basis of clinical categories already in use in the profession. This brings up the semantic issue, that is, the categories are based on the ways in which psychology views people, and not necessarily on the ways people view themselves, nor does it reflect the T.A. perspective. The categories are limited to the language of the diagnostician and are made on the basis of the symptoms as seen from the world view of the clinician. This factor has serious implications for issues in politics, civil rights and for treatment strategies because it gives the diagnostician an unusual and unfair power advantage.

At Cathexis, the MMPI is used as an adjunct to the clinical and the Transactional Analysis diagnoses. It provides a baseline profile for comparison over time of the individual with himself. In this study it is used for categorizing the individuals as schizophrenics and nonschizophrenics. It is used to demonstrate change in "personality profiles" over time. It is used for descriptive purposes as it sets parameters within which the persons in the study fall.

Semantic Differential Test

The Semantic Differential is a combination of controlled association and scaling procedures. The subject is provided with a concept to be differentiated and a set of bipolar adjectival scales against which to do it (Osgood, 1957). His only task is to indicate, for each item (pairing of a concept with a scale), the direction of his feeling about the concept and its intensity in a seven-step scale. From the myriad linguistic and nonlinguistic behaviors mediated by symbolic processes a sample is selected which is indicative of the ways that connotative meanings vary and are largely insensitive to other sources of variation. The measurement model allows the subject to judge a series of concepts (myself, my mother, etc.) against a series of bipolar, seven-step scales defined by verbal opposites (e.g., good-bad, strong-weak, hot-cold). The concept is given at the top of each sheet. The subject judges it against each successive scale by putting a check mark (x) in the appropriate position (e.g., +3 very good, +2 good, +1 slightly good, 0 neutral or neither, -1 slightly bad, -2 quite bad, -3 extremely bad). These particular quantifiers have been shown by Norman Cliff (1959) to yield approximately equal degrees of intensity. The term "concept" refers to the "stimulus" to which the subject's checking operation is a terminal "response." Although single words must often serve, a concept may require a noun phrase such as "my ideal self." It is evident that the concepts judged against a semantic differential may be varied in nature, and the type selected depends chiefly on the interests of the investigator (Osgood, 1957: 77).

When a sample of subjects judges a set of concepts against a set of adjectival scales in the semantic differential, a "cube" of data is generated. The rows in the cube are defined by the adjectival scales. The columns are defined by the concepts evaluated and the slices, from front to back, by the subject's responses. (See Figure 2-1) Each cell in this matrix of data represents the judgment of a particular concept against a particular scale by a particular subject. Each of the n slices represents the complete judgments of a single subject; each of the m columns represents the judgments by all subjects against all scales for a single concept; and each row represents the complete data for each of the k scales, all subjects ratings of all concepts against this scale (Osgood, 1957: 86-87). The Semantic Differential measures the connotative meanings of concepts in "semantic space."

"Semantic space" may be viewed as a three-dimensional space like a room. Imagine three sticks at right angles to each other, meeting in the center of the room and touching the walls, the floor and the ceiling. Each stick or axis is labeled x, y, z (Figure 2-2), and each axis is numbered from +3 to -3. The three dominant and independent factors which appear most often in factor analysis of such data "cubes" are an *Evaluative factor* (good-bad, pleasant-unpleasant), a *Potency factor* (strong-weak, hard-soft) and an *Activity factor* (slow-fast, excitable-calm). This means that there are three "directions" in semantic space which are regions of relatively high density, in the sense of many closely related modes of qualifying. These three "directions" tend to be orthogonal to each other. They are inde-

THE MEASUREMENT OF MEANING

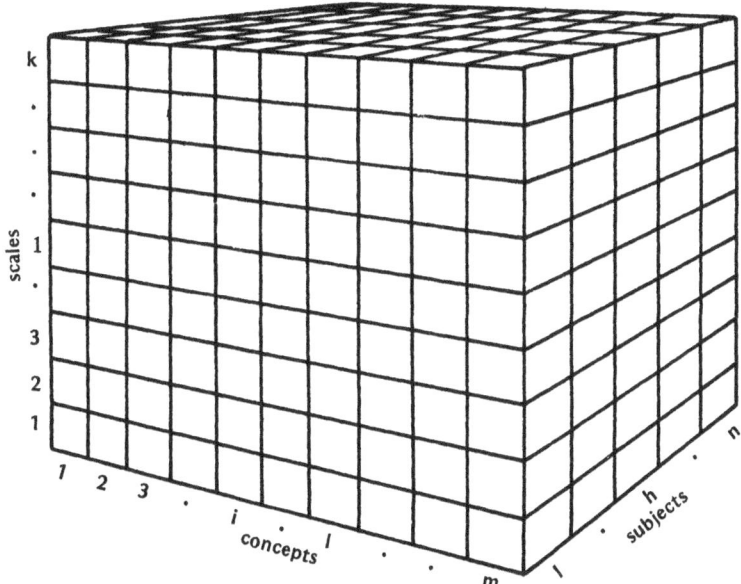

Figure 2-1. RECTANGULAR SOLID OF DATA generated by the semantic differential (from Osgood, THE MEASUREMENT OF MEANING, 1957:86-87).

pendently variable dimensions of meaning. These factors are also more reactive in nature than sensory, more broadly affective than discriminatively cognitive; thus, they are closer to the connotative than to the denotative aspects of meaning. The Semantic Differential then gives a view of the affective or emotional meaning, that is, the *feeling* sense of the concept to the subject.

In this study, the Semantic Differential was used descriptively. It was employed to show the change in the connotative view of certain concepts for the subjects. The expectation is that the connotative meaning of symbols such as myself, my life style, my mother, etc. would show change as a result of a twelve-month exposure to the Cathexis Community. Semantic Differentials were filled out by the subjects at the beginning of the study and one year later. It was also employed to show whether the world view and view of self as given in the life history questionnaire is the same as described by the

Semantic Differential. Differences will indicate a change in self system and in world view.

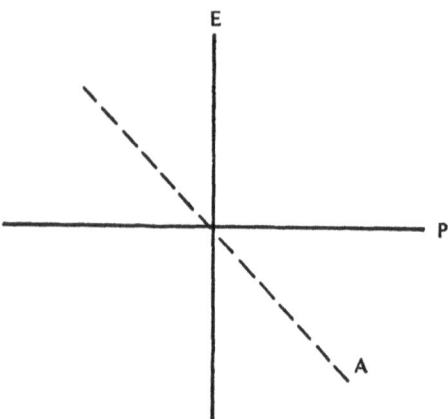

Figure 2-2. SEMANTIC SPACE (Osgood, 1964:171-200).

Life History Information and World View

Another source of world view and presentation of self is the Life Script Questionnaire. The questionnaire used in this study consists of 72 questions. Each question is designed to evoke specific information from the individual about his possible childhood view of himself and of his world and his family (known as Script or Protocol). The questions are arranged so that the subject will respond to each question in one sentence or less. The Life Script Questionnaire is constructed to follow the protocol suggested by Eric Berne (1972: 425-427). It is designed to be used as a shortcut to treatment. It gives a "quick way of finding the active elements in a person's script so that its tragic progress can be headed off as quickly and effectively as possible" (Berne, 1972: 426). Accompanying the questionnaires were interviews with selected individuals. Further information on life history and world view was obtained during the participant-observation periods with the study group when they were in their groups and at drop-in and in their living situations, in other daily experiences at Cathexis.

In general, the Life History Information was devised to complete the following information:

1. Prenatal and conceptual information—pregnancy planned, unplanned, parents' attitudes towards the pregnancy.

2. Birth data—family myth about the birth, ordinal position, parent's attitudes, health and needs, finances, other persons in the family, siblings, grandparents, and extended family attitudes about the subject.

3. Family membership—descriptions of personality of family members, attitudes towards the world, the subject, major life goals.

4. Developmental history, description of self, major life crises, minor life crises.

5. Life span, plans for life, fantasies about life span, projected successes and failures, suicide and thoughts about death, personal mythical hero or heroine, and protocols.

6. Self-protective and self-destructive experiences. Major illnesses, minor illnesses, periods of activity and lack of activity in life.

7. Education and occupational history, past experiences, and future plans.

8. Housing experiences since birth, present living circumstances, future plans for life style.

9. Summary of experiences of the Self at present, and projected expectations of the experience of the self in the future.

One of the criteria for including persons in the study was their initial willingness, and capability to fill out one of these questionnaires. This stipulation eliminated persons who were too incapacitated at the time to be able to respond with any paper and pencil test materials.

EXPERIENTIAL SOURCES OF DATA

Participant—Observation

One of the key practices of traditional ethnography is to learn about the culture by observing it, and to some degree, while observing, to participate or vice versa. The anthropologist lives among the people themselves, establishing himself within the physical surroundings of the people. He makes himself as much like them culturally as they will permit, and as is compatible with the maintenance of this objectivity. Often the subjective materials he gains are as important as the objective materials obtained. Participation often has the advantage of helping the investigator establish good relationships with the people so that the channels of communication will be maintained (Cohen et. al. in Narroll, 1973: 220-245; Mead, 1955: 245-258; Read, 1965). By actually taking part in, and experiencing the culture with the native actors, the ethnographer gets an inside view that is not possible otherwise. Whiting and Whiting (1973: 259) point out that merely interviewing people about their behavior will give the ethnographer a different picture than will be acquired if the behavior is witnessed as it happens. Hence by being with the actors as they unfold their daily drama, the opportunities to witness events of the daily experience are many. The role of the participant-observer allows the ethnographer to hear, experience and record events which he would otherwise miss or which would be redefined by an informant. The experience of participating supplies the ethnographer with a wealth of clues, many of them subtle, by which can be inferred the existence of dynamics which may be covert. Although the ideal is never fully realized because of the limits of time, and limits set by the subjects, much is gained by this method.

One major difficulty of the participant-observation technique is that the participant may identify so fully with the local values that he will lose his detachment, and not achieve an accurate and objective description of the culture. Another problem of this method is that of *culture shock*, if the value system one is observing is too dissonant with one's own.

The use of language may be considered a key aspect of participation; although it is not imperative, it is often useful if the ethnographer knows the language of the people he is studying. Not being able to communicate about one's daily needs can add to the stress and dissonance of being in a strange value system. In this study, the argot of Transactional Analysis is being treated as an *exotic language*. It is also common for ethnographers to use informants. This is done because there is not the time nor energy in a usual field-work tour to see and do everything that the culture offers. Also, often translation is necessary where the ethnographer is learning, or not fluent in the language. In interviewing informants it is useful to use a list of questions or a standard questionnaire to elicit answers to key problems which the ethnographers find important. These questionnaires can often be verified through participating in casual conversations and through being present at some of the selected community experiences. As will be seen, I found the participant-observation method valuable throughout the period of study.

Culture Shock and Cognitive Dissonance

One of the phenomena which makes record keeping difficult and sometimes takes the data collection out of the realm of objectivity is the experience of cognitive dissonance and consequent *culture shock*. This condition has been acknowledged and described by ethnographers for some time (Bohannen, 1964; Fernea, 1969; Read, 1965). It is the anxiety state which results from the ambiguity and insecurity of one's position in an unfamiliar cultural environment. Some ethnographers can stand more of this kind of stress than others. Some undoubtedly conceal the fact that this has happened to them. Whether culture shock actually affects the objectivity of the investigator or not has been given little attention. This is, in fact, a universal phenomenon. It is experienced by most aware and sensitive human beings when they find themselves in strange and unusual surroundings where demands are being made upon them which they believe for the moment they cannot meet. The major dynamic in this phenomenon is *cognitive dissonance* (Festinger, 1957). Human beings will make a supreme effort to bring what they are experiencing into the definable limits of their own world view. If this effort does not meet with success fairly consistently and fairly soon, the individual will begin to put a great deal of energy into defending his internal world view, and denying the stimulus which is creating the dissonance. The stress of this attempt in some cases will "overload the computer" and it will "crash."

Culture Shock is explainable in the Transactional Analysis systems theory in the following manner. The person who is experiencing cognitive dissonance will have an Adult Ego State which does not have sufficient information about this particular set of events which is consonant with familiar events. The information in the Parent is limited to the value and belief system of the individual and may not be consonant with the new environment. The Child may feel or experience that its survival is dependent upon its adhering to the value and belief system put out by the Parent. The Adult does not have enough information to contradict this and archaic systems of behavior are instituted (see T.A. definition of psychopathology in Chapter I). This is defined in standard psychiatry as an *Anxiety State* (DSMII, 1968). Theoretically (T.A.) while the person is experiencing the internal dialog between the Parent and the Child, the Adult is not able to function because the psychic energy has been drawn into the dialog and is not available for computing. This means that input of information about the environment is interrupted until the person can reestablish equilibrium and the psychic energy flow between all three Ego States is reestablished. Once equilibrium is reestablished, the ability of the Adult to compute data input, and deal with it, returns. In at least one instance, I myself did not realize that I was in culture shock until I left Cathexis for a planned break. On return to my own familiar environment, after an interval of immersion in the Cathexis community, I found myself in an acute anxiety state. As I rethought the experience, and talked with a therapist in my own community, I realized that I had made so intense an effort to adapt to the Cathexis expectations of heavy confrontation of behavior that I placed myself in a situation where I was defending everything I said and did. I had Overadapted to the community demands in order to avoid the confrontations. The standard strategy of being highly reactive to Discounting, and the intense investment in noting every detail of participants' behaviors was threatening to me. In my striving to become a *perfect* participant in the community, I lost my perspective.

Since culture shock is often the outcome of the individual being disengaged from his usual cultural spheres, it follows that the person's internal world view is the pivotal concept in this dynamic. World view theorists (Foster, 1967; Kearney, 1975) indicate that it is the basic cognitive orientations which shape the uniformities in all spheres of cultural behavior. If the basic cognitive orientations are not consonant (cognitive dissonance) with the environment, then the individual will do something to adjust himself or the environment.

Recording, Taping and Confidentiality

Most of the information about the community was gathered in a series of notebooks. In some situations I was able to take notes while the events were unfolding. Most of the time I had to write notes after the events because of the community stipulation that any tape recordings of actual therapy was not permissible due to the need to keep confidential all that transpired in such sessions. Tapes were obtained of some interviews of the didactic sessions and of the seminars.

In writing notes, I made an effort to synthesize my experiences and write down everything I could remember and, time permitting, was physically able to write. Whatever came to mind as I was writing was recorded. I made an effort to follow a structure in terms of time in my mind. Starting with the most recent event of the day, I described it and went back through the day or period in terms of the key events. I would write everything that came to mind in a type of free association process. Activities, objects, behaviors, characteristics, interactions and setting would be described. What toys the two-year-olds were playing with, how a caretaker gave a bottle or changed a diaper, who said what when a dish was out of place, were all recorded as they were recalled. I recorded as much of how everyone was behaving as I could. Although I thought about giving all items equal value in my notes, I found personal antipathy, personal distress or loss of recall entering into some of the observations and some of the personal experiences. My notes represent a journal of daily experiences.

I brought to the experience of observing this community several elements of preprogramming: three of these are of note in terms of record keeping:

1. I was a public health and psychiatric nurse for several years and had learned a phenomenological approach to record keeping. Recording precisely what I saw and what I felt about behavior I was observing had been a long practice of mine.

2. I had training in Transactional Analysis and had earned my Clinical Membership. As a consequence, I perceive the T.A. model as a set of "rules for behavior." I was intrigued with how these rules for behavior were learned and experienced. I wanted to know what the patterns of behavior were that the subjects in the study expressed before and after learning the rules.

3. I was born in Angola, West Africa, of missionary parents. My father was an Anthropologist and earned his Ph.D. when I was 10 years old. My early years were influenced by family discussions of cultural anthropology and visits to the villages where my father was interviewing informants. My early childhood friendships were with African children. Some of my parenting experiences came from the extended family of the household staff and other missionaries in the field.

Since the issue of "psychological and cognitive validity" will be raised, I bring to attention Keesing's (Naroll, 1973: 423-453) points. Ethnographers will have to limit their focus at some point for heuristic reasons because: (1) the selective focus will be bound to create a gap between the ethnographic account and the cognitive ordering of the actors; (2) a cultural description will be ordered in a single linear (written) sequence, rendering an ethnography different in basic structure from the cognitive organization of cultural knowledge; (3) the ethnographic description is written in a metalanguage foreign to the world of the actor; (4) levels of consciousness (Bateson, 1968) provides for a coding of lower levels of consciousness in terms of higher metalanguages (Surface Structure/Deep structure of Chomsky, 1957).

> The point then, is that "cognitive validity" cannot be a realistic hope
> in ethnographic description if it is taken to mean that the description is to
> replicate on paper what goes on neurophysiologically or perceptually in
> the heads of our subjects. (Keesing, 1973: 444)

Personal Involvement

The decision to work within one's own culture should not be
made without appreciation of the problems peculiar to this type of
experience. Holloman (1974: 268) points this out in her article on
the experiences she had at the Esalen Institute in Big Sur. The problems raised by the relationships between personal values, the assumptions about the nature of man, and human society and the fieldwork
context is likely to be of crucial importance. As I pointed out in the
section on Culture Shock, and as Holloman found out, she was a
participant in a more personal sense than she had anticipated. She
was to find the experience rewarding however painful. It spurred
her on to further assessment of her role as a teacher, and to personal
change.

In my own case, I was prepared to become involved experientially
in some of the usual experiences at Cathexis. I had had a personal
association with Cathexis through a member of my family and, as a
student of T.A., I knew that I would be making therapy Contracts
for personal change and planned to become involved personally in
selected parts of the healing rituals offered in the program. I realized
that I would be confronting developmental lacunae in my own personality structure. Beyond those experiences where I had Contracts
for change, I was as much as is possible the observer.

Anthropologists have long been defensive about the charge that
the quality of their work is not replicable. The standard argument is
that "beauty is only in the eye of the beholder." All of the judgments arise as a result of the idiosyncracies of one person's perceptions. Among ethnographers who have used exceptionally intense
personal involvement as a means of acquiring data are Marlene Dobkin de Rios 1972a), Carlos Castaneda (1968: 1971), and Michael
Harner (1972). As Harner says (1972: xv):

> As more anthropologists undertake field research . . . it will be inter-
> esting to see how "participant-observation" influences their understand-
> ing of the cultures studied, and affects their personal, theoretical and meth-
> odological orientations.

He points out that "words alone never adequately convey the realities of shamanism. These can only be approached with the aid of *natenia* and the chemical door to the otherwise invisible world of the Jivaro shaman" (Harner, 1972: 26). De Rios says:

> I also took *ayahuasca* in ritual context. In most investigations of drug use, it is believed that the researcher must have some subjective experience in order to understand the nature of the informants' reports. This was particularly applicable in the *ayahuasca* study, as culturally reported visions which filled notebooks seemed difficult to comprehend until a subjective experience clarified the veracity of reports about seeing unidentified persons appear in living color, etc. Recounting my own experience with *ayahuasca* provided an excellent entry into the world of informants' personal experience, since they were more apt to discuss their own visions with another person who had participated in their ritual. (De Rios, 1972: 73)

I support these points of view since this was essentially my own experience. The ineffable sense of *communitas* would escape me entirely if I had not had it myself. Nor could I really understand the visceral sense of integration one has after resolving an emotional impasse, if I had not myself experienced the "magic" of the rituals.

Transactional Analysis theory supplies an explanation for the value of the experiential approach. Given that the Adult Ego State is that part of the integrated individual which collects data, makes decisions and computes facts, then, theoretically, the Adult is not emotionally involved in the scenes in which the Child and Parent are involved. When the Adult is not Contaminated (overridden with Child or Parent energy), or drugged, it can make clear assessments of the unfolding events. Even when there is no emotional objectivity, it is possible to sort the facts from the feelings by Cathecting Adult. In conventional terms: given that the brain is analogous to a computer, then all data or information is taken in and stored and is available at a later date for review and for objective evaluation. It is important to note that there are certain drugs which slow down or distort the functioning of the data retrieval system in somewhat the same way in which biases and value systems may distort information.

Having decided to involve myself experientially, I went about finding out actually how the various rituals feel, as well as how they work. I will supply an insider's view of some of the healing rituals used in the treatment community in this study. Following, in Chapter IV, will be excerpts of fractions of my own personal experiences with Cathecting Little.

As a consequence of the decision to involve myself in the treatment process, it was necessary that I accept the diagnostic criteria used at Cathexis. This process is described in part by Ehrenwald (1966) as "doctrinal compliance." Doctrinal compliance seems to be an unconscious process which occurs both in "magical" and "modern" therapies. Unlike suggestion, it seems to be an unconscious process where the patient appears to comply with the therapist in validating his theories. I accepted Agitation as a major diagnostic issue for my own treatment very early in my exposure to Cathexis' model. Agitation is described as a set of behaviors which have significance for competitive personality structures. It is characterized by mostly nongoal-directed activities such as finger-tapping, pacing, wriggling, rocking, smoking, snacking, etc. Sometimes, Agitation manifests itself in the attacking of repetitive jobs such as some aspects of housework or handwork (knitting, crocheting, etc.). My own experience with Agitation manifested itself in speech blocking, nervous body movements signifying inner discomfort, competitive behaviors and Escalations to temper tantrums. The treatment contracts I made generated the experiences of rituals which involved regression (i.e., Cathecting Little). At the various marathons and groups in which I was involved, I had the opportunity to cathect age five, age three and, in a guided fantasy, I experienced being nine months of age. Group and Marathon experiences allowed time to rethink old views and values which were no longer useful to me in the present. Much information was gained and personal change occurred as a result of vicariously experiencing others' Working. Being exposed to other people Working through specific issues, provided me with empathic learning and further information on the nature of the ritual processes. Cathexis also structures a large amount of cognitive feedback and learning for its participants. Every time a treatment issue is raised, or a ritual is experienced, the therapist or staff give information in the language of T.A. on what is happening and what might be learned from the experience. Much of the information on the operational aspects of specific rituals was gathered in this way.

Further validation of experiential data-gathering comes with input from others who have had the same experiences will be used in the descriptions of the rituals and results of ritual experiences. Personal experiences of the participants in the study as well as my own will be explicated.

SUMMARY

Methods used in this study include experiential data-gathering techniques and clinical data-gathering techniques. Clear understanding of the methods includes a discussion of the diagnostic approaches and the modes of classifying people and behaviors. The difference between the classical psychological modes of classifying psychopathology and the T.A. model were discussed. The instruments used in the study for collecting information were described: they are the MMPI, the Semantic Differential, the Life Script Questionnaire, Interviews and a semantic analysis of MMPI questions. The traditional role in anthropology in participant-observation was discussed, as were other types of experiential sources of data. Questions around studying one's own culture were discussed and examples of intense self-involvement in foreign settings were quoted.

Chapter III

CATHEXIS: THE DIALECTIC BETWEEN "REAL" AND "NOT REAL"

Don Juan slowly walked around me ... he finally said: ... "you now have the need to live like a warrior. You have always known that, now you're simply in the position of having to make use of something you disregarded before. But you had to struggle for this knowledge; it wasn't just given to you, it wasn't just handed down to you. You had to beat it out of yourself." —*(Casteneda: 1971: 263)*

CALIFORNIA MYSTIQUE

Oleanders! Large, clumpy bushes smothered in pink. The blossoms exude a heavy spicy incense. The low brown foothills of the Diablo range rise humpbacked behind the gnarled old trees and the houses nestled below. The Castro Valley, home for the suburbs of several large urban areas, is about as California as California can be. Here, too, is some of the mystique from my African childhood. I smell the oleander's spicy odor. I see the brown and green. I remember the African bush. The vegetation is reminiscent for me. Many of the plants of central California are the same as those in the highlands of West Central Africa. I am a child again. Hot sun and dust. Oleanders are poisonous. Delicious smell, exotic look, danger! Oleanders are a paradox as is California. A paradox for all who do not live there. It holds a certain power over the rest of the world. Many things start in California, later to become custom in other states and other countries. California is "magic" to many with its continuous stream of offbeat, outrageous aspirations. The occult generation; the flower children; the arch conservative; center for the beginnings of the Human Potential Movement; Hollywood and stardom; television giveaways; the gold rush; the drug market; "go west young man!" . . . go to California!

In many parts of the world I have been told by people: "when I go to the U.S. I am going to go to California!" Fortunes are made and lost all over the world, but it is "special" if it happened in California. There is a mythology about California, perpetrated by literature and film. "California Style" is pandered to by Madison Avenue. The California mystique is unmatched as far as the unusual in art, music, film, life style and education are concerned. The mystical, magical, powerful, unusual and blatant seem to happen more easily in California. George Leonard wrote *The Transformation* in California. This is a book which contains a mystical essay about a climb up Mount Tamalpais. You have to have done it to know what he is talking about!

Many, although not all leaders in the Human Potential Movement, have been inspired in California. Carlos Castaneda, Claudio Naranjo, Robert Ornstein, Alan Watts, Ram Das, John Lilly and others have a piece of the California mystique in their writings. Bateson's work on the "double-bind" was developed in California. Is it because California is a "power center?" Is it the San Andreas Fault? Is it because people are living dangerously? The mystique and the "magic" of the fountain of youth have a long history in California. People seem to believe that somehow, sometime, someday, their dreams will all magically come true in California. California is where Eric Berne developed the Transactional Analysis Theory of Scripts and Fairy Tales.

People have a need for explaining their misery and their lack of control over their environment with recourse to "magic." Fairy tales, personal myths, individual heroes and heroines figure in the determining of people's Scripts.

> The first and most archaic version of the script, the primal protocol, is conceived in the mind of the child at an age when few people outside his immediate family are real to him. We assume that his parents appear to him as huge figures endowed with magic powers, like the giants and giant-esses, ogres and gorgons of mythology, if only because they are three times as tall and ten times as big as he is. (Berne, 1972: 39)

Fairy tales, archetypal myths, personal mystiques—all of these figure in the ways in which people manage their relationships. The Real and the Unreal are a part of the dialectic of being sane or crazy. California's mystique seems to provide an ecosystem which permits the germination of new and unusual ideas—ideas which at first seem out of line to the established ways of viewing the world. Cathexis[1] Community is one of these places.

HISTORY OF CATHEXIS COMMUNITY

The dialectic between "magic," the Not Real, and "Science" the Real; between thesis and antithesis, find a synthesis in some of the Growth Centers which have originated in California. Cathexis community, which is described here, is in the Castro Valley, near Oakland, California. The history of this community goes back to the Eric Berne Seminars in Carmel, California and at the Langley Porter Clinic in San Francisco. Here Eric Berne developed his theories in collaboration with those who are now well-known names in Transactional Analysis: Steve Karpman, who developed the Drama Triangle idea; Claude Steiner, famous in the Radical Therapy Movement, developed the Script Matrix; Jack Dusay, the Egogram Theory; and many others were involved in these seminars. Among the members of these seminars was a young woman, Jacqui Schiff, who was to become a social worker. Jacqui took the theory and philosophy of Transactional Analysis with her to graduate school. Working with other professionals, with her husband, Moe, a social worker, and schizophrenic patients, Jacqui came up with a unique approach to the treatment of psychotic persons. This treatment involved regressive techniques. The chronicle of her early experiences in developing the Reparenting Theory is expressed in a book written by Jacqui Schiff and Beth Day, *All My Children* (1970). There is also a series of articles written by Jacqui and members of her community which have appeared in the *Transactional Analysis Bulletin* (1969) and in the *Transactional Analysis Journal* (1971) describing each step in the early development of this approach.

In 1965, the "Schiff Family" approach began with the taking into their home of a schizophrenic young person. It was not long before the "family" had increased to fifteen persons. The defining of Reparenting started when "the family" began to experiment with the Decathexis of the Parent Ego State. The early results were encouraging and this group pursued the collection of information about the pathological and environmental needs of the children and the kinds of interventions needed to treat the schizophrenic. Unique in the "Schiff family" approach then, and now, is the requirement that the person who is experiencing the Regression keep the caretakers informed about his inner process; and, also, to keep informing the patient about his behavior. The information gained from these regressive experiences is used in refining the interventions in the setting.

Transactional Analysis promised to become a powerful tool for understanding human interaction. The "family" took the process offered by Transactional Analysis and continued to develop it as a tool for curing the schizophrenics who came to the program. To date the process has transformed a considerable number of anomic, alienated, psychotics to "normal" functioning persons. Some of these people are now many of the warm, loving and exciting people who can be seen functioning well in their own communities and at the T.A. Association meetings. The power of the T.A. model, the acuity of mind of Jacqui Schiff, the intellect and energy of the patients and their belief in the process have combined to create a powerful and transformative set of interventions.

In the sense that the theories developed in the Cathexis community have resulted from the collaboration of all of the persons involved, this is not a program where the professional practitioners *do* treatment *to* patients. In this treatment environment, each person who enters a treatment or a training Contract has been integrally involved in major therapeutic and theoretical decisions. Close scrutiny of the Regressive patient and constant input from the patient himself is a part of the process. As each new theoretical issue arises, there is a sharing of the information gained in institutes, conferences, the journals and in seminars. Even data gained around failures is shared. Each step taken in the treatment process is on the basis of actual data collected experientially. This type of sharing of information is not new. Freud, Jung and Reich shared with their students in seminars. The difference at Cathexis seems to be in the sharing and involvement of the psychotic person himself in the development of interventive techniques and hypotheses.

At Cathexis, the reality of an *infant* with *urgent* needs for regressive experiences has been fully recognized as part of the problem of schizophrenia. This is the basic assumption on which the T.A. model of schizophrenia and Reparenting has been built.

As a consequence of the controversial nature of reparenting approach, it became necessary for the "family" to function under circumstances which were inimical to the survival of the early program. The neighborhood in which they were living experienced discomfort with the "weirdos" and "hippie types" and the "crazies" living next door. Also, the psychiatric establishment has not recognized T.A. or Reparenting as valid psychotherapy. (In some parts of the United States this is still the case.)

In 1971, in order to increase communication with and facilitate the training of professionals, the Cathexis Institute was established in Oakland, California. The Cathexis and "Schiff Family" approach is of growing interest to practitioners of psychotherapy from all over the world. It allows for the continuing development of theory and practice. Professionals are now keen to involve themselves in learning more about Reparenting. The inclusion of persons with professional degrees and training in institutes provides a climate for dialog and theory development between patient and practitioner. Along with the institute as an alternative to hospitalization for some of the otherwise incapacitated persons, the Cathexis School was also established. It is a laboratory outpatient program which provides research input and learning facilities for both patients and trainees. Together, the Institute and the School form a setting for the development of new theory and a climate for learning.

CONTEXTS

There are several transactional contexts in which the healing processes occur at Cathexis. Each one is separated out under the broad headings of philosophical structure, physical structure, temporal structure, social structure and psychological structure. More finitely they are delineated as places, activities and processes. The fabric of the transactional context is woven of many threads. These overlap and intertwine. The linear method of describing them may not give as multidimensional a view as exists in reality.

The Cathexis Social Structure
  (Staff and Participants)

No formal hierarchical structure[2] is immediately obvious. There are, however, several levels of authority. In the final analysis, although the director of the program is Jacqui Schiff, all responsibility is shared. Jacqui is a tough-minded, clear-thinking woman, whose small voice and childlike appearance belie the fact that she is meticulous in the manner in which she applies the process they have developed. No deviation from the rules of "undefended relating, being responsible and no secrets" is tolerated. Jacqui provides a role model for the Passivity Confrontation interventions. Even the slightest infringement of the rules on Discounting is immediately reacted to by her. Many practitioners and professional persons find her level of confrontation on this issue frightening. Since her behavior is becoming legendary, some choose not to relate to her either socially or professionally. There are also those who are highly critical of her methods. Others avoid exploring the learning opportunities in the Institute setting because of the general need of most persons to relate from Defended[3] positions (i.e., using their customary Rackets and Games). An individual's investment in learning to become Undefended has to be a strong one to remain at Cathexis. The person must be undefended to maintain communication with other persons in the community. The propensity on my part for instance to Defend (project past fears on Jacqui) became a major issue in my experience in the program.

Responsible for directing the School, and in close communication with Jacqui and the rest of the people is the Director of the School. This person is in a dual capacity as trainer and trainee in Transactional Analysis. Generally this is a person with some professional education who has a training contract with Jacqui (who is a Teaching Member of the ITAA). The contract is for training towards membership as a Clinical Member or as a Teaching Member in the International Transactional Analysis Association. At the next level is a number of persons designated as "staff." These are generally persons who have training contracts for Clinical Membership also. They are persons who have an interest in furthering their knowledge and skills in Reparenting as a treatment model. Their educational backgrounds range from those with professional degrees, preprofessional training, to paraprofessional. Some of the staff are "graduated" or are near graduation from "Patient" status. Graduation may mean having completed a series of treatment contracts, being "cured" of schizophrenia and/or having demonstrated a readiness for a training contract. Other participants in the program may occasionally take on "staff" or "caretaking" responsibilities depending on their level of responsible interaction or functioning in the community and in their life styles. Functioning means that the person had adapted well to the rules of the community and the larger society. It means that the person is reacting in an Undefended and honest manner. This person has been found to be sufficiently dependable to be accorded a given level of responsibility in the running of the community. Some of these persons will have achieved the designation of "caretaker" in their residential setting. Further discussion of the concept of "responsibility" as it arises appears in the section on group experience.

The organizational structure is fluid and not fixed. Movement from one position to another is possible as needs and skills change. In this type of structure, each individual who demonstrates the capability for differing tasks takes the opportunity to propose his need for the experience. He is able to fulfill that need depending on the context and on his presentation of himself in his group and to his therapist. This flexibility of movement was observed on several occasions. The position of "person in charge" is undertaken in any situation where responsible action is necessary by whomever may be on the scene. The apparent flexibility of this structure in terms of position and power is misleading. In actuality there is within the T.A. Reparenting model a highly structured and meticulously delineated mode of transacting. There can be no misunderstanding at each moment as to what is going on in a transaction, unless one or more of the individuals is Redefining the issues.

Jules Henry (1975: 1-15) addresses the issue of structure in what he calls I-E Factor—the ideo-emotional factor. By Henry's definition, these are the "emotionally toned ideas and beliefs that govern interpersonal relations and man's relation to the rest of the world." He points out that in most therapeutic environments it is relatively easy to distinguish between the rationale of therapy and the I-E Factors because there is a sharp separation between staff and patients. In most settings there is a prohibition on mutual emotional involvement between staff and patients. (Perhaps this is because of the need of mental health staff to maintain the myth of their own "excellent emotional health.") If the lives of staff and patients are intimate and the mutual involvement of staff and patients is central to the healing process, emotional and interactional problems of all involved are acknowledged and verified as realities of every day life. The distinction between therapeutic rationale and the I-E Factor is obscured. There is no sharp distinction between these two factors at Cathexis. This is evident from the structural outline of the community and from its philosophical charter. Jules Henry describes a similar situation at the Orthogenic School (Bettleheim):

> ...the children are the centre of therapeutic and emotional interest...
> this central position comes as a consequence, in part, of the properties of
> the social system itself, and hence the children cannot be left out of an
> analytical description of it. The children are present not as objects, which

is what patients are in most psychiatric institutions, but as dynamic parts of the system, exerting an effect within it at all times: the counselor's entire position in the school is determined by the nature of her involvement in the children. This is a concrete expression of the general proposition that persons are members of the same social system to the degree that they are involved with one another. . .in most psychiatric hospitals most of the time patients and personnel are simply not members of the same social system. (1973: 6)

Mutual responsibility is a key factor in this type of social structure.

At Cathexis, each individual is responsible for his own program which must be worked out with his group therapist and with the director of the School. His psychotherapy and learning program are not split between different departments as happens in most therapy institutions. The process by which he learns the "language" and learns to think is largely dependent upon the Contractual Arrangements between himself and the other persons in the setting. In order to get into the therapeutic program, the person must make a Treatment Contract[4] with the director of the school; show willingness to take some minimal responsibility for his treatment; show motivation to deal with the issues involved in his contract. Once the person has joined the program he is expected to meet his therapy group once a week and participate in the Drop-In Program at the School on a regular basis. Further, he must keep up with the "program" he has set with the director and with the treatment contacts he has made. These are all elements of the social structure.

(Philosophy of Cathexis)

The philosophy of the program at Cathexis is expressed in the following poem which is printed on the stationery, brochures and announcements for the Community:

> Let not young souls be smothered out before
> They do quaint deeds and fully flaunt their pride
> It is the world's one crime its babes grow dull,
> Its poor are ox-like, limp and leaden-eyed.
> Not that they starve, but starve so dreamlessly,
> Not that they sow, but that they seldom reap,
> Not that they serve, but have no gods to serve,
> Not that they die, but that they die like sheep.
> —*Vachel Lindsay*

The treatment philosophy is also reflected in the metaphors characteristic of the community argot, such as "starving baby," "parenting," "being responsible," "undefended relating" by all involved, "lack of secrecy," "babies," "dealing" and so forth. Basic is the belief that schizophrenics received such poor Parenting at so very young an age, that their socialization is radically incomplete and that a treatment program must provide an environment in which they can fill in these gaps. According to Schiff:

> Underpinning our interventions with patients is a consciously formulated and experientially supported philosophy. Two major components are that patients know cognitively and/or viscerally what they need to do to get well, and that they can take responsibility for their functioning during treatment if they have a supportive environment while they develop new internal structures and options for behavior. Our treatment structure and interventions are programmed in relation to these ideas. (1975: 98)

The focus of the philosophy is that the Parent in the schizophrenic's head must be amended, the Child renurtured and retrained so that the person finally comes to the realization in his Adult that he can be responsible for meeting his own physical and emotional needs. The problem is seen to lie in four Parent messages that come predominantly from the Controlling Parent. These are:

1. Parent's needs come first
2. The world is a scary place (the Goblins will get you)
3. People are not to be trusted
4. You are not a person without me (the Parent)

Schiff says (1972:21):

> The process we call "reparenting" involves erasing the Parent Ego State completely . . . and replacing the Parent messages with healthy messages about the child's self, what the world is like and what he will do with the world.

The fourth message above, "you are not a person without me," describes the theory of Symbiosis on which the Reparenting program is based. Further discussion of this theory will appear in the section on the Transactional Analysis Basis of Reparenting.

Physical Contexts

There are two Cathexis communities—one in the Oakland area, the other in India. The current study deals with Jacqui Schiff's community in California. Ms. Schiff's home is a modest, modern house set on a large tract of land with a cottage next door. The home was built to accommodate her and her natural children, and one or more of the Children in Regression. The cottage houses some of the other Children. (Children means specifically persons who have structured a Reparenting Contract with Schiff and staff.) Other important loci of this community are the School, a small, single-family dwelling in Oakland about 20 minutes by freeway from the Schiff "family" residence, and a Residential Treatment Home known as Gladman House, where a number of the persons who are in treatment in the community live. (Since the time of this study, Gladman House has been closed and the residents now live in various group and individual arrangements.)

Most of the transactions and decisions which affect the operation of the community are made in a group setting either in the "family," the "residential group" or in a gathering of the Seminar at one of the physical locations. The major dynamics occur wherever the people of the community are together through their interpersonal relationships for that time and that place. The entire community is transactional. The processes of current transactions are what define the program for each individual involved.

The period during which I was involved in Cathexis, I determined the major physical components of the community to exist in the following manner: "the family" (located physically at the "House" and at the "Cottage"); the "School" (located in Oakland); the "Institute" (located where the staff and director were teaching outside professionals); the Residential Treatment Home—Gladman House (located in Oakland; the "groups" and Drop-In Center (located in the School); the T.A. Seminar; and the individuals who are involved in all or some of these components. All of the persons who are involved in these components are persons who have some type of Contract (treatment or training or both) with the staff and faculty of the Institute. The total community is organized around a structure of rules which can be applied in any setting, whether they are at a picnic, at home or in the laboratory. (Childs-Gowell; 1979)

The Seminars at Cathexis are a part of the structure of the International Transactional Analysis Association. The ITAA and its affiliates function as an educational institution for people in the broad field of social psychiatry: psychiatrists, psychologists, psychiatric nurses, social workers, correctional officers, social scientists, educators and clergy. The teaching by Teaching Members of the ITAA is primarily oriented toward group therapy, social dynamics and personality theory based on Transactional Analysis. The Association is now in its 20th year, it is self-supporting through tuition and membership fees. The affiliated T.A. Institutes and Seminars and Study Groups are open to those in medicine or the social sciences who are engaged in professional and paraprofessional work in those fields, or are registered for advanced study at recognized universities. At Cathexis, all members of the community are expected to attend and involve themselves in the Seminars as part of their program. The Seminars are the locus for the presentation of T.A. Theory and for the working out of new ideas.

Theoretical Basis (The Transactional Analysis
  Model as Applied at Cathexis)

Symbiosis is the key to the pathological manner in which schizophrenics conceptualize their world. Bowlby describes this dynamic in his two volumes on *Attachment* and *Separation* (Bowlby, 1969: Chapter II, vol. I). Bowlby follows Spitz among others. Spitz (1965) did research on his observation of the fact that completely neglected infants die even though their physical needs may be adequately met. He called this condition *marasmus*. In the normal childbearing cycle, the infant's dependence on the mother for nurture (for her breast, her breath, her heartbeat and responsiveness) and the mother's need to supply it, bind mother and infant together. Bowlby's theories also build on the research done by Lorenz on *imprinting* (Lorenz, 1935). Bowlby builds his theory on *instinct*.[5] He postulates that the child's tie to his mother is the product of a number of behavioral systems that have proximity to the mother as a basic factor. He regards attachment behavior as a class of social behavior equal in importance to mating and parental behavior. He holds it to have a biological function specific to itself. Attachment develops within the child as a result of its interaction with its immediate environment; especially, through interaction with the principal nurturant figure in the environment—usually the mother. Out of this interaction with the mothering figure develops the infant's first cooperative relationships and its first models of social life. Spitz (1965) was later to document this in his series on hospitalized infants.

Attachment behavior as described by Bowlby essentially underlies the theory of Symbiosis. Bowlby's ideas are supported by the research of Harlow (1958; 1961) on the behavior of monkey infants exposed to different kinds of maternal figures (cloth and wire mothers). Human infant studies by Ainsworth (1963: 1967) and Schaffer and Emerson (1964a) indicate that in all but a small number of Ganda children, attachment behavior is clearly present by six months of age. The age at which attachment behavior is fully developed in Ganda as observed by Ainsworth, does not differ greatly from the age at which Schaffer and Emerson found it to develop in Scottish children. According to Bowlby (1969: 201) most human infants have a fully developed attachment to the mothering person some time up to the period of from six months to twelve months of age with the peak months being at about nine months.

Symbiosis is described as a "normal condition of the oral stage in the development of the child. It is experienced by both the mother and the child as a merging or sharing of their needs" (Schiff and Schiff, 1971:71). Symbiosis is seen as necessary for normal early development and for the survival of the child. When the symbiosis is broken or impaired in early months, or when it is prolonged beyond periods of life when the child could be experiencing and experimenting with separation from the mother, pathology arises.

The Transactional Analysis clinical approach based on the theory of Symbiosis is as follows: The patient's time in the treatment program is structured towards his learning to become aware of the ways in which he manipulates people into entering Symbiotic Transactions with him. He becomes aware of the ways in which he gets other people to think, feel Feelings and solve problems for him. His time is also structured towards increasing awareness of the other behavioral options which are available to him. Persons who are Symbiotic have expectations that other people can be made to think for them. They will use "passive" (nonthinking, nonfeeling) behaviors to reinforce this expectation. Passive behaviors are seen as resulting from unresolved dependency needs (i.e., Symbiosis).

Passive behaviors are seen as manifesting themselves in four modes of transacting:

    1. *Doing nothing*, and waiting for someone else to do the thinking, feeling or doing that the current situation demands

    2. *Overadapting*, i.e., being overcompliant and attempting to second guess the other person's thinking, feelings or wants before doing so oneself

    3. *Agitated behaviors*, manifested in frantic, confused, overreacting activities to avoid thinking, feeling or problem-solving

4. *Escalation to incapacitation or to violence*, to avoid the responsibility of thinking, feeling or problem-solving, of which the person perceives himself incapable

As can be seen, these are all ways in which a person shifts responsibility for thinking, feeling or doing to the other person in the Symbiosis. The major mechanisms in passivity are *Discounting* (= denial of the stimulus, the problem and the options for behavior), *Redefining* (= distortion of the stimulus, the problem and the options) and *Grandiosity* (= aggrandizing or minimizing the environmental cues). These mechanisms are all ways to ensure the preservation of defensive mental sets (i.e., Frames of Reference or world view).

With Discounting the individual reduces the impact of the three parts of any Transaction. These parts are the stimulus, the problem and the options for solving the problem. The impact of the stimulus is reduced by the individual in four ways (see Figures 3-1, 3-2, 3-3, 3-4).

According to Schiff, et. al. (1975: 16-17):

1. Generally, for each type of discounting, a discount in any of the four modes involves discounts in all those below it on the chart. For example, people who discount a stimulus generally also at the same time discount the significance of the stimulus, the changeability of the stimulus, and their ability to react differently to the stimulus. (See vertical arrow on Figure 3-1.)

2. Generally in any row on the table the discount of a type involves discounts of all types to the right. For example, people who discount pain (stimulus) will discount the existence of a problem as well as the existence of options to solve the problem around the pain. (See horizontal arrow on Figure 3-1.)

3. Discounting occurring at any point on the table also involves discounting in the row below it in the type to the left, and in the row above it in the type to the right (see diagonal arrows on the table.) For example, if a mother discounts the significance of a baby's crying (stimulus) by shutting the door to the baby's room, she is also discounting the existent problem for the baby. Similarly, if the mother said, "The baby always cries; there's nothing that can be done," she is discounting her own and the baby's ability to react differently to stimuli, discounting the solvability of the problem, and discounting the significance of options. ("It won't make any difference.")

Schiff believes that children raised in environments where Discounting is always in or near the upper left corner of the Table in Figure 3-1, develop the most incapacitating pathology.

According to the Charts (Figure 3-1), the Treatment issues then follow:

T_1 Awareness (internal and external)

T_2 Significance of awareness, problem definition

T_3 Awareness of change, defining problem significance, defining options

T_4 Awareness of personal change, defining problem solutions, defining relevant action options

T_5 Awareness of personal abilities for selecting viable options

T_6 Awareness of ability for action, and to take action

Mode	Type of Discounting		
Existence	T_1 Existence of Stimuli	T_2 Existence of Problems	T_3 Existence of Options
Significance	T_2 Significance of Stimuli	T_3 Significance of Problems	T_4 Significance of Options
Change Possibilities	T_3 Changeability of Stimuli	T_4 Solvability of Problems	T_5 Viability of Options
Personal Abilities	T_4 Person's Ability to React Differently	T_5 Person's Ability to Solve Problems	T_6 Person's Ability to Act on Options

Figure 3-1. RELATIONSHIPS BETWEEN TYPES AND MODES OF DISCOUNTING (Schiff et al., 1975:16).

The healing rituals which include use of the chart and the confrontation of Passivity and Symbiotic transactions are all initiated by the
practical goals of providing the individuals in the program with the
opportunities to *"reality test."* Each individual is repeatedly
encouraged to consensually validate his awareness and, through use
of the chart as one tool, to identify his level of Discounting. This
process is structured to the individual recognizing Ego States which
are involved in the Discounting. It is structured to the individual's
identifying the Discounting behavior as it fits into his own developmental experience. This assists the individual in identifying developmental lacunae in his own childhood. Once the person knows
something about his patterns of behaving, he has a tool for correct-
ing them.

Type and Mode	Area	Example
Stimuli	Self	"I don't feel angry (hungry, pain)," said by an angry (hungry, injured person.
	Other	"You didn't stroke me," said by someone who was just stroked.
	Situation	"I can see perfectly," said by a driver in a thick fog.
Significance of Stimuli	Self	"Don't take any notice; I'm always angry," said in response to a specific provocation.
	Others	"You didn't want to stroke me; you thought you had to."
	Situation	"I always drive at 50 mph in thick fog."
Variability of	Self	"I'm always angry; my father and grandfather were too. It's genetic."
	Others	"It doesn't matter what happens, you'll always stroke me that way."
	Situation	"I know the fog's thick, but I've got an appointment."
Ability to React Differently	Self	"I know people change, but I'll always be angry."
	Others	"I don't like what you do, but you won't change."
	Situation	"I can't (they won't) change the appointment because of the fog."

Figure 3-2. DISCOUNTING STIMULI BY AREA AND MODE.

Type and Level	Area	Example
Problems	Self	Someone is sick or injured and proceeds as if nothing is wrong. "I'm OK."
	Others	People ignoring another person's distress. "He or she is OK."
	Situation	A person driving a car with bad brakes as if they were OK.
Significance of Problems	Self	"There's nothing seriously wrong with me, I've always been in pain (sick) since . . ."
	Others	"He or she is always crying (sick, angry) . . . ," said in response to another's distress.
	Situation	"The brakes are usually bad after 30,000 miles."
Solvability of Problems	Self	"No one can do anything for my pain (sickness)."
	Others	"Nothing can be done for (about) him/her."
	Situation	"The brakes always wear out, nothing can stop that."
Ability to Solve Problems	Self	"I can't do anything about my pain (sickness)."
	Others	"I (he/she) can't do anything about my (his/her) distress."
	Situation	"I can't do anything about the brakes, I'm no mechanic."

Figure 3-3. DISCOUNTING PROBLEMS BY AREA AND MODE.

Type and Level	Area	Example
Options	Self	"I have to keep my anger (thoughts) to myself."
	Others	"He was going to hit me; the only thing I could do was hit him first."
	Situation	"We need money for carpets; we can't afford a vacation."
Significance of Options	Self	"It won't make any difference to talk about my anger (thoughts)."
	Others	"If I'd talked to him, he'd still have hit me."
	Situation	"I'll still be tired, even if I have a vacation."
Viability of Options	Self	"No one can talk about their anger (thoughts) if they've never done it."
	Others	"No one can just talk when they are going to get hit."
	Situation	"People in our position can't take vacations."
Ability to Act on Options	Self	"Others may get something from talking about their anger (thoughts) but not me (him/her)."
	Others	"A person who is going to hit someone isn't going to talk."
	Situation	"I'm (he's/she's) not the type of person who takes holidays."

Figure 3-4. DISCOUNTING OPTIONS BY AREA AND MODE.

Passivity Confrontation involves a group dynamic, in which all of the individuals in the therapeutic community are held responsible for the transactions in which they are involved or which they are observing. They are accountable for all their thoughts and feelings arising from any transaction which is occurring, either between themselves or others in their immediate vicinity. Each is responsible for Undefended Relating, for not keeping thoughts and feelings secret or for acting in a Sneaky manner (see philosophy, pp. 10-11). Consensual validation is only possible if there is accountability. Each individual checks out what he *thinks* is occurring inside himself or in his environment. Each activity and behavior which seems inappropriate for the immediate circumstances is questioned, challenged or confronted as to its validity in the current transaction. A basic expectation in this behavior is that the confrontation is done in a Caring manner. The confronter is not expected to leave the confrontee personally diminished. Character assassination or attacking the person's personality is generally not considered a part of the Caring confrontation. Transactions that are Caring (I'm OK, You're OK, let's see what we can do about your Not OK behavior) are an important aspect of the Passivity Confrontation model. The philosophy and expectations around the Passivity Confrontation model create a highly Reactive environment for the individuals who are involved. Both the staff, the patients and any visitor involved in the community at any given moment may expect confrontation. Further discussion of the Transactional Analysis model used in this community will occur in conjunction with specific discussion of the ritual processes, healing experiences and "typical" experiences described as occurring at Cathexis.

Temporal Contexts

In the temporal context, and on a macroscopic level, the total experience at Cathexis fits the definition of Ritual Process. The individual enters, experiences and leaves the program via specifically structured processes. Descriptions of entry, experiencing and leaving as they are "typical" for any one individual follow.

(Entering)

Usually the person who comes to Cathexis makes an appointment with one of the staff or with the Director of the "School." He is allowed to visit for an agreed upon period of time, during which he is interviewed for goals, motivation for change and diagnosis. Often the interview is unassembled—the individual participates in the Drop-In program and everyone is involved in assessing his level of pathology and his usual Games. The diagnostic process involves at some point an MMPI and an intake interview by one of the salaried personnel, and/or all of the people in the program who interact with him during his visits to the Drop-In. When the general diagnosis has been made, often a subdiagnosis of type of pathology (type of schizophrenia) is also decided upon.[6] At this point a consensus is often reached by all who have talked with the prospective patient on his Games. The prospective patient is also interviewed for a Treatment Contract. Often a joint decision is made by staff and patients and the person is then admitted, or not admitted, to the program. In order to enter Cathexis' program, a diagnosis of schizophrenia is not necessary but is usual. The thrust of the program is towards curing schizophrenics. If the prospective patient is unwilling (or unable, too incapacitated) to make a firm Treatment Contract on a life change matter, he is admitted with a Minimal Contract. (An example of this would be an agreement to appear at the Drop-In center on a stated scheduled, and/or to come to a group to which he has been assigned.) When a Treatment Contract, which is agreeable to both staff, group members and the client, has been established the new patient works out a "program" with the director of the school. Patients usually come to Cathexis by self-referral, by referral from other professionals, on the advice of friends who are already in the program or of persons who have successfully completed the program.

(Experiencing)

"Healing and Dealing"

A typical week will include attending a Therapy Group for two hours weekly, attending the Drop-In daily for four hours each weekday and carrying out the elements of the "program" priorly agreed upon. Persons live in a residential treatment home, such as Gladman House, in the "cottage" as a part of the Schiff "family" or in some other arrangement in the area such as their own apartment, a nursing home or a halfway house. Most of the living-in arrangements involve the persons with others who use Passivity Confrontation. It is a general policy for persons in this program to be advised that they not live with their own families. This policy is based on the belief that the family-of-origin is heavily invested in the Passive behaviors which form part of the patient's pathology. Change by the patient will be blocked by the family's investment in maintaining their own Passivity and the Symbiotic ties. Those who are in a total Regression with a Reparenting Contract often live with the person with whom they have the contract.

Responsibilty—Learning to "Deal"

The daily activities for persons involved in the therapeutic community begin in various ways. This is consonant with the dependency needs, employment status and living arrangements of each individual. The household responsibilities are carried out by the members living together in any one of the above arrangements. There is no hired "household help." Most of the living arrangements are communal. Housekeeping tasks are agreed upon during the house-group meetings. The carrying out of responsibilities around daily life activities in a consistent manner is seen as part of the healing ritual process. The house-groups will use Confrontation in a consistent and highly reactive manner in order to bring about compliance with house and group standards. The expectation in each household is that the persons will become increasingly "responsible" in their daily experiences. An example of one person's view of "being responsible" follows.

> Sonny D.: (#4): "How I become a responsible person is when I show that I can take responsibility in caring and in confronting other people, and in doing something about the confrontations. Being responsible for things I get myself into is important. How I react to people and how I act ... settling matters as they happen instead of letting them go by. What I do now is hassel (defend)—I do not respond directly to what is going on, I mean, to the immediate problem. I do not deal."

The following exchange occurred between Sonny D. and Brenda R. in relation to a household problem:

> Brenda: (#11): "Sonny, the dishwasher did not get turned on last night and now we do not have any dishes for lunch."
> Sonny: (#4): "Well, I did turn it on."
> Brenda: "The dishes are still dirty. The machine must not have cycled. We still have a problem of dishes for lunch."
> Sonny: "What are you telling me?"

Brenda: "There are not enough clean dishes for lunch."
Sonny: "I'll turn the machine off now and we can put the lunch dishes in because it is not full."
Brenda: "That does not solve the problem."
Sonny: "I'll take care of the dishes, now, and after lunch."
(taking responsibility for the current problem).

This type of exchange is the source of information that the community members use as data in making group decisions about issues having to do with whether a person is being "responsible" in his daily living experiences. The persons in the community will exchange frequent information throughout the day with one another over the various matters involving running and living in a household. The expectation of each member is that the confrontations will end in the problems being solved and the differences being resolved. Where one member of the community is found by several of the other members to not "deal," their ability to function in a responsible manner is then brought into question. "Dealing" is an important concept in the framework of the Passivity Confrontation model. It is one of the key symbols in the adaptational strategies being learned by the participants in the program. "Dealing" is a concept whereby persons decide the amount of energy they are willing to invest in another member of the community.

"Dealing" is in some ways synonymous with "problem-solving" but has more impact because it is a "Martian" (Berne, 1972: 100-104) word—a word that a four-year-old would be able to absorb and use readily and a word that a Martian first coming to earth would be able to understand. In Cathexis community it has a more literal meaning than "problem-solving" and is understandable by the Child. A number of issues which have reality for the community members come together in this word, and this gives it multivocality (Turner, 1969). Following are a number of excerpts from interviews and written materials obtained from persons at Cathexis:

#2 DK: To deal means to get something settled.

#5 HI: It is peace after the storm. To deal is to relate again to a person I have been feeling uncomfortable with.

#6 EC: To deal means to take responsibility for my actions, good or bad, and to do something effective about solving the problems which arise from my actions.

#8 JP: I think that dealing is an important factor in living with other people. I feel good about dealing with others and others dealing with me because by dealing I get close to people and dealing is inviting [sic] for a more meaningful relationship.

#9 AC: Dealing means recognizing what I and the other person do to solve an uncomfortable feeling between us.

#10 KH: To deal is to take account of the situation, the other person's feelings, your own feelings and to solve the problem between us.

A high value is placed upon being able and willing to "deal." Value rests upon being aware of one's own inner reality, of the outer reality and in checking out the discrepancies between the two, as they relate to any transaction. When a person does not "deal," he is being Sneaky, i.e., is using defensive modes of relating and is not taking responsibility for what he is thinking or feeling.

The structuring of each day is done by the individual in relation to the treatment contracts and programs he has worked out with the "school." If the person has a job, that will be involved in his time structure. If he is in residence and not supporting himself, he will be involved in some type of schooling, household responsibilities or in activities which meet his dependency needs. Basic theoretical issues upon which this total program is based is that people in the program are encouraged to recognize their dependency needs and to learn to take responsibility for getting them met. All of the persons in the program are expected to plan some time-structure throughout his day; this may be plumbing, carpentry, gardening, homemaker, housekeeping, caretaking activities or Cathecting Little, and doing the activities which are commensurate with the age at which the person is experiencing the regression. The late afternoon of each workday is spent at the Drop-In Center. Therapy groups occur afternoons and evenings during the week. All group experiences, including the house-group meetings, make it possible for the individual to utilize a protected setting where he can check out discrepancies in his inner and outer realities and where he can experience Being Little. The patient experiences confrontation on his inappropriate behaviors. He can learn to be actively confrontive himself and learns to be caring. Manipulative and Symbiotic behaviors are talked about and dealt with; individual problem-solving is possible throughout each day. There will be more about transactional contexts and experiential settings in another section of this chapter.

(Leaving the program)

Leaving the program can be effected in a number of ways. One of the ways to leave the program is to get hospitalized. The use of hospitalization as a problem-solving strategy is frowned upon; a person who uses such an avenue is apt to get expelled from the community. It is believed that persons who need to use hospital structures for dealing with life crises do not do well in the Cathexis type of program. Hospitalization is a form of shifting responsibility to others without the appropriate structure for dealing with the problem. The hoped for and expected way to leave the program is to stay until one has completed one's Treatment Contracts and is ready to make Contracts for functioning in society or in another program. This is *graduating*. A number of the participants do accomplish this goal. Some movement in and out of the program occurs. Some leave takings are planned and some are not. A person who wants to change his program, who wants to get out of therapy, is expected to present a plan for leaving and to do this in his Adult Ego State. When he is able to do this, and show that he has given up some of the destructive and Gamey behaviors, he emancipates from his group and from the "school." Many of those who do leave too soon come back to complete further psychotherapy at Cathexis or find another therapist. Occasionally an individual will leave precipitously and impulsively over an unsettled problem (i.e., without "dealing"). This is called "running away." Coming back to Cathexis and the program is quite difficult if the person has left under such circumstances, or if he has been expelled. He must "deal" with everyone who was affected by his leaving in that manner. Ten percent of the clients leave the program without coming to terms with the staff and other participants.

If the person's manner of leaving is seen as fitting into "Third Degree" category of Game his coming back to the program may be impossible. His relationship with the program is severed completely. "Third Degree" Games involve what are known as "Tissue Transactions" which arise from Life Scripts with a violent Payoff. The Currency in Third Degree Transactions and Games is usually human flesh, blood and bone. The meaning of this is that in some way the person's life and limb is threatened through suicide, homicide or carelessness about others' or one's own life. Any such gestures are regarded as highly significant and are treated with great concern, i.e., they are reacted to with a high level of Confrontation.

Transactional Contexts

A portion of the transformative nature of the Cathexis experience occurs as a result of the Healing rituals. These are transactional experiences which are either structured or spontaneous. They occur in a number of physical contexts which have been discussed previously, namely, Groups, Drop-In, etc. A selection of the ritual experiences are described here, followed by examples of these transactional experiences as they occurred in the various group and transactional contexts.

(Healing rituals)

These are repeated, structured experiences which are used to provide the person with an opportunity to integrate the affective, the behavioral and the cognitive aspects of the learning they must experience in order to fill in their developmental lacunae. Transactional Analysis provides a common language built around the theory of Ego States and through it these three aspects of learning are effected. Richard Erskine (1975: 163) gives a careful explanation of this.[7] The healing rituals are apt to occur in a number of different aspects of the program. They were observed in the "family," in group therapy, in Drop-In, in Marathon groups, in the residential setting and in other informal gatherings. In fact, the rituals may be said to occur wherever persons are interacting in this community. Following are descriptions of some of the healing rituals which I observed and experienced at Cathexis.

The healing rituals which I observed at Cathexis can be said to fit the definitions given by Rappaport (1974) and Turner (1969b). That is, they are "a standardized system of stereotyped behaviors and communications which manipulate human emotion toward a preset end result," and "invariant sequences of formal acts and utterances," and "patterned processes in time" which are both diachronic and synchronic. They are phases in broad social processes and serve as cybernetic feedback loops for deviation correction and anticipation. The Rituals at Cathexis can be divided into three general categories: (1) *Thinking Rituals*, (2) *Feeling Rituals* and (3) *Doing and Being Rituals*. The rituals are structured so that each individual has the opportunity to experience each ritual repeatedly according to his own learning and dependency needs. This makes it possible for the person to incorporate the ritual as an integral part of his new system of transacting. As time goes on, he finds that he is "safe" using the rituals. He finds that transacting with people becomes less threatening to his old Frame of Reference. With the help of the rituals he can check his inner reality and find that it becomes more and more congruent with the outer reality. In time he finds more and more consensus in his transactions with people and, as this is increasingly rewarding to him, he transfers these abilities to the greater society.

(Thinking rituals)

Thinking rituals take a number of forms. These rituals are based on the belief that people who have psychopathology have not had appropriate experience in the use of their ability to think. This issue has been discussed under Diagnosis in Chapter II (page 63). The *Thinking Rituals* push the person to check out both inner environment and outer information in a standard fashion: for example, the person may be told over and over; "check out the stimulus," "what is going on inside your head?" "what is happening in the immediate environment?" "how about you *listen* to what Joe said?" "*LOOK* at _____, what do you see?" "paraphrase what I just said," "what do you HEAR Mary say?" Persons are required to use all of their sensory apparatus for information intake. They are told repeatedly "you can THINK," "how about you *Think*," "sit in that chair until you have *thought* about what is going on," "stand in the corner until you *think* about what you did," "you are Redefining —now *think* about what I just said . . . ." There is a constant demand placed on each person to "THINK ABOUT . . . ." The first step, then, is to check out the stimulus (see chart titled Discounting, Figure 3-1, page 97). The second step in *Thinking Rituals* is to encourage learning to define the problem. Persons will be asked repeatedly until they start asking themselves: "What is the problem?" Is the problem significant?" "What can I do about the problem?" "Who is the problem?" "Why is this person a problem to me?" "Where is the problem (inside me? outside me?)" "Is it my problem?" and so forth. All kinds of imaginable questions are raised about *the problem* to elicit thinking on the issues involved in "the problem." The third major aspect of the Thinking Rituals is the series of questions designed to elicit thinking about Options (see Discounting charts, pages 97-101) which are asked repeatedly until the individual starts asking the same questions of himself before resorting to his archaic and automatic modes of interacting. The participants practice identifying the Discounting mechanism in themselves and in others. By raising awareness of the mechanism the patient is progressively able to Think clearly. The "locked system of messages in the Parent corresponding adaptations in the Child, and an Adult which is mis-informed ... " (Schiff, 1975) which characterizes psychopathology begins to become unlocked. *Thinking Rituals* are an integral part of the total program at Cathexis. This type of awareness seems to have been omitted from the socialization process of many people in Wes-tern Urban Culture. It may be the result of what Mary Douglas (1970: 84-85) describes as a "low grid, low group" cultural experience. It is most blatant and more significantly absent in the socialization of persons with psychopathology.

Another *Thinking Ritual* which is a repeated process in the Cathexis program is based on a major Transactional Analysis concept, the Karpman Drama Triangle (see Figure 3-5).

> Drama in life, as in the theater, is based on "switches," and these switches have been neatly summarized by Stephen Karpman in a simple diagram he calls "the Drama Triangle" starts off in one of the three main roles; Rescuer, Persecutor or Victim, with the other principal player (the Antagonist) in one of the other roles. When a crisis occurs, the two players move around the triangle, thus switching roles. (Berne, 1972: 186)

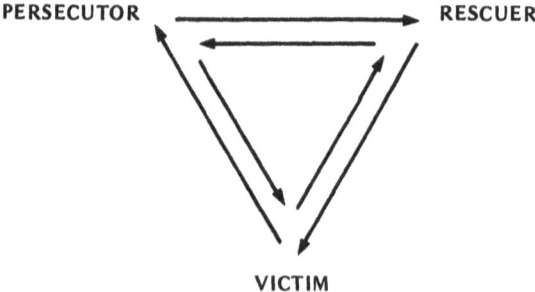

Figure 3-5. KARPMAN'S DRAMA TRIANGLE.

The Drama begins when these roles are established or are anticipated by those involved in the transaction. Manipulative roles are a part of people's manner of interacting with each other. Only three roles are necessary in drama analysis to depict the emotional reversals that are drama. These are action roles. They are the Persecutor, Rescuer and Victim (Karpman, 1968: 39-43). The Drama begins with the establishment of two or more of these roles by the persons involved. It can begin also when they are anticipated by those involved. No Drama occurs unless there is a switch in roles, between the protagonist and the antagonist. Every person from time to time plays all three parts of the Persecutor, Rescuer and Victim. However, each person tends to confront life more frequently from a favorite role. The primary role that is played is not always immediately clear. The player may *act* one way and *feel* another way. For example, it is not uncommon for a person who feels like a Victim to act the Persecutor. Each person in a Life Drama will be playing the role from both a social level and a psychological level. The *Thinking Ritual* built on the Drama Triangle requires that the person *thinks* about the roles he has just played in a transaction. He identifies the key positions in which he has just engaged. He *thinks* about and owns up to the payoffs: (Triumph, Pity, Guilt, Self-pity, etc.) both social and psychological, gained by him through the roles he has played. The Redefining Hexagon (see Chart Redefining, Figure 3-6) is a further *Think Structure* based on the Drama Triangle. Awareness of the Redefining Roles and the behaviors involved in Redefining provides another series of *Thinking Rituals* for understanding psychopathology, and for changing one's cognitive and affective frames of Reference (Figure 3-6).

> Redefining refers to the mechanism people use to maintain an established view of themselves, other people and the world (frame of reference, world view) in order to advance their scripts. It is the internal mechanism people use to defend their frames of reference and redefine the stimuli to fit in . . . it appears that whenever people redefine, their behavior is gamey or scripty; . . . redefining is used with the four passive behaviors to confirm or enforce the symbiotic relationships people require to advance their scripts . . . when people redefine, their options are limited by the structure of the symbiotic relationships their redefining and behavior established; when not redefining, people can determine and act on their own options without these restrictions. (Schiff, 1975: 54-55)

The process of Redefining is confronted in such a manner that the person becomes aware that this is what he is doing. The person quickly becomes interested in not Redefining. Participants are asked to focus repeatedly on the Symbiotic basis of their Redefining. This focus clarifies the three distinctive Redefining transactions: (1) the internal components of the mechanism, (2) the transactional aspects of Redefining and (3) the behavioral aspects. It also clarifies the six different roles adopted when people redefine. It points up the competitive nature of Redefining. People usually Redefine because of a current insecurity (dissonance) based on unresolved past experiences. These roles automatically carry out the Script Decisions and establish unresolved dependency. People present themselves to the world through each of these six major roles: Caretaker, Woeful Righteous,

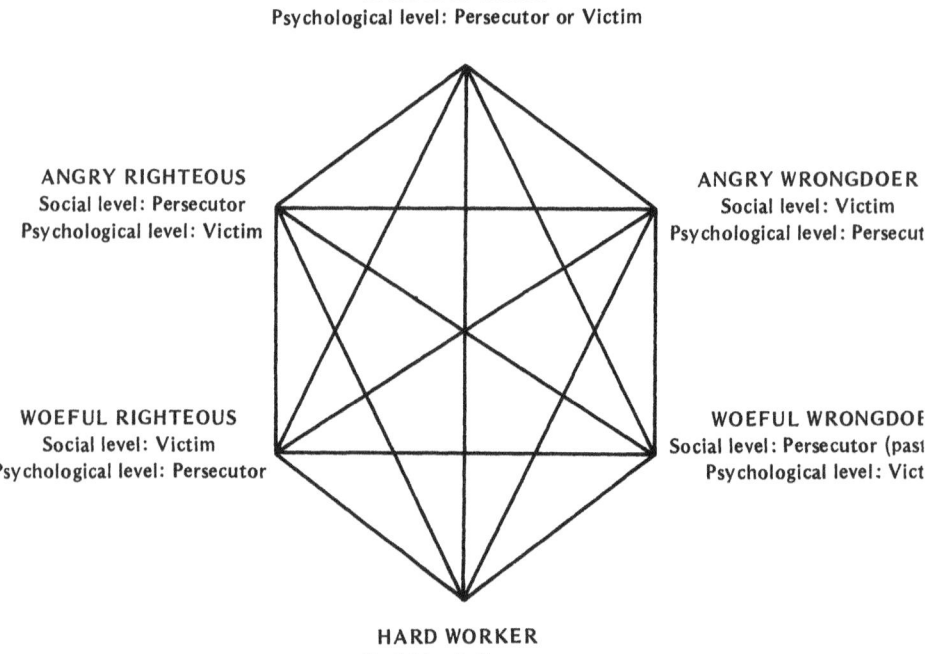

Figure 3-6. Redefining hexagon showing redefining roles and positions.

Angry Righteous, Woeful Wrongdoer, Angry Wrongdoer and Hard-worker. They are carried out and exchanged between players in order to make the players' Scripts work according to the protocol (Berne, 1972: 100-104).[8] Clear and repeated confrontation on Redefining and competitiveness comprises another of the Thinking strategies among the Healing Rituals in this program.

Thinking about feelings

Thinking about feelings comprises another series of rituals within the Thinking Ritual set. It is evident that a common Western Urban Cultural expectation is that when people are being emotional they are not able to think. The O'Neills discuss this characteristic in their book *Open Marriage* (1972: Chapter 7). The common belief is that being emotional excludes the ability to be clear-headed. Also, *being emotional* is often confused with *having a feeling*. Thinking is also confused with feeling in the common phrase: "I feel that . . . " and a statement of fact is added. At Cathexis, the individual is required to carefully differentiate "feelings" from "emotional rackets." In Transactional Analysis, emotions are defined as diffuse and are used to manipulate other people to achieve one's own ends. The repeated expectation is that the person will learn to make this distinction. It is planned, also, that he will learn to distinguish the difference between feelings.

People are often confused about the difference between fear and anger, for instance. This confusion often ariscs in early childhood when the child explodes into a "temper tantrum." It is labeled immediately as "that child is angry," Frequently no one has checked out what the child is actually feeling, which may be fear. Although a tantrum may *look* like anger to an unperceptive grownup, it may actually be a panic reaction. An important part of the Thinking Rituals is the process of awareness of the energy in the body—the ability to distinguish the source of that energy and categorize it as *mad, sad, scared* or *glad*. The notion about feelings is intentionally simplistic. Participants are taught that there are only four feelings expressive of emotion and also, only four sensations expressive of physiological states. The four feelings are *mad, sad, scared, glad*. The four physiological states are *pain, hunger, hot/cold, sexy*. These are purposefully oversimplified because theoretically it is the 0-5 year-old child who has not learned the differences. Many children are not confronted with the fact that they know something about

their feelings.   People then begin to learn at Cathexis that they are
expected to be able to tell the difference between a feeling, a sensation and a Racket (the TA term for emotion).[9]   A suggested
"Think Structure" appeared in the *TA Journal* in an article by
Pam Levin (III: 2: I/73: 38-40):

I am _____
                                      Feeling
That if I _____
                              Behavior I initiate
I will be _____
                          unhealthy Parent response
So I _____
                    problem justifying behavior
                    Game, Drama Triangle, Redefine, etc.

     Instead of thinking or feeling appropriately for this moment. I will
think about what I am feeling and think about my options.

An example of this is:

     I am *scared* that if I *ask for love*, I will be *rejected*, so I *act stuck up*
instead. /OR/ I am *sad* that if I *try to talk to my girlfriend*, I will be
contradicted so I *sulk* instead. I will think about what I am feeling and
check out my options for thinking and feeling.

Related to this process are ways in which persons can learn to experience awareness of and express feelings. These are designated as
Feeling Rituals.

(Feeling Rituals)

    Feeling Rituals involve actual practice in recognizing feelings and
encouragement in identifying and practicing the *mad, sad, scared*
and *glad* appropriately. This practice may be effected through a
number of the modern psychotherapeutic techniques such as psychodrama, roleplaying, tickling, fantasy exercises, rage-reduction experiences, gestalt techniques and various other imaginative approaches
including the Cathecting Little experiences. Cathecting Little has
been covered more fully elsewhere. It will be described in the
sections on the group, Drop-In and Marathon settings. All of the
above types of experiences allow the individual to spend some time
in the therapy setting actually *"being"* mad, sad, scared, glad. Participants are expected to *think* about the ways in which they would

expect to gain experience in the particular feeling and to structure such experiences into their program. For instance, a Rage Reduction Ritual requires that there be from eight to twelve strong, competent persons on hand to hold the individual's arms, legs, body and head so he may have a cathartic rage experience and not harm himself or others. Each person is expected to define his goals and the outcomes he has for the particular Feeling Ritual. He is to gain the assistance of the number of persons needed to be on hand. In many of the Feeling Rituals, the person will start with going through the motions of the structured ritual "as if" he were a certain age, or "as if" he were feeling a specific feeling, or "as if" someone significant such as "mom" or "dad" were actually present. The participant often finds that the "as if" disappears and he is transported into the actual situation, as in an altered-state-of-consciousness. This involves, for the participant, a transformation of the metamessages around the original experiences. Participants will stage these rituals in any of the appropriate settings such as at Drop-In, in Group or in Marathon. The *Feeling Rituals* often allow for a cathartic experience. If there has been a good cognitive framework set up ahead of time for the experience, the individual then finds out that he is able to express a feeling such as *mad* appropriately. The scare about being lost in an uncontrolled sea of emotion is dealt with and the patient can integrate the experience into his learning process. *Doing and Being Rituals* integrate the Thinking and Feeling learnings.

(Doing and Being Rituals)

Doing and Being Rituals overlap the two previously described rituals. These can cover any and all activities from the situational therapy experiences, to the structured therapy experiences, to those how-to-get-along-in-a-job-interview, etc. experiences. The individuals have an opportunity to role-play, to do psychodrama. They can learn to fantasize how they are going to behave in a specific situation and to gain structure from this.[10] They can do the same thing with old experiences where things "went wrong," or situations where things "went right." There is constant practice on the "how to" aspects of their daily lives. *Doing Rituals* involve the practical aspects of practicing of thinking—practicing feelings and practicing thoughts and feelings which are appropriate for specific times and places.

An interesting fact about persons with severe psychopathology is that they tend to keep their eyes out of focus. They see the world as a foggy blur. This is a defense against seeing and hearing things which were threatening to them when they were little. The schizophrenic is thought to have an inefficient way of sifting out all of the information which comes into their Nervous System. This theory is the basis of treatment with the antipsychotic drugs such as Thorazine. Recognizing that many of the individuals in the Cathexis program have visual and motor difficulties related to this incapacity, the Dolman Delcato treatment program has been instituted with some of the individuals (Delcato, 1974: Chapter X). This is a series of exercises calculated to assist the individual with visual-motor and gross motor retraining. It is similar to the Slingerland Dyslexia treatment program. Each individual's visual-motor functioning is evaluated and he is assigned specific exercises to do which will allow for the restructuring of the neuromuscular system around the person's deficit. Many of the *Doing Rituals* are structured around the theory of "recapitulation" which is described by Delcato:

> Treatment is based on recapitulation. If a developmental stage has been missed or short-changed,... the opportunity to go through the experience again to see if the child can profit from it by thoroughly re-experiencing it. We know that the brain can become better organized if the significant developmental milestones that have been skipped are retraced and re-experienced... we take the children back to a function typical of a much younger age. We have them practice the related motor functions that re-enforce their sensory development. (1974: 153)

Another aspect of the *Doing and Being Rituals* is that of the planned Regressions which are staged by each individual at some time or another. Some of the Regressions will be Spot Regressions with the person electing to experience a Regression to a specific age for only a few minutes or momentarily in a fantasy exercise. Another type of planned Regression is the total Regression which is only planned within a Reparenting Contract. Those individuals who have experienced a total Regression will actually become small infants biologically. They will follow through with developmental stages in a progressively structured manner. Ms. Schiff estimates that it takes about three to six weeks for each year of chronological age of the individual experiencing a Total Regression to return to their present chronological age with most of the developmental lacunae completed. Each age has its developmental tasks and its particular socialization experiences. Each individual will experience each of these as though he never has had the experience before. They even look as youthful as the age they are experiencing.

One of the "children" who is about age 14 in his regression, but who is actually in his late twenties chronologically, asked me today to show him how to shave himself. I took the request seriously and the ensuing teaching session was done in earnest as though this was the first time for this adolescent. He told me that he had never seen anyone shave in his family, nor had anyone taken time to teach him how when he was fourteen the first time. He learned how to shave himself under my direction and guidance as if he were actually fourteen and doing it for the first time. It was a pleasant experience for me. He told me later that he also enjoyed the experience and that he liked the way in which I sequenced the learning. (Field notes for August 11, 1974)

This episode points up the importance in the socialization of children that they see their elders modeling and doing things that are a part of daily life. Also it points up the fact that in many young persons' socialization grownups take for granted that their children will automatically know how to do certain tasks because they themselves do them. (A blatant example of this kind of default in socialization is how children are "taught" about the sexual experience in western societies.) Very often what happened in these persons' experiences as children was that they had long been "shut out" by the grownups and they no longer asked to be shown things they did not know or understand.

(Acting Out)

"Acting out" is no excuse for not knowing what to do or say in a situation. A basic expectation held in the program is that persons will ask for what they need, and will not "act out" around uncertainties in their daily lives. Behaving in a manner which is inappropriate to the setting, becoming hysterical, laughing when crying is called for, having tantrums, etc., are termed "acting out." Participants are expected to talk about problems as they occur and to "deal" with them. The expectation is that they will Function in their daily lives in a coherent and responsible manner; that they will take responsibility for what they need to know and what they need to do. If a person is aware that his Child Ego State needs to be expressive over an issue, or a series of issues, then the rule is that he will make arrangements to behave in that manner. Staged tantrums, rage reductions, psychodramas or other such extraordinary experiences are appropriate in "Protected" settings. The program proceeds on the basic assumption that each person has all three Ego States available to him at all times, however Contaminated, and is capable of planning and programming his life and his activities for the appropriate experiences.

Doing and Being Rituals are too numerous to detail completely. Some of them are further described in the sections on Drop-In, Groups and Marathons. These experiences fit the definition of Ritual. They are used to anticipate deviations in the patient's self-system and to correct deviations in behaviors. They are situational and processual. All of the rituals have their symbolic language. Some of them have symbolic implications for the participants. They are all closely related to basic bodily and physiological functions, such as birth, death, eating and elimination. Among the symbolic objects are items associated with childhood and with daily living activities in western cultures, such as chairs, corners, baby bottles, diapers and toys of various types. There is a ritual-like structure of form and meaning for the participants in all of the rituals and in the various other activities which are a part of the structured setting at Cathexis.

Learning to Cathect each Ego State separately (Uncontaminated) and at each developmental stage is not just a cognitive tool. It is a reality, and occurs through all Ritual Processes and in all transactions in the program. This means that one can objectively observe the person using a specific Ego State in any one moment. The experiencing of an Ego State is not just something which is going on in the other person's head. Continuing the discussion of Transactional Contexts, we will look next at the places in which the Healing Rituals occur and the descriptions of the settings and the rituals. These are the Drop-In Center, the Groups and Marathons.

(The Drop-In Center)

Drop-In occurs two hours a day on weekdays in the late afternoons at the "School." This setting consists of a modest single-level dwelling in an urban residential area. There are two group rooms, furnished with chairs and sofas, a kitchen area and a dining-living room area. The dining/living area of the house is well carpeted and furnished with large pillows, toys, children's books and playthings. All persons coming to the Drop-In have treatment or learning Contracts with the director. Generally "no contract" means not being allowed to use the facility. The cost for Drop-In is a part of the total charge for being in the program. During the two-hour period, the participant has the option of deciding how he will structure the two hours. He decides which Ego States he will be Cathecting during Drop-In. He then proceeds to interact with the other participants from that Ego State. Those electing Adult Ego State usually attend a problem-solving group where they have the opportunity to deal with current problems and to make changes in their programs. The usual rituals used in this type of group are Thinking Rituals. However, if the therapist and patient become involved in a gestalt experience about an inner dialog, or feelings, then Doing and Being Rituals may be used.

Those electing to Cathect Child will select the age they plan to experience. They will proceed to actually *become* that age and, with toys or games or other activities appropriate to that age, proceed to play. Participants in Drop-In who have "Bottle" and "Being Nurtured" Contracts will spend time during the Drop-In actually being held as an infant and being fed a bottle of formula. The bottle ritual is as follows: the individual negotiates with a staff member directly and without being ulterior—to be held and bottled for a specific time. If the negotiation in any way involves Redefining, Discounting or a Game of any kind, the transactions are confronted and "dealt" with before the Ritual may proceed. When the patient has settled down in the arms of the nurturing person, it is expected that he "fuss" or "cry" to get the bottle in his mouth.[11] Doing this permits the Child to learn that he is in charge of getting his needs met. He learns that small persons can ask directly for what they need and get it. He learns that the grownups do not mindread. They do not anticipate what he is thinking. He must make clear what he wants. This is an important issue with persons with thinking disorders. They often act as though others "know" what they are thinking and feeling themselves. They assume that they "know" what others are thinking and feeling. The bottle and nurture rituals and other rituals in the program force the patient to experience the fact that he must take responsibility for his own body and his own awareness and thoughts, he must be aware of his own needs, how to meet them and to state clearly his thoughts and feelings around those needs. Persons are also expected to be able to identify the physiological expression of hunger. The bottle ritual should not be undertaken if the stomach is full or if the patient has recently eaten. This process involves the patient in recognizing his bodily reactions to need and nurture.

The Drop-In is a locus in the community where the emotional Rackets (the buggy, unproductive, bratty and irresponsible behaviors which are manipulative instead of direct) are expressed and then confronted. Nastiness, giddyness, hasseling, fighting, whining, complaining and pouting and others kinds of Agitated or provocative behaviors are reacted to and dealt with. Persons who Cathect Child during Drop-In will do Play Therapy. They will play with the tinker toys, blocks, games, small stuffed animals, cars and trains. They may play with each other depending on the developmental stage involved. The staff engage with the children, holding, playing with, bottling, stroking, answering questions and defining appropriate behaviors for them as the need arises. The problem-solving goes on as a part of the process of Being Little. Each individual who is Cathecting Little is treated as though he really is a three-year-old or whatever his stated age for the Drop-In period. He is given the New Parent messages relative to what is occurring. He gains Adult information about the process as it happens. For example:

> Andy (age 26) and Wanda (age 22) were being four and five years old. They started skipping and jumping around the dining room. There were several smaller children playing on the floor. They were told to "stop bouncing around and think" about why this was inappropriate behavior for this time and place. Andy started to sulk (Racket), he was told to stand facing the corner until he had thought about what had happened, and what he could do about his behavior. Wanda said that she thought that it was because she might step on someone, and stated that she would not do that again here. The staff person who was reacting to the behavior responded by commending her for thinking, and for taking responsibility for her behavior. She settled down to play with the blocks. Andy spent most of the remaining time in the corner sulking. When he said he was ready to come out, a staff person agreed to listen to him. He said that he was jumping up and down because he liked to do it, and couldn't see why he had to stop. He was reminded that this was "justifying" his behavior. Rationalizing doesn't solve problems. He had to go back into the corner and think further about what had happened. Andy continued to sulk, producing no solution to this problem. He continued to use explanation and justification for behaving the way he had. By the end of the afternoon, he was reminded in a matter-of-fact manner that the rules require that he would have to think through the situation and find a solution to the problem, or stand in the corner each day until he did. (Field Notes, August 9, 1974)

This is an example of a Parenting episode which occurs often at the Drop-In. It is a therapeutic strategy which is described in the literature as spot Reparenting (Osnes, 1974).

Parenting and Reparenting are an aspect of most of the transactions which occur each day in the program. The patient knows what his Contracts are. He knows what changes he is intending to make in his own inner structure. In discussion and negotiation with the staff, he makes requests, or is given instruction, for the kinds of New Parent information he may need to incorporate. These New Parent messages then become a part of the rituals and daily process for the individual. A variety of issues are addressed in the Parenting process. Andy was learning new behavior and learning to take responsibility for it. Others may gain New Parent messages on issues of body care, nurture, sexuality, appearance, etc. The Drop-In program is geared to keep the clients out of the hospital. About ninety percent of those persons remaining at Cathexis for one year or longer remain functional outside of hospital settings. Over a longer period about seventeen percent become highly functional and involved in the world, many of them becoming highly productive members of society (personal communication, J. Schiff).

At the Drop-In, I observed and talked with persons who were in the traditional diagnostic sense: "very sick schizophrenics." They were behaving from time to time in the classic manner of persons with such thinking and feeling disorders. There was hallucinating, catatonia and occasional inappropriate behavior. The difference here was that each of these persons was confronted with a kind but firm request to "stop that behavior and think and talk about what is going on with you." Invariably the behavior would stop and dialog would ensue. The "very sick" person is still seen as able to think, to talk and to make some sense out of his environment. No one is ever treated as though he is incapable of doing something appropriate in a given situation.

(Reparenting)

Reparenting and Nurturing Rituals are rituals which occur throughout the program and which fit all the Ritual categories. These activities were observed in each of the settings including Drop-In. As explained previously, Reparenting can be done in a "Total Regression" or it can occur in "Spot Regression." An important point is that it is always a part of a Contractural agreement. The usual persons who do Parenting are staff. Sometimes Caretakers will also do Parenting functions. The first responsibility of the Parent is seen as a protective and nurturing responsibility. The information to the Child is: (1) take care of yourself and (2) you are important. The premise is that a child who had to take care of Mother, grows up believing then that Mother's needs are more important than his own. Consequently, the Child will be Sneaky about meeting his own needs. The second responsibility of the Parent is to encourage thinking and problem-solving. The information given to the Child is: (1) you can think, (2) you can solve problems and (3) you can do things for yourself. Both positive and negative reinforcement are viewed as important in conveying this information. Schiff sees that conditional reinforcement (Strokes) is important after age two for facilitating social awareness. The schizophrenic is seen as being a person who has been misinformed and reinforced for being different, unusual and devious (Sneaky) but not reinforced for being a real human being (authentic). Conformity is seen as an important developmental task and it is expected of all participants in their Reparenting. The "family" value system has to be conformed to. The "children" are expected to be able to do things they do not want to do without suffering over the tasks. With each individual, the decision to Reparent is based on the developmental issue with which he is dealing at the time. Much time is spent in Group sessions and in the Drop-In exploring developmental issues. Each person thinks through the history of his own childhood. Each person has to be clear in terms of the age at which he requires the Reparenting. Each person has to be specific about the information he requires. This process is effected through the frequent giving of diagnostic information about the usual growth and development issues and what the individual's current behavior is indicating to the observer. Information about developmental issues that persons are displaying in their behavior is fed back to them. Often suggestions such as "you think about what it was like in your household when you were three years old" are offered. Total Regressions are not dealt with in the Groups or in the Drop-In. They are only structured in the home settings of the person taking the Parent contract. Every time a Contract is made, both the New Parent and the person who is in treatment have to be entirely clear as to their joint expectations from the experience. Within the overall Reparenting experience are a number of rituals around being Nurtured.

(Nurturing)

Being Nurtured involves a Patient and a Caretaker (or staff). An agreement is worked out for any type of nonsexual[12] physical contact. This means that the individual will ask for, and get, experiences of being held in a Caretaker's arms or lap, being massaged, getting his head Stroked and any number of other kinds of touching and grooming types of behavior. Sometimes being held includes being fed a bottle. I asked a number of individuals what it meant to them to get a bottle, to be held and to "Be Little." The following are quotes from several individuals in the program.

Person #1: It means that I get caring, and get my needs met. I get things I think I didn't get when I was really little. I don't have to act inadequate to get my needs met. I feel safe, when I am being held.

Person #2: I am just *Being* for awhile. I do not have to DO what others expect. After being held I am not confused and I can think and solve problems and take responsibility for myself.

Person #3: The bottle experience is one of the ways of getting some of the bad stuff in my head worked out.

Person #4: I become aware of parts of my body like my mouth and lips and the feel of the milk in my throat as I swallow. I hear the heart beat of the person who is holding me and I am comforted.

Person #5: I feel safe, I don't hear anything of what is being said around me. Everything recedes and people's voices become unspecific and don't matter.

Person #6: I think that getting a bottle is like a programmed experience where I can get closeness and caring.

Person #7: It is like not being here at all, but in a warm, safe faraway place where I do not have to be tense and tight all of the time.

Person #8: I feel warm and safe, I don't have to do anything to be OK.

Person #9: Being little is important to me, it gives me a chance to see the problem where it started and work it out.

Person #10: Being held and getting a bottle gives me a chance to find out what I am like at one or two years old. Some of my old Parent gets replaced with new messages.

Person #11: My insides slow down and the tightness in my chest goes away.

The Drop-In playroom will often look as though there is a room full of toddlers all of whom are over five feet tall and weigh over 100 pounds each. At the end of the Drop-In period of two hours, the "little ones" will be told to put the toys away and help clean up. When everything is put away they are told: "Okay, Cathect your Adult now." The transformation is startling. The two, three, four and five-year-old behavior disappears and each person suddenly becomes a grownup. Some of the participants check out their programs with staff before leaving. Business that remains to be finished is cleared up. In a few minutes most of the participants have gone home. Some of those remaining for group therapy sessions socialize with one another while they wait for their group to begin. Drop-In is over for another day.

(Group Therapy)

The group therapy sessions involve five to eight persons who have been assigned to that Group and one or two therapists who are staff persons. The group rules follow the same cannon as in the philosophy of the community: undefended relating, responsibility for thoughts and feelings and no sneaky behavior. Persons are expected to think and talk about their thoughts outloud so that the discrepancies between inner and outer reality can be reconciled or resolved. The capacity to think, to think about feelings, to feel feelings and to do something about the feelings is expected of everyone, no matter what the level of their disability. The recurring expectation is that Group members will be prepared to raise the problems they are having and to find solutions to their problems through the group dialectic. They learn to "deal." A major learning from Group is that participants come to know what their needs are and how to get those needs met. Many of the same issues which arise in Drop-In and in the House Groups are dealt with in the same manner in Group Therapy. The process in this treatment lies in identifying personal needs, the problems related to the needs and how to seek the solutions to these problems so that the needs are met. The mechanisms of Discounting, Grandiosity and Redefining are confronted over and over consistently and precisely. Group may begin typically with the individuals wishing to "work on a problem" saying so. A hearing of the problem ensues with training in learning how to state a problem clearly and concisely. Following this, clarification of issues may be addressed. Finally, how the invidialual proposes to solve the problem may be

discussed. Usually this procedure raises Game behavior and investment in Script issues through Redefining and Discounting or Grandiosity. These behaviors are dealt with as they happen through a
variety of techniques. There is ample opportunity for reinforcement
and feedback during the interactions.

Transactional Analysis offers a common language which includes
the recognition of the actuality of the Ego States. The person who is
working on a problem may state it in terms of the internal conflict
between Ego States. Such an example follows.

> Sue D said that she needed to do something about increasing her
> sources of Strokes. She stated that she was having an inner dialogue which
> condensed basically into statements from her Controlling Parent; "it is
> dangerous to get love outside the family"; and from the Child: "I need to
> be loved I can't trust anyone." Sue was involved in checking out the
> Facts: i.e., the reality about the opinions of her Controlling Parent and the
> needs of the Child, and the sources of Strokes. She asked permission from
> the other members of the group to reject the Parent opinions and to think
> about trusting the members of the group and the therapist for Strokes.
> She acknowledged that she was very fearful about getting love from stran-
> gers, and could not let herself accept the caring from people outside of her
> family. When she went into the fear she recalled an incident in her child-
> hood that was clearly a Decision point for her. The two ritual activities in
> this situation involved Sue in experiencing the childhood incident in a
> fantasy replay, and allowing herself to be held by the therapist. (Notes
> from August 15 , 1974)

Both of the rituals Sue experienced come under the rubric of
"Cathecting Little." The participants in the Groups learn that they
can become aware of the gaps in their socialization and development
and, also, that they can request to structure experiences which will
promote the reexperiencing of ages, scenes and empty spaces in their
early years. Later Sue stated that she did not believe that she had
ever been held by her mother. Her history indicated that this may
well have been the case. She made an in-group Contract to request
Nurturing and to structure "being held" experiences in her house and
in Drop-In. She agreed that she would use the experiences for up-
dating her Parent and her Adult about herself and other people and
about the suitable sources of Strokes in her current life.

Group therapy experiences at Cathexis usually are structured
around Talking and Thinking Rituals. Contracts are made, problems
are solved and the transactions inside the group are focused upon.
The Doing and Being and Feeling Rituals enter into the group process, but generally more frequently occur in the other experiences

outside of group therapy. It is believed in Transactional Analysis
that if Group members resolve their in-group dynamics, they transfer
the learning to the out-of-group activities. If Sue was willing to
change the view she had about herself and her ability to get close
to people within the group, then she would begin to transfer this new
learning to her outside activities. The group process is based on the
Contracts for change that each participant has made. The Rituals
in the Group occur as a result of these Contracts. No two group
meetings are the same although the people are the same.

(House Group)

House Group involves all of the persons who live together in any
of the Residential Treatment settings. These are generally held once
a week. They may last from fifteen minutes to three or four hours,
or may even go on into the night until all issues have been resolved
among the members for that period. Sometimes an individual will
be left sitting in a chair in the Living Room when everyone else
goes off to bed because he has not "dealt." House meetings also
occur at the "family" residence. These include the persons who live
in the Cottage and all other people who have Contracts with the
"family."

There are a number of kinds of House Groups. One of these is
the formally scheduled weekly meeting for all of the persons in the
household. One kind of group consists of small groups of three and
four persons who have chosen to work together to solve daily
problems. This kind of group will meet spontaneously at any time of
the day. These meetings are impromptu and are called together by
one or more persons who have something to settle. They are set up
to allow two individuals to "deal" and a third person to be an objective hearer of the issue. These small groups allow the individuals
to clear their day of resentments and, also, unfinished business. A
major part of the enculturation to this community and the Passivity
Confrontation model involves practice in dealing with problems as
they arise. A third kind of group consists of the "Caretakers" meetings which are also apt to occur as need arises, but which may also
be scheduled. Caretakers are persons who have Contracts to develop
their abilities as Nurturing Parents. They are to learn to care for
others appropriately.[12]   Throughout any of the group meetings, or
in any of the daily activities of the participants in the community,
it is expected that no one will circumvent, ignore or accumulate

thoughts or feelings (see Stamp Collecting). In the example cited earlier, where Sonny D and Brenda R were discussing the lunch responsibilities, should Sonny have continued to "hassel," i.e., avoid the problem, Brenda would have called in a third person establishing an impromptu group for "dealing." Alternatively, Brenda may have set the goal of calling a small group before the end of the day to "deal" with Sonny about his behavior. The purpose of the group would have been to elicit a responsible stand from him. Further, if Sonny would not "deal" because of his defensive behavior, the matter would be brought up in House Group Meeting and more serious discussion covering his general behavior would have been raised. In House Group, when a person does not "deal," he may end up losing his house privileges until he "deals." This is called "being put on restriction" or "being put on supervision." When a person is restricted, he has to stay within the bounds of the restriction which is usually a physical one. Being on Supervision means that the person has to be within the vicinity of a Caretaker at all times, day and night, through all activities. Where a person is suicidal, sometimes Supervision includes the distance between patient and Caretaker being maintained by a short length of clothesline tied to both of them.

Restriction in the Houses, as in Drop-In and in Group, may range from being excluded from joining in House fun to having to stay in the living room all of the time when not engaged in chores or business. The person on restriction might have to sit in a chair until ready to "deal," stand in a corner, be put on supervision or experience some other kind of restriction of his activities. It is expected that he does some thinking towards a plan or program which implies responsibility for his actions in the future. Others in the community might also choose not to relate to (invest energy in) that individual until he settles the matter. This latter behavior is not synonymous with "silent treatment" of boarding school days; persons do talk to the individual on restriction, but the conversations are as a rule strictly business.

> Martha has a Contract to relate to Jacqui during the time she has come to Cathexis for a short-term experience. She has done nothing to fulfill this Contract in the first week of her stay. She is restricted to the Living Room of the residence until she comes up with a plan as to how she is going to carry out developing a relationship with Jacqui. People in the House are talking with her at meals, and during the day only if she initiates the conversations. (Field notes, August 6, 1975)

This experience usually results in the individual agreeing to, or adapting to, group pressure or coming up with a plan to meet his contract, or in some cases, may result in the individual choosing to leave the program rather than "deal." Maintaining one's place in the community is very important to most of the persons in it.

In the House Group meetings all household responsibilities are openly discussed. The financial arrangements of the House are carried out by a house finance committee or group. Gardening, kitchen and cleaning activities are mutually agreed upon in keeping with each person's schedule and level of responsibility. Each person is expected to take responsibility for his own needs. He is to consider carefully before taking on some task that he will later sabotage because he has not maintained awareness of his own limits. In House Group meetings, each person is expected to report on his progress with his own life and the parts of it he is Reprogramming. Each one gives information and feedback to each of the others in the House on their perceptions of one another's activities. An example of House Group business is as follows.

> In the House meeting I observed tonight, Jerry B was told by several people that they care for him and do not like to see him withdrawing as much as he has been observed to do lately. It was pointed out to him that they would like to see him do something about this problem, or leave the House. Aileen was asked by several people to remove herself from the group circle and sit apart and think about why she was giggling. It was noted that she did a lot of inappropriate giggling, and that the current behavior was an example of this. She was asked to make a commitment to stop this type of behavior. Joe was informed by several persons that if he continued to stall about making a decision to go into Group and get therapy, and stop his lack of responsiveness at the House, he would be asked to leave. Teresa's acting out hysterically earlier in the week was confronted. She made a behavioral contract for the remainder of the week to not use hysterical behavior as a problem-solving tactic. Andy told Brenda that he did not like the negative manner in which she approached him. Several people spoke up and corroborated Andy's experience with Brenda. She made a plan then and there for eliminating this behavior and asked for confrontation around being negative. A couple of people had broken in-house contracts that they had made with each other, and they decided with the group that they would spend their evenings on restriction in the living room until they had resolved the specific issues involved in the contracts. Two persons were commended on improvements that they had made around specific issues having to do with self care and housekeeping. They were praised by several who had noted these changes. Other discussion had to do with plans for a picnic and decisions about admitting a new member to the household. The staff

persons entered into the dialogs as peers, or from time to time provided an additional objective or theoretical piece of information. The ideo-emotional climate was maintained in this meeting. (August 5, 1974)

There are often bids on the part of participants in these meetings to cast the staff or house parents in authoritarian roles. The staff are reactive to these transference issues. They will ask for clarification in the language of Ego States, or use other therapeutic interventions to point this up. A frequent intervention involves the statements of fact: "I am hearing you ask me to tell you what to do." A variety of questions such as: "Are you asking for my permission?" "Do you want my Parent or my Adult to respond to that?" Patients will also feed back to the staff with "Hey John, that sounded like a very heavy Parent, is that where you meant to come from?"

A person wishing to live in any of the Houses must spend three days in that household and must be accepted by a majority of the residents before a decision to admit him is made. This gives every-one time to gain more knowledge of the person and to get an idea as to what his Games might be. With three days of interaction, he is better able to decide whether he himself wishes to live here. The residents are also able to decide if they wish to invest energy in this person. Many decisions are made on the basis of *energy*, whether persons who are already in the house wish to expend that kind of energy the new person might require of them as housemate.

(Marathon Groups)

According to Bach (1966:18, 995-1002), Marathon groups are a group practicum in intimate, authentic human interaction. One of the unique aspects of the Marathon Group is an intensification and acceleration of transparency (Jourard, 1967) and genuine encounter by a deliberate instigation of group pressure focused on specific behavioral change over a protracted period. The Marathon provides a natural gestalt, that is, a unit of learning experience which is not broken up into bits and pieces. Marathons can occur as a whole living experience, providing the participants with peer pressure, therapeutic interventions, time to practice changes and to experience new perceptions. At Cathexis, Marathons are one part of the healing ritual process. Many of the elements in the Marathon are the same as in the therapy group and in the Drop-In. The participants in Cathexis have an opportunity to experience as many of these Marathon groups as they need during the course of their treatment. Marathon Groups are generally conducted at a retreat or at the home of a staff member, where the facilities are adequate for comfort and for encounter. The Marathon lasts from two and one-half to four days. It is basically an extended group session. The two-hour group therapy sessions are microcosms of the Marathon and of the Ritual Process as described by von Gennep (1969).

All of the experiences at Cathexis fit the description of Rites-of-Passage in one way or another. Participants are in an overall *liminal* phase as long as they are experiencing the program. More specifically, a Marathon is a good example of the Ritual Process because all of the elements as described by Turner are there. Turner points out (1967: 93-111; 1969: 94-130) that Rites-of-Passage constitute transitions between states. By "state" Turner (1967) means a relatively fixed or stable condition" such as "married or single state," "the state of infancy," or an office or calling, rank or degree. He goes on to say that it can refer to the "physical, mental or emotional condition in which a person or group may be found at a particular time." He refers to any type of "stable or recurrent condition that is culturally recognized" (Turner, 1967: 94). The people in the Marathon are in the patient or participant state. The Marathon Group experience fits von Gennep's context in the way in which Turner defines it as follows.

Separation and Isolation. The individuals are separated from their daily lives and routine circumstances. There are no contracts permitted with the outside during the marathon. No phone calls are allowed. No one may live outside the house where the Marathon is being held. No one may communicate with anyone outside of the group of people who are either running the Marathon or are participating in it. During the marathon no one may isolate himself and be alone. All things are to be done in twos or threes when the group process is not in progress. There is a status-stripping and leveling in the beginning hours of the marathon. People are addressed throughout by first names. No regard is taken of a person's status, educational level or professional position in the regular world. During the sessions there is no socializing allowed. During meals and breaks, the socializing is kept to a minimum. Superficial socializing is not condoned, i.e., what is called "Victorian Socializing." The marathon is a guided experience based on Contracts for change made by each individual in the first hours of the marathon. The separation and isolation continues throughout the two to four days of the marathon. At the Cathexis community the marathon participants are not all members of the current patient population. The participants will include persons who used to be in the program. There may be outside therapists participating as patients. Other persons, such as educators who are interested in the experience of a marathon on the Cathexis model, will be participating also. Some of the participants come from very distant cities to be involved in working with Ms. Schiff. Marathons involve between fifteen and twenty persons, including the therapist and the two or three staff who may be assisting her. The marathon group becomes a world of its own for the period of its existence.

Leveling and Status stripping. This occurs as soon as the marathon begins. Prohibitions on using titles, last names and "being Nice" reinforce this. These prohibitions also tend to increase the sense of separation and of norm suspension. One is apt to be confronted and restricted for any of the behaviors which break the basic marathon rules. Some of the behaviors which are "normal" for some individuals will be seen as deceptive, sneaky, defensive or in many ways not responsible behavior. The unequivocal confrontations of these behaviors quickly strip the individual of much of the usual supports of his outside life. This creates for the individual a *norm suspension and inversion* of the usual and expected. He experiences a dissonance between the outer world and his inner world. Almost all of the rules which constrain interaction in the dominant society seem to be either suspended or turned around during a marathon. Men and women hold each other as one would hold a baby. Sexual connotations to holding, which would be usual in the larger society, do not enter into these types of interactions. The marathon is a prototype family. During its process, all the members are relating in such a manner as to increase their awareness of the Parent, Adult and Child. The incest taboo is in force for all participants, as it is in any normal family. Aside from the ethical issues the observation of the taboo provides a climate where problems related to the expression of sexual energy may be clarified Parent to Child and Adult to Adult in a nonthreatening environment. Bottles and Being Little are used by persons of differing ages. Persons who have contracts to be very Little (babies) are diapered and fed as babies are usually cared for, regardless of their chronological ages and greying hair. Direct Confrontation on thoughts and feelings are the order of each day. If face-saving mechanisms are used there is immediate reaction and demand for honesty. Every aspect of the developmental cycle may arise for someone at some time during the marathon. It will be experienced and discussed in terms of what the individual can gain and how he may grow. The developmental issues form the symbolic basis for the Contracted changes proposed by each person. Many of the rituals experienced during the marathon are taken from culturally defined life crisis situations such as birth, death, weaning, toilet training, menarche, etc.

The liminal phase. The liminal personae are defined by the contracts they make at the beginning of the marathon. The following are examples of some of the different types of contracts made at various Cathexis marathons in which I participated between 1972 and 1975.

1. I will be two years old and resolve the controlling and omnipotent behavior I did not complete when I was two.

2. I will resolve the smart-mouth competitive issues I have around being nine years old which interfere with my functioning now as a grownup.

3. I will find a new direction in my life and examine the issues which are keeping me stuck at this time.

4. I will take responsibility for being defensive and will listen to and deal with any confrontation of the defensiveness.

5. I will resolve Decisions I made at age five which cause me to believe that I am responsible for other's suffering.

6. I will be three years old, and differentiate between feeling mad or scared, and stop mixing them up.

7. I will be three years old and fill in the gaps in knowledge and in feeling on the issues of sex and my sexuality.

8. I will confront the difficulty I have in defining myself as separate from others. I will do this as a one year old.

9. I will accept confrontation on all aspects of my behavior which are perceived as seductive and/or provocative.

10. I will be a tiny baby and experience being reborn again so I can get a new perspective on the world and find it a safer place this time.

The liminal period proceeds entirely on the basis of the Contracts for change which the participants have made with the therapist and the staff. These commitments are maintained by the group canons which have been discussed in the section on Philosophy. All liminal personae are held responsible for discussion and definition of all transactions on the basis of what each person has Contracted to change in himself, or what his job is at the marathon. The staff usually Contract in terms of the service they are providing. Some of them function explicitly as therapists, Caretakers or facilitators of the process, and the Contract each one makes is implicit in the role they have taken for the time period. Nevertheless, a staff person may Contract for confrontation on issues that will improve his learning to become a good therapist. Some examples of contracts made by staff are:

> I will entertain confrontation on any interventions I make which are from the Rescuer position.
> I will listen and be reactive to each problem that arises.
> I will accept and deal with confrontation about my Bossy Parent.
> I will work on improving my Nurturing Parent skills.
> I am working on increasing my listening skills.

"Dealing" continues on all levels at marathons just as in the other settings. There will be spontaneous "dealing" and there will occur situations where "dealing" is planned and structured. Everyone is expected to "deal." One of the characteristics of *Liminality* is the statuslessness of the participants. In a Marathon, as in the total community at Cathexis, the persons are defenseless. They have agreed to desist from neurotic and psychotic defenses which characterize their usual manner of transacting. Since defense mechanisms are unconscious, this Contract results in direct and often acutely unpleasant confrontations of behavior which is seen as defensive. If a person smiles when he is angry, laughs when the topic is not amusing, his behavior will be discussed in detail. For the person who "suffers" this can become an extreme hardship.

The first time I experienced a marathon was an anguished and extremely difficult time. This fact of confrontation of all defenses raises questions about social control power, why persons are willing to put up with this kind of treatment and, what is more, pay large sums of money to involve themselves in it. Complete discussion of this issue of social control, and others of group norms, power and communitas occur elsewhere in this work.

The setting of Contracts is the first part of the Ritual Process experienced as the Marathon group gets underway. The plan is that each person will be able to achieve a resolution of the problem represented by the making of the Treatment Contract. Contract setting involves considerable dialog between the therapist, the group participants and the individual setting the Contract. It involves an exploration of developmental issues and a careful consideration of the appropriateness of this Contract for this person, at this time and in this place. During the Contract-setting process, there may be a number of questions raised for eliciting information about the individual's developmental history, family history and previous treatment history. When the Contract-setting process is complete, each individual will have arrived at a Contract which is reasonable for him and ascribed to by a consensus of the people present. At this point each person writes his Contract on a blackboard, or on a large piece of paper, where it is visible to all and can be referred to from time to time throughout the Marathon. Occasionally during a Marathon a Contract will be amended by discussion with the therapist.

Once all of the Contracts have been set, each person goes into the particular group which will provide the setting for his working on his Contract. One group consists of those who are going to Cathect Little. The other group is made up of those who will problem-solve in Adult. The "little ones" are supervised in play and interaction by staff therapists. The others enter into a problem-solving, group-process oriented group where talking therapy will be the major mode used. The "children" move in and out of the group room listening to the process and occasionally asking questions about what the "grownups" are experiencing. Occasionally, a "child" will cathect Adult with the therapist's permission and join the group process. The healing rituals in a marathon are the same as described in all of the other group settings in the Cathexis structure. There are people Being two year olds, Being nine months old, Being "naughty," and Being "nice"; all of these experiences provide the individuals themselves with insights and the therapists with information for feedback.

One of the Healing (Doing and Being) Rituals is the "rebirth experience." This experience takes the form of a symbolic reliving, or reexperiencing, of the moments of conception, gestation and parturition. It is enacted in the form of a psychodrama. One of these psychodramas is described below:

> The protagonist curled up under a blanket or quilt. She was held and touched over the whole of her body by the hands of the other participants in the group. Before beginning, the baby-to-be, assigned meaningful (to her) phrases and statements to the other persons present. Roles such as Aunt Jane, Mother, sister Susan were also assigned. This patient's goal was that the "baby" inside her would be born again with a new and safer perspective on the world. She assigned phrases and statements to the group members which were as follows: "I love this baby," "I am glad I am pregnant with this baby," "I'm glad she is a girl," "the world is a good place to be." A number of similar statements were to be made which would imply to the "baby" that the world was a safe place and that she would be loved, and that she was really wanted by the New Parent. She stated that she would "hear" the statements, and that she would "accept caring this

time" instead of reject it. She stated specifically that she would be allowing herself to grow up feeling safe. The statements about her health, and
her sanity were couched in positive terms. The whole experience is planned
and timed by the "baby," and when she emerged from the blankets she
was treated just as a newborn baby would be treated. She experienced
being held, fed a bottle, and cared for in every respect as a much-wanted
baby would be treated. The New Mother who was the Therapist on this
occasion held the "baby" and gave the "baby" the information she had
requested. Other family personae did the same. She spent the next several
hours being a "baby" and being cared for, including being diapered and
bottled, and tucked into a crib, and being held. Her reflexes and reactions were very similar to a newborn infant's. I noted that after that phase
of the marathon was over she moved her body and limbs with more grace,
and in a more relaxed manner than she did before the experience. She also
had a calmness of face, and a glow in her skin which was not previously
present. (Notes from January 11, 1975)

Although in this experience reported here, the Mother was the therapist, occasionally she may be some other person in the group whom
the patient chooses. This surrogate-mother gives the "baby" new
information about his existence. He gets new messages about the
world into which he is being reborn. All of the messages are picked
by the patient to counter the Old Parent information which has
been destructive or belittling. The messages are always constructed
to counter the four messages described in the chapter on the
Cathexis philosophy.

Peak experiences. Throughout this rebirth ritual and the other
ones in which I have participated, there is a sense of joy and high
excitement and expectancy in the group. In talking with participants
and assessing my own experience, it appears that for some of the
participants there occurs a "peak experience" in this ritual. The
descriptions given me resemble descriptions found in the literature
on religious experiences. It follows closely Maslow's (1967: 71-92)
description of "peak experiences."

> ...may be seen as a fusion of ego, id, superego and ego ideal, of
> conscious, preconscious, and unconscious, or primary and secondary
> processes, a synthesizing of pleasure principle with reality principle, a
> healthy regression with fear in the service of the greatest maturity, a true
> integration of the person at all levels.

We experienced a communication of high energy and excitement
during and following the above rebirth ritual. Throughout the Marathons there is movement from pleasurable peaks of excitement to
extremely unpleasant and personally painful experiences. Each

Ritual may often represent a phase in the process of the dialectic between thinking, feeling and behaving: the thesis, antithesis and, finally, the synthesis. The high experiences and the low experiences are each followed by a period of structure, when Redecisions are most often apt to be made. The obstacles in the person's movement toward change are examined and reprogrammed. Redecision theory is one of the Transactional Analysis notions developed by the Gouldings (1972: 62) based on Berne (1965: 269-278). He states that healthy Decisions are adaptable statements of purpose: "I will be thoughtful and devote myself to living a fine life." A pathological decision is a verbal absolute, a determination of conduct in psychiatric patients (and that is what makes them patients) that leaves no room for adaptation because of its absoluteness: it is "never" or "always." "Never again will I love anybody," or "I will always hate women." "I'll be mad forever." Because the Child made the Decision, it is possible in the therapeutic ritual process to uncover the old decision in the Child and provide the environment for the individual to make a Redecision about the conduct of his life in the present. After making a Redecision about himself, the individual usually experiences a surge of energy. In the group experience this may be transformed for use in lucid thinking and in planning for one's life in the world. The sharing of this surge of energy results in the sharing of *communitas*, of an *I–Thou bond*. Each experience for each individual, whether his own or that of others, creates a sense of power in the face of his Script (which at times seems overwhelming). From the sharing of these experiences, each individual in the marathon comes to gain insights into his own motivations and is able to make plans which are more reality oriented. Turner points out (1976: 19-39) that:

> Spontaneous communitas has something "magical" about it. Subjectively there is in it, the feeling of endless power. But this power untransformed cannot readily be applied to organizational details of social existence. It is no substitute for lucid thought and sustained will. On the other hand, structural actions swiftly become arid and mechanical if those involved in it are not periodically immersed in the regenerative abyss of communitas. Wisdom is always to find the appropriate relationship between structure and communitas under the given circumstances of time, and place, to accept each modality when it is paramount without rejecting the other, and not to cling to one when its present impetus is spent.

The Marathon experience is a Rite of Transition. In it, both structure and communitas occur. It represents a guided experience which offers the participant a protected environment where "the bubble of perception" (Castaneda, 1974) can be broken out of. It provides a protected environment where therapeutic rituals can be tested. It provides an environment where new learning can occur. It provides the setting where personal power comes with the discovery that one can transform archaic Decisions to Redecisions about oneself and one's world. *Communitas* provides the "magic" and the energy to perceive oneself, one's world and others in a different way. From this experience the individual gains personal power (Casteneda, 1974). The "magic" and the power gained from the experience allow the individuals the ability to think about their experiences, in the past and in the present, and fit their views to present "reality." The Marathon is a microlevel rite-of-transition of which the total Cathexis community is a macrolevel rite-of-transition. The individuals in the Cathexis community pass through all of the various rites of transition in the process of transforming their World View from the psychopathological one to the "normal" World View.

Reintegration. In moving from the world of the Marathon back into the larger community, the individuals involved experience aggregation (Turner, 1974). For those who are from the Cathexis community there is little change in their larger experience for the community rules are the same as the Marathon rules. For those going back into the greater society and reintegrating into their old networks, aggregation is sometimes a problem. Since the "bubble of perception" is different, and the sense of personal power has changed, sometimes there is difficulty in adjusting to the persons who expect to play the same Games as before. Also reverse-culture-shock is apt to occur. In general, for the Cathexis patients, reintegration into the larger society occurs for them on a daily basis and they have the opportunity to test their new skills of perception and power over a long period of time.

SUMMARY

In this chapter I have described the Cathexis healing community, its setting, structure and function. I have shown the various ways in which an individual experiences the community in the process of self-transformation. I have examined the Healing Rituals and their definitions and the settings in which they are experienced. I have discussed and described the various group modalities through which the individuals at Cathexis gain the new cognitive framework which is the essence of the healing process.

Following is a presentation of the self-systems of selected individuals in the program. A discussion of the transformation which the participants in the study experience as a result of their stay in the Cathexis program makes up the text of the next chapter. The results of the analysis of participant-observation materials and test materials are used to show that people do change in the Cathexis treatment model.

NOTES AND REFERENCES

1. The word "cathexis" is defined by Berne (1966: 298): "a concentration of energy on a given object; to put all one's energy into one ego state." Parsons (1965: 5, 10, 11) defines "cathexis" as "the attachment to objects which are gratifying and rejection of those which are noxious, lies at the root of the selective nature of action."

2. The community and its components break down in a flow manner with direct communication occurring between all of the parts of the system as follows (at no time was their structure in a formal hierarchical order):

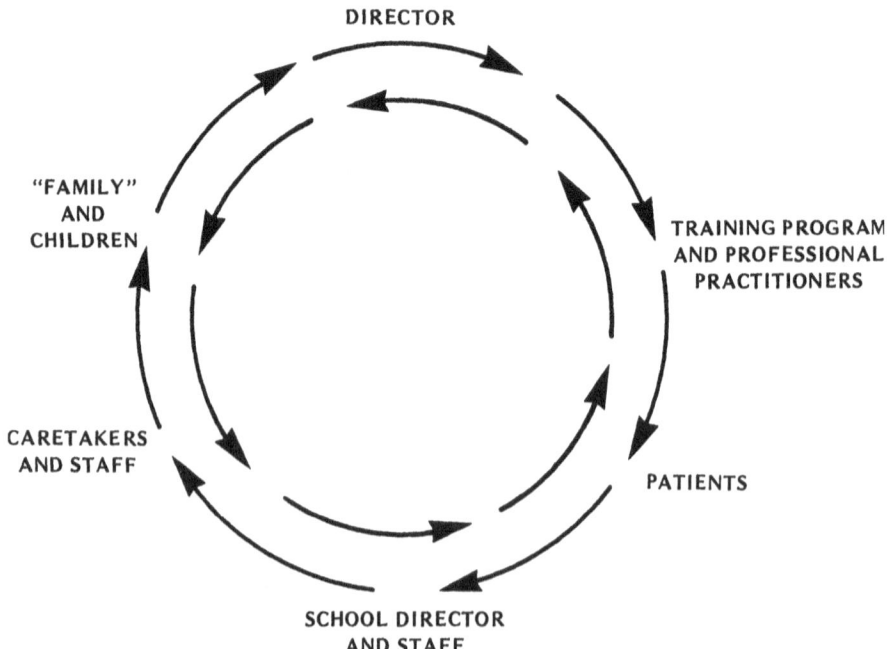

DIRECTOR

"FAMILY" AND CHILDREN

TRAINING PROGRAM AND PROFESSIONAL PRACTITIONERS

CARETAKERS AND STAFF

PATIENTS

SCHOOL DIRECTOR AND STAFF

3. With regard to defense mechanisms, Freud's definition of these underpins the T.A. Theory of Rackets and Games. The mechanism of projection of archaic experiences is a part of Redefining. Carlos Castenada (1974: 237) refers to Don Juan's demand that he "stop indulging," "stop the inner dialog" as part of the process of becoming a warrior is probably a related process. Don Juan says:

> Take self-pity again. It was useful to you because you either felt important and deserving of better conditions, better treatment, or because you were unwilling to assume responsibility for the acts that brought you to that state that elicited self-pity.

4. Contracts—see Chapter I, pages 46-47.
5. Instinct: Bowlby uses this word himself. It is a controversial and little used word in the social sciences. So far as a set of behaviors it has been applied to animal studies, but not to human studies. Bowlby states that the paradigm used in his works is based on current evolution theory and is the same as that of modern biology. Its main features are inherent in a model of motivation summarized as follows (Bowlby, vol. II: 81):

— behavior results from the activation, and later the termination, of *behavioral systems* that develop and exist within the organism, and are of very varying degrees of organizational complexity;
— the behavior that results from the activation and termination of certain types of behavioral system is traditionally termed *instinctive* because it follows a recognizably similar pattern in almost all members of a species, has consequences that are usually obvious value in contributing to species survival, and in many cases develops when all the ordinary opportunities for learning it are exiguous or absent;
— the *causal factors* that either activate or terminate systems responsible for instinctive behavior include hormonal levels, the organization and autonomous action of the central nervous system, environmental stimuli of particular sorts, and proprioceptive stimuli arising within the organism;
— the *biological function* of a system responsible for instinctive behavior is that consequence of its activity that promotes the survival of the species (or population) of which the organism is a member, and does so in such degree that individuals endowed with the system leave behind them more progeny than those not endowed with it;
— the *environment of evolutionary* adaptedness is the environment in which a species lived while its existing characteristics, including behavioral systems, were being evolved, and is the only environment in which there can be any assurance that activation of a system will be likely to result in the achievement of its biological function;
— behavioral systems develop within an individual through the interaction during ontogeny of genetically determined biases and the environment in which the individual is reared; the further the *rearing environment* departs from that of the evolutionary adaptedness the more likely are that individual's behavioral systems to develop atypically.

6. The Cathexis subdiagnoses are based on MMPI data, clinical information and their own observations about the developmental experiences of the patients. They have developed several categories of classification which are: Hebephrenia, the most regressive of the schizophrenics; Catatonia, characterized by a gross behavioral slowdown often interspersed with periods of violence or running; Paranoia, where the patient habitually escalates anger over fear and developmentally the disturbance occurs as lack of socialization in the 8-15 month period; Hysteria, the personality which is characterized by emotional outbursts, over-adaptation, an apparent, often feigned shallowness and exaggerated attention to appearance issues; Manic-depressive, which occurs as a result of competition between the nurturing person and the Child over who is going to avoid the Agitation; the Obsessive-compulsive which is characteristic of persons with family backgrounds where there are long distance quarrels, little nurturing, and anger and fear are not differentiated. The other diagnoses which are touched upon are Depression, Character disorders, inadequate personality, and phobias (Schiff et. al, 1975: 78-87).

7. According to Richard Erskine (TAJ 5:2: April 1975: 163) one of the reasons TA is such an effective psychotherapy is that it incorporates *cognitive*, *affective*, and *behavioral* approaches to problem-solving. TA fuses the three approaches in the following manner: the cognitive in teaching TA theory and identifying with the client why he or she is having a problem; the affectiveness in the work done on removing old blocks and establishing new ways of experiencing feelings; and the behavioral in the negotiation of a contract for treatment, which specifies what the client wants to change, how he or she will behave differently, and how other people will know he or she has changed.

8. Redefining: Each of the characteristics of the Redefining roles can be seen in the related Game. For example, Woeful Righteous and Woeful Wrongdoer may be seen in the Game of "If it weren't for you," and in "Wooden Leg"; the Angry Righteous Role in "Now I got you S.O.B." Aside from redefining roles there are three types of Redefining relationships. These are the Symbiotic type, the Parent-competitive type and the Child-competitive type. In the first type, the persons:

> ... generally expect B to take care of A, define situations and do the thinking. They also expect A to express feelings, make demands around needs, and take only token responsibility for perceptions, thinking, and feeling, behaviors and meeting his or her own needs. B discounts his or her Child needs and feelings; A discounts his or her own Parent and Adult abilities. (Mellor, 1974: 306)

In the second type of Redefining relationship the basis of the relationship is on a:

> ... competition for the Parent/Adult position in the symbiosis. The stakes of the competition are the "survival issue" because the symbiosis is threatened. Each person attempts to get the other to overadapt to his or her definition of the situation, issue or event. Both are discounting feelings and needs, and are collecting stamps to justify the escalations they will use to establish the symbiosis in the Parent/Adult position. (Mellor, 1975: 306-307)

In the third type of Redefining relationship the main ingredient involves competition for the:

> ... Child position in the symbiosis. Again the symbiosis is threatened, and the stakes revolve around the "survival issue." Both are demanding that the other person "take care" of them symbiotically and are discounting their responsibility for themselves ... the favored positions on the Karpman Drama Triangle appear to be Victim and Persecutor, and both people usually attempt to occupy the same position simultaneously. The most intense competition thus tends to develop around the Victim position.

9. *Webster's Dictionary* describes emotion as:

> ... an agitation, disturbance, or tumultuous movement either physical or social. Any such departure from the usual calm state of the organism as includes strong feeling, an impulse to overaction. synonym: feeling.

10. A key issue in the mental illnesses, and particularly in schizophrenia, is the assumption by the schizophrenic in "magic." That is that people can "magically" tell what he needs without his asking for or taking responsibility for stating his needs. Training the person out of these assumptions requires frequent confrontations of the issues around the assumptions that other people's powers of perception and of mind are exceptional and "magical." The patient's Grandiosity allows him to assume that he does not have to inform others of what he is thinking or feeling because they just "know," nor does he need to find out what they are thinking and feeling because some sort of ESP or "magic" will provide the information he or they need. This type of assuming of power and of expectations of transfer of thoughts often leads to expressions of rage and impotence. This type of behavior in the Passivity framework is known as an Escalation to violence or to Incapacitation. Training in informing others of one's thoughts and feelings, and checking out what is going on in other people's heads is basic to every interaction. This is not to say that ESP does not exist, or that the crazy person's powers of perception may not be exceptional. The issue is that of the Grandiosity which goes with *assuming* one "knows" without actually checking the facts.

11. Observation of the Incest Taboo is a key treatment issue in all psychotherapy. Many therapists who are not clear on the power exchange in the transference and countertransference (Parent Child Symbiosis) phenomenon break this taboo. Recent examples of this have shown up in the news media where patients have sued their psychotherapists for malpractice and won the suit. This issue of patient-therapist exchange of sexual favors is an ethical issue being raised in professional associations also. It is a problem that deserves careful study, without the pronouncements of morality (Controlling Parent) or the fear inherent in the breaking of any Taboo. Careful study of the implications in psychotherapy of the Incest Taboo have yet to be done. A preliminary discussion occurs in my article, "Implications of the Incest Taboo for Nursing Practice" (Gowell, 1973b).

12. Parenting is a caring and limit-setting function. Many of the individuals in psychotherapy are there because they did not experience caring, and have not introjected these functions into their own psychological structure. Learning to be a Nurturing Parent is a part of the process of learning to take care of oneself and getting one's own needs met.

Chapter IV

MADNESS: IN THE BEGINNING
AND AT THE END

When I was mad, (crazy) I did not think, I reacted to everything and everyone automatically. I believe that one has to be able to think in order to derive benefit from life. Learning to use the think structure of Transactional Analysis assured me of finding a way to move from dependence on a kind of magical intervention in my life to independence and to interdependence. Resolving my madness made it possible for me to acknowledge consciously my essential unity and connectedness with all of life. It also made clear my unique separateness. Being able to think has become an essential part of my education for survival and fulfillment. (Cara, d. 1974)

World View (changes in cognition) transformation is the topic of this chapter.   In it I describe the World View of the patients at Cathexis.   The material on world view which I collected at the beginning of the study is compared with that collected at the end of the study. The period of data collection spans twelve months, August 1974 to August 1975.   There were fifteen people in the study to start, nine female and six male.   At the end there were twelve, seven female and five male.

The purpose of this part is to respond to the questions about the efficacy of the Transactional Analysis model in changing World View. This chapter will show that:

Persons with psychopathology known as schizophrenia do show some changes in (1) personality profiles, (2) World View and (3) personal constructs about Self and Significant others.

Further, this part will demonstrate that the Cathexis community approach to the treatment of schizophrenia is effective.

141

Interview Techniques

The subjects were asked to fill out a questionnaire comprising 72 questions (see Appendix). Each incomplete and complete questionnaire was completed with a face-to-face interview with the person. Each question was answered with one sentence. Selected individuals were talked with about their current lives and their selves. The face-to-face interviews were open-ended interviews conducted in conversational manner in the setting in which the individual was at the time. Some of the questions were taken from the Life Script Questionnaire and some of them from the special group of questions which were chosen from the MMPI.

Schizophrenia as Psychopathology

Etymologically, schizophrenia means schiz = broken, phrenos = soul or heart. A schizophrenic is literally one who is broken-spirited or broken-hearted. One wonders about the subjective experiences of individuals whose spirits are fragmented. In order to survive in spite of this fragmentation, those labeled schizophrenic appear to have developed an adaptive strategy which Haley terms "the art of being schizophrenic." This "art" covers a broad spectrum of behaviors. Haley says that the schizophrenic has to come from the:

> ...right sort of family...as individuals the family members are unrecognizable on the street, but bring them together and the outstanding feature is immediately apparent, a kind of formless, bizarre, despair, overlaid with a veneer of glowy hope and good intentions concealing a power-struggle-to-the-death coated with a quality of continual confusion. ...He must have learned to manipulate and balance complicated, conflicting family triangles, and he must be perceptive enough to keep his feet in a morass of trickery and despair .... As a consequence he must become skilled in concealing his emotions, he must learn to indicate that whatever he did just happened and he is not responsible for it, he must perceive the threats in every situation, and he must achieve skill in stabilizing whatever system he is in by being a willing scapegoat to support the inadequacies of those around him. (Haley, 1967: 156-157)

It is widely recognized that parents of people who experience psychopathology are less stable and consistent than parents in general. However, they are not so unstable as to be unable to maintain themselves in society. A number of dissertations and other studies indicate parental instability as a key factor in childhood emotional disorders (Hafner et al., 1969: 185). If parenting is the "medium for the message" of psychopathology, then parents themselves are transmitting a similar (crazy) experience. Henry's *Pathway's to Madness* (1965) studies the fact that no matter how well intentioned the parents may be, they themselves experienced so many double-binds in their own enculturation, they are simply passing that experience on to their children.

Laing (1967: 104) states that about one-fifth of mental hospital admissions in the United Kingdom are diagnosed as schizophrenic. He believes that there are hard data to indicate that "we are driving our children mad more effectively than we are educating them. Perhaps it is the way we are raising our children that is driving them mad." How this is being done is one of the questions in Henry's study (1965) and in this study.

Studies of family networks of schizophrenics conducted at Yale, Pennsylvania Psychiatric Institute, the National Institutes of Mental Health and the Palo Alto Psychiatric Institute, among others, have shown that the person who is diagnosed as schizophrenic is part of a wider network of *disturbed and disturbing patterns of communication*. In cases studied at the Tavistock Clinic regarding the social events surrounding schizophrenia, it was concluded that the behavior so labeled "is a special strategy that a person invents in order to live in an unliveable situation" (Laing, 1967: 114). Haley (1967), who is quoted earlier, supports this opinion. Those labeled schizophrenic are beset by contradictory and paradoxical pressures and demands. The pressures are from inside himself, and from those around him. He is as if in the position of checkmate in a game of chess. One of my own clients expressed to me that as a child the choice was to be "trapped or slapped." Following is a description of the Cathexis sample, which comprises this study.

The Cathexis Sample: Life Script Questionnaire and Interview Data

The information gained through interviews, Life Script Questionnaires, observation and participation in treatment and living settings follows. Most of the persons who agreed to participate had been in a previous treatment in other settings and had been at Cathexis for from six months to three years at the time of my first contact.

Cultural and Family Data

The racial, religious and family backgrounds of the persons in this study showed the following breakdown: most of them were from "Old American" families of Western European extraction (Figure 4-1). The majority (over 50 percent) of their antecedents were of Anglosaxon heritage. Most of them came from German (40 percent) and English (13 percent) backgrounds.

Country of Origin	Number	Percent
German	6	40%
English	2	13
Scotch	1	7
Polish	1	7
Irish	1	7
Danish	1	7
French	1	7
None designated	2	12

Figure 4-1. Ethnic Origin of Subjects in Study.

Religious backgrounds of the subjects (Figure 4-2) indicate that most of them came from Protestant families (10 = 67 percent). Those from Catholic family backgrounds represented 20 percent of the sample (three persons). There was one of Jewish family background and one person did not designate religious affiliation for the family.

As far as *family size* is concerned, all had one or more siblings, the family average number of children was 3.5 children. The distribution of family size was three families with two children (20 percent); six families with three children (40 percent); two families with four children (13 percent); one family with five children (7 percent); and two with six children (13 percent). *Ordinal position* among the participants in the study indicates four individuals were the oldest (27 percent); two were second (13 percent); five were third (33 percent); and one was fourth (7 percent) and one was sixth (7 percent).

There was one twin, and one not designated. The *ages* of the subjects range from nineteen years to thirty-nine years. The mean is 25.7 years at the beginning of the study, the median twenty-five years and the mode twenty-one years (Figure 4-3). Educationally, these persons had achieved considerable number of years of schooling. The range was eleven years to seventeen years of primary, secondary, college and graduate school. Occupations represented were teaching, nursing, psychotherapist, trucker, carpenter, student, artist, educational consultant, sales and wholesale specialist.

Religion	Number	Percent
Lutheran	3	20%
Catholic	3	20
Protestant	3	20
Episcopal	2	13
Baptist	2	13
Jewish	1	7
None	1	7

Figure 4-2. Religious Background of Subjects.

Major life threatening experiences, such as suicide, hospitalizations, surgery, birth experiences, etc., were represented as follows: nine of the subjects (60 percent) had experienced at least one hospitalization of some kind for surgery or for severe illness during their childhood. Psychiatric hospitalization for psychopathology was admitted to by ten (67 percent) of the individuals, five of them (33 percent) denying psychiatric hospital experience. All of them had had some experience in psychiatric treatment in other modalities. Some of them used were gestalt, psychodrama, bioenergetics, z-therapy, classical psychoanalytic, counseling therapy and encounter group experiences. All of the interviewees denied any outstanding traumatic experience during their childhood. They all claimed a repetitive type of abuse or neglect from persons in charge of their lives when they were small. One of them claimed birth trauma or family stories about difficult or unusual births. Two persons reported that their mothers had characterized their births as a "nuisance" and "irritation," or "I came at the wrong time." All of the subjects stated that they were not truly welcome to their parents, but were "tolerated." Those who had older siblings stated that they were welcome to the older brothers and sisters though not necessarily to the parents. One of the subjects reported mother and father who were totally "devoted." Subsequent information indicated that this stance was a part of the denial system of this person. The facts were that there had been a series of nursemaids and this person was sent to boarding school at an unusually early age.

Range	19-39	years
Mean	25.7	years
Median	25	years
Mode	21	years

Figure 4-3. Age Breakdown of Subjects.

Relationships in the Family

The subjects reported that their relationships with parents and older persons were of a consistent type. Interviews corroborated one mother in the descriptions of the ways in which each perceived "big people" as talking to them as children; they consistently reported experience with significant persons who "talked down" to them when they were little. They reported that these particular persons still do that. Some examples:

#1 C.M.: "They talked to me as though I was stupid and not worth talking to and didn't matter."

#7 I.E.: "They talked *at* me not *to* me."

#8 J.F.: "They talked to me as though I wasn't a person, but as though I were a thing, an animal, or a complete baby."

The consensus was that all big people whom they experienced were condescending, used teasing, joking and mocking modes of communication.   A repeated point made was that these "adults" saw the children in the study as objects and not as human beings. When queried about subject matter when the "adults" did talk to them, a frequent response was that most of the material covered in conversations had to do with superficialities like weather, clothing and food. No one reported discussions or conversations on topics that were intimate, close or authentically related to the child's own concerns.

My impression from the questionnaires, observations and interviews is that to be a child in these families was to experience one's self as an object and as a burden to the older generation. Another impression was that the family members had little skill in relating in a "real" or transparent manner (Jourard, 1967) with these subjects as children.   It appears that their humanity was largely negated. The sole models presented to these children were limited in scope. My presumption is that it would be difficult to develop a language of communication, or skills in interpersonal relationships from imitating or modeling the persons who were responsible for these patients as children. Excerpted below is one of the personal accounts:

> When I think about it, I don't believe that there ever was a time when I got my needs met on my terms. I cannot recall for instance, ever feeling satisfied after a meal even though there was always plenty of food. My memory of meals was of always having to eat something I did not want or like. My mother considered it a personal affront to her ability as a cook and as a mother if any portion of the food was not eaten. She would get hysterical, beating her breast verbally and tearing her hair figuratively. A typical example of the sack-cloth and ashes "woe-is-me," "what-did-I do-to-deserve-this-child," kind of behavior. Other times she would resort to silent suffering and I never knew specifically what had set off this episode. In some deep inner sense I always believed that I was being reproached for the act of my birth. I think that deep down, my mother could not stand to have a baby at that time, and I was living reproach to her of her lost youth.   She would get stiff when her mother, my grandmother, came around too. My grandmother was very pushy, domineering and always got her way.   I stayed away from her, I needed to make this wall to survive when she came, I thought I would disintegrate into many pieces if her energy got to me. My dad was always angry. He was apt to be violent without warning. He was always blaming his circumstances, my mother, his boss, the kids, his brothers, or anyone who was in his line of vision. I thought I was guilty of some horrible secret and that he knew what it was. I made him mad by just *Being*. I learned to stay out of people's way and not say anything. My mother says that I was a "good, quiet child." That is until I was fourteen, then I broke all of the rules. I really showed them. (#13 TS)

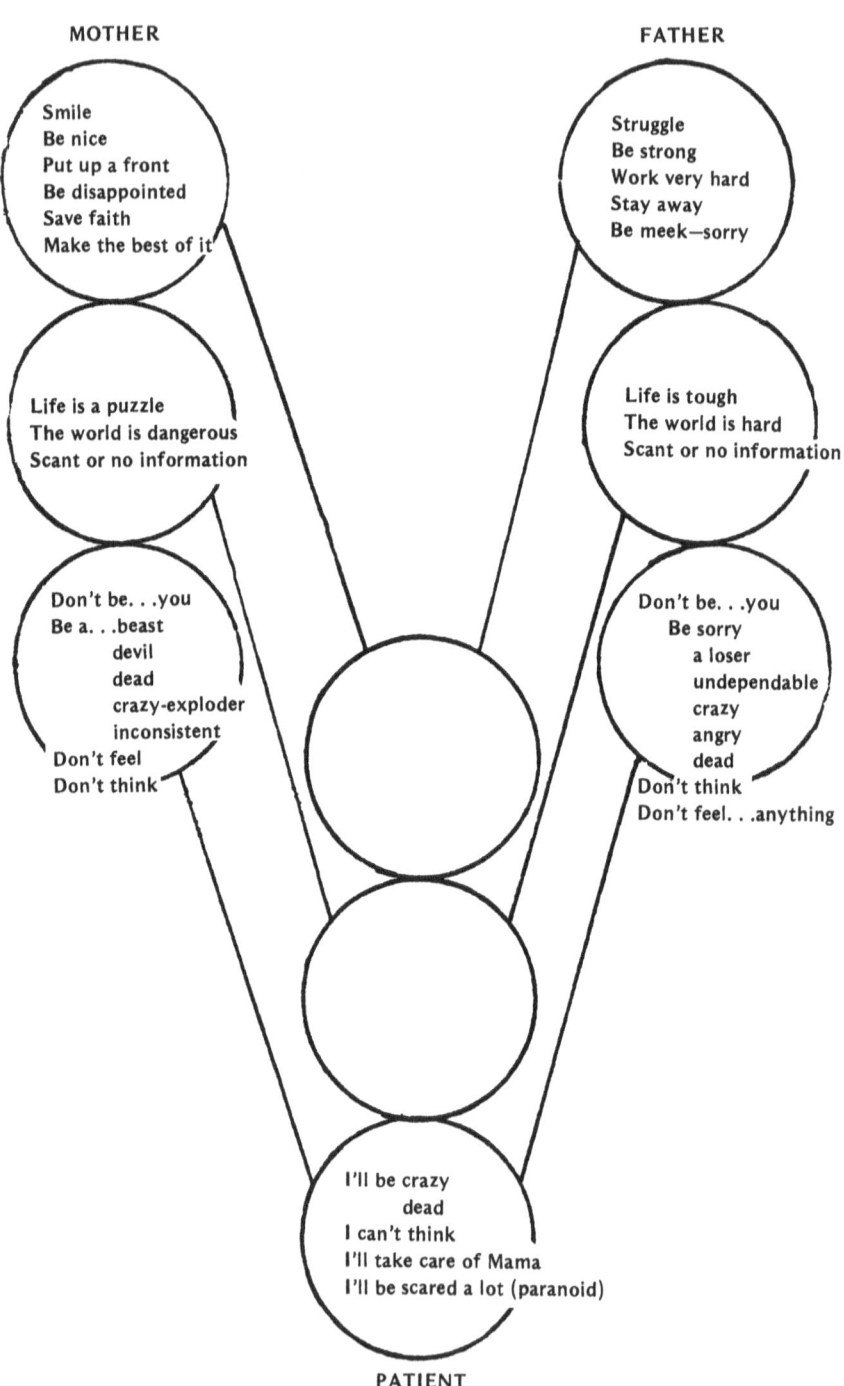

MOTHER

Smile
Be nice
Put up a front
Be disappointed
Save faith
Make the best of it

FATHER

Struggle
Be strong
Work very hard
Stay away
Be meek—sorry

Life is a puzzle
The world is dangerous
Scant or no information

Life is tough
The world is hard
Scant or no information

Don't be. . .you
Be a. . .beast
devil
dead
crazy-exploder
inconsistent
Don't feel
Don't think

Don't be. . .you
Be sorry
a loser
undependable
crazy
angry
dead
Don't think
Don't feel. . .anything

I'll be crazy
dead
I can't think
I'll take care of Mama
I'll be scared a lot (paranoid)

PATIENT

Figure 4-4. Typical Script Matrix for Subjects at Cathexis.

Family World View

The patients' interpretations of their parents' World Views and their parents personalities are considered Family World View.

Responses to questionnaires brought out descriptive material about mother and father as they are now and as the patients remember them when children. Each person was asked to provide a short sentence describing mother, father and their favorite or most common saying about life.

Mother

Two of the patients (13 percent) saw "mother" in a positive light, at least describing her as a "kind, quiet" type of person. Thirteen (87 percent) gave only negative or derogatory descriptions. Commonly used words were: "cranky," "crabby," "cold," "rigid," "distant," "unpredictable," "ignorant," "easily depressed," "easily upset," "high strung," "hysterical," "overprotective," and "withdrawing." The descriptions of "mother" changed hardly at all with each subject from the beginning of the treatment at Cathexis to twelve months later. Interestingly, characterizations of "mother" before and after treatment were similar.

BEFORE	AFTER
#1. C.M.: "Cold, rigid and angry, she put up a good front."	#1. "Cold, rigid (sic) angry, doesn't show affection, gives material things."
#2. D.K.: "Scared, angry, depressed, crazy."	#2. "Nice, hysterical, overadapted."
#3. F.A.: "Crabby bitch."	#3. "Nasty, deceitful, sneaky, dishonest."
#4. G.J.: "Most of the time quiet, the rest of the time yelling and/or arguing."	#4. "Very withdrawn or yelling."
#5. H.I.: "Quiet, sad, or yelling, unpredictable."	#5. "Quiet, sad, yelling and jumping up and down."
#6. E.C.: "She cries, she's fogged out."	#6. "Fogged out, cries a lot. New Mother is strong, caring, independent."

#7. I.D.: "Unpredictable, explosive, vindictive, sadistic, incapable of showing affection or loving children."

#7. "A murderess, a witch, a monster, abusive, never happy."

#8. J.F.: "Flighty, hysterical, out of touch with feelings, gallows laughter, always busy, high society, bridge and Chanel #5."

#8. "Out of control, agitated, busy, sudden outbursts."

#9. A.G.: "Cynical, seductive, superficially caring."

#9. "Agitated yes-person, over adapted, manipulative, hysterical."

#10. K.H.: "Good, hard working, quiet, uncomplaining, helped old and sick and homeless, etc., she was matter-of-fact."

#10. "Good, never complaining, nice."

#11. B.C.: "A kind woman who means well but is ignorant and needs more information. She would get agitated and hysterical and scared."

#11. "Kind, absent-minded gentle woman, satisfied with her own life. Hysterical when things went wrong."

#12. M.E.: "Cold, distant, ungiving of herself, overprotective, hysterical, religious withdrawing and sulking."

#12. "Cold, ungiving of herself, religious fanatic, self-sacrificing, martyr, artistic and withdrawn.

Patients were asked "what was your mother's favorite saying about life?" The following list of sayings is indicative that these women had a World View of a difficult, demanding and uncompromising existence. These mothers were characterized as being persons who would put up with a lot before they would do anything about it. Patient G.J. said that mother was "quiet and unassuming and uncomplaining until something happened, and then she would explode and yell a lot." I. D. said that mother would just use "words, words, words, until there was nothing left." Five (33 percent) of the subjects stated that "mother" was a victim and a martyr, and she saw the world from a hopeless, powerless position, totally at the mercy of their husbands and families. Favorite sayings about life were:

#1. C.M.:   "Look good even though times are rough."

#2. D.K.:   "It's a challenge."

#3. F.A.: "What a crock of shit, I might as well kill myself, I'd be better off dead."

#4. G. J.: "I don't know if she had one."

#5. H. I.: "Make the best of it" (meaning that there wasn't anything good about it).

#6. E.C.: "With my luck . . ." (anything or everything will turn out badly, including me).

#7. I.D.: "Life is a disappointment, you can't get what you want."

#8. J.F.: "She had no saying, except Be Nice."

#9. A.G.: "Life takes away as much as you get."

#10. K.H.: "Life is unpleasant and puzzling and it is best to not think about it, just live it. Have faith."

#11. B.C.: "This isn't the end of the world. It would be easier if people did what they were supposed to."

#12. M.E.: "Have faith and don't think about it. It's not safe."

#13. T.J.: "Don't think life will be handed to you on a silver platter. People are no good and they'll take advantage."

#14. H.R.: "You'll be the death of me." and "Whatever you do, do it well."

#15. R.C.: "Be strong, and keep up a good front, and look at things positively."

Further descriptive information about "mothers" was elicited through the Semantic Differential. This material is included later in this chapter.

Fathers

In characterizing "father" there were thirteen (87 percent) who gave negative description, one (7 percent) who offered a positive one, and one (7 percent) who was neutral. Words used to describe father were: "beaten down," "always angry," "mean," "severe," "cruel," "homocidal," he "kills with words," "overbearing," a "violent man." A content analysis of the words used to describe "father" showed the word "angry" coming up in more than half of the descriptions (53 percent). Other words which were similar were "violent" (27 percent) and "argumentative," and "blaming" which came up along with these two above. In an overall analysis, other words indicating a grownup who was out of control as opposed to a pleasant and considerate person were expressed. Out of a total of sixty words which were used to describe the fathers, forty of these (66 percent) were of a violent, or forceful nature, sixteen (25 percent) of them were complementary, and seven (9 percent) were neutral. There were at no time any words which would indicate that these fathers were seen as "warm, loving, kind or close" or that they related in any way to the children as human beings. The "father's" most favorite saying about the world follows:

#1. C.M.:   "It's a dog-eat-dog world."

#2. D.K.:   "There has to be some purpose and some way to be happy" (but it'll never happen to me or you).

#3. F.A.:   "It takes a lot of hard work, but you can do it if you try hard" (but watch out, because I don't see how).

#4. G.J.:   "That he had to walk ten minutes to school so why couldn't I. That it's a hard world."

#5. H.I.:   "It's a hard life, and you'll never make it."

#6. E.C.:   "The little guy doesn't have a chance. Get as much as you can since nothing else is worth living for."

#7. I.D.:   "The world is too tough, you'll never make it."

#8. J.F.:   "Be prepared for death, people are not O.K. and I don't trust anyone."

#9. A.G.:   "You'll never make it, it's a hard place."

#10. K.H.:   "Don't trust. Be honest, be dependable."

#11. B.C.:   "It's an angry, sad and scary place and you might get eaten."

#12. M.F.:   None

#13. T.J.:   "Life is a struggle for everyone."

#14. R.C.:   "They leave me alone and I leave them alone."

#15. H.R.: "What you put into it is what you get out of it."
(since you're shit, you'll get shit).

The overall picture is of a group of bitter, angry, hardworking, downtrodden, unfeeling and alienated set of men who were the "fathers" in this study. Most of the descriptions of relationships with the parents were on the basis of punishment. Transactions reported as children were expressed in terms of punishment. The indication was that getting noticed meant getting punished. Questions about punishment elicited comments about kinds of punishment and the remorse and guilt that followed the parental outburst. Typically "father" would get drunk, withdraw or explode; and/or "mother" would withdraw or explode. Someone in the family (usually the subject) would get or feel punished, or experience guilt about the explosion.

Punishment

Subjects were asked to define the use of punishment in their family as to type and degree of punishment. Eight of them claimed that punishment was the only mode of communication in their family. This represents 53 percent of the respondents. The patients characterized punishment as "mild," though I would have characterized the descriptions as "severe" at best. The punishments described are as follows:

#1. C.M.: "I would be restricted, sent to my room, I couldn't have friends over, I would have to do extra work. I would have to stay in my room a long time" (moderate, sometimes severe).

#2. D.K.: "Whipping and hitting. They would not talk to me. They would ignore me for days" (mild).

#3. F.A.: "I would get hit with a clothes hanger, a belt, flyswatter, spatula or a hand, they would hit a lot, a lot of yelling and cursing" (mild).

#4. G.J.: "Sometimes spank. Yell and scream. Tell me I was no good" (mild).

#5. H.I.: "Spanking, hitting, being ignored, slapping, yelling" (mild).

#6. E.C.: "Beatings and noncommunication" (severe).

#7. I.D.:   "Isolation, spanking and abusive and cruel and crazy behavior. Burned with cigarettes and fire.   Thrown off the stairs" (severe—required physician's care).

#8. J.F.:   "Put in room alone in bed for the day. Shaming me in front of people. Leaving me alone by walking away. Laughing at me. Using lots of words on me" (severe to the mind not to the body).

#9. A.G.:   "Used spanking and escalating anger at me.   Beating and acting superior" (moderate).

#10. K.H.: "Spanking and scolding, yelling" (moderate).

#11. B.D.: "Very little notice of what I did. Punishment might have been better than nothing" (mild maybe, but a vacuum is severe).

#12. M.E.: "Slapping, hitting, a face slapping, forced to go to room" (moderate).

#13. T.J.: "None, no notice at all" (mild).

#14. H.R.: "No punishment, no nothing, never made to do anything" (physically mild, mentally severe).

#15. R.C.: "Spankings, restrictions, abandonment" (severe).

In a few of the subjects' experiences, the spankings, and verbal abuse were better tolerated than the total rejection and not being noticed. Such behaviors as belittling, ridiculing, rejecting and active destruction of the person's dignity such as mocking, jeering and blaming were claimed. Three of the persons claimed that they would rather have been beaten to "get it over with" than the constant verbal abuse which was reported. Also, isolation was reported as being most severe. Subjects were queried about what "did you do when your parents acted 'upset'?" A typical response was made by #13. T.J.: "Making myself scarce was the best way to deal with it, but if I couldn't do that, or get away, I would try to melt into the wall." Three-fourths (10) of those interviewed responded to the effect that it was their responsibility to try to make the upset parent feel better in some way, to "try to get them to forget the problem" (#5.H.I.). As to "how you did that?", the responses varied; but all talked with implied that the taking on of responsibility for the feelings, actions and even thoughts of the "adults" was something they tried to do. Four (27 percent) claimed that getting the "adults" to focus on them was often a relief and cut the tension in the family. The scape-goating, or focusing on the subject, would eventually be a part of the individual's identity. It would be one of the ways in which he would be able to distinguish himself as Real or Not Real, i.e., as existing. As long as the subject was getting the energy from one or both of the parents, he could know that he was alive for that moment, however painfully so. Being isolated was like being dead.

World View and Self Concept

The excerpt on page 147 gives a flavor of family life for one of the individuals in the study. This section will describe some of the typical statements concerning themselves and their ideas about the world given by informants. The quotes are representative of the types of statements they made about themselves in response to my request that they describe themselves, and "describe how you experience yourself as functioning in the world as you see it." In general, the picture given is dismal. About 66 percent responded only with uncomplementary adjectives about themselves. The other 33 percent gave either neutral or mildly positive evaluations:

#1. C.M.: "I am anal, sensitive. Not functional."

#2. D.K.: "Scared, angry, depressed, crazy, no good."

#3. F.A.: "An O.K. person, sometimes negativistic, not very caring, scared."

#4. G.J.: "I am a bad guy; the black sheep of the family. An H-addict. No good for myself."

#5. H.I.: "Quiet, and sad, a baby. I don't like myself any."

#6. E.C.: "Evil, distant, clumsy, do not relate."

#7. I.D.: "Battered abused child. Evil. A devil. I am just a person, maybe with some ability."

#8. J.F.: "Gentle, angry, violent, false energy and motivation. A dead child unborn. Very little inside, anal, turnwords (sic) giddy and invested in getting well."

#9. A.G.: "Potentially brilliant, energetic, crazy, humorous, angry, bitter and a shithead."

#10. K.H.: "Sad, lonely, have problems getting along at work which I don't understand; problems relating to men, want to be a baby; am maintaining myself precariously."

#11. B.C.: "I am externally angry and not caring but responsible. Internally scared, sad and very young. Negativistic and fault finding. Destructive."

#12. M.E.: "Changeable from very functional, caring and giving to destructive immobile, scared, dead."

#13. T.J.: "Hysterical depressed, sensitive, intelligent creative, and distant. I hate myself."

#14. H.R.: "Grandiose, paranoid, phony, scared, intelligent. Destructive, mostly scared."

#15. R.C.: "Domineering, cunning, powerful. Scared a lot. Still a baby. Easy going. Restricted and ungiving. Unrelenting."

Words which seemed to come up often in the discussions of self and evaluations of self are "violent," "destructive," "clumsy," "giddy," "dead," "a devil," "anal," "restricted and ungiving," "rigid," etc. I found that most of the responses were given with considerable nonverbal evidence of discomfort as though giving a description of oneself were a painful experience. The bulk of the material on self was overwhelmingly self-deprecatory or self-destructive. There were a few positive self-evaluations which came out in the interviews. Some of these were slipped into the general overall statement of self-dislike: "generous," "creative," "intelligent," "humorous" are some of the adjectives used. The person who described self as "quiet" added: "and maybe I'd have been better off if I had not been so quiet, and kicked up some dust once in a-while" (#5.H.I.). Whatever the response to the questions, most of the individuals indicated nonverbally that talking about themselves was not a comfortable act. On being asked to explain the discomfort, a typical response was as follows:

#3. F.A.: "I don't know, I'm just not supposed to."

#8. J.F.: "I just don't feel good about myself."

#10. K.H.: "If I talk about myself I'll get into trouble."

#13. T.J.: "I'm supposed to stay out of the way."

#5. H.I.:   "My mother told me that it was unlucky to talk about myself."

#7. I.D.:   "If I talk about myself I'll get bashed."

Included with these responses were such statements as "We're not supposed to talk about ourselves in my family" (#1.C.M.). The consensus was that the person would find self in some kind of trouble. When asked "with whom," the response was generally vague. Three of the subjects were not visibly uncomfortable. This comprises about 21 percent of the sample. The subject who characterized self as "an abused and battered child" (#7.I.D.) indicated that further abuse would be incurred if she talked about self any more.

Self System: The Scare

The subjects were asked to elaborate on their use of the word "scared" and what they thought of the question #352 from the MMPI ("I have been afraid of things or people that I know would not hurt me"). The following selections are descriptions by four individuals of their responses to the stimulus question. Five of the fifteen subjects were asked to respond to these selected MMPI questions. Of the five persons, four of them follow. The fifth declined to respond to this question.

#1. C.M.:   I have seen strange creatures and entered into dialog with them, not of the human race. I have multicolored science fiction dreams sometimes that scare me. I have made spiders move by my will. I think that my whole life has been strange and unusual and horrifying. This makes me horrifying to others so I keep away.

#5. H.I.:   I believe that some people can get to me with their minds. I think that Jacqui can send her mind in the night and hurt me. It doesn't make sense, but I believe it is so. I am afraid of crosses. My family used Jesus Christ and the cross to abuse me, they really dumped a lot of scary stuff on me, and I don't know that I think that these things won't really hurt me.

#7. I.E.:   I have been scared of everything and everybody. I have had times when I found I had done things that I had no sense or memory of doing. I have seen and heard things that other people didn't or that I later found out weren't there. I have lost track of me. It seemed like I spread out all over and what's left breaks up. I find I don't have any armor for the barrage of noise, sense smell and sights and it seems my feelings

with equal force bombarded me from inside. I get lost. I
don't know many people, I don't know how to take care of
myself. I find most often my body is so full of holes, if I
were made of a light film balloon, the wind would fill me to
the point of exploding but I wouldn't explode. I would
deflate all over the city and wonder where and what and who
I was, and whoever "I" was.

#14. H.R.:   I have been extremely afraid of people and had no physical
reason for this, psychologically afraid. I don't think of myself
as being bigger or stronger than people (this is a very large
person). I have thought I was going to disappear. I think that
sometimes there is no space between minds, and I have supernatural powers.

Related to the questions of being scared a lot, and of scaring themselves about strange and unnatural events, the above responses are
similar to responses given about self-destruction.

Self System: Life, Death, and Suicide

The question of suicide:[1] Not only was the view of self both
negative and fragmented, but also the view of the future, the world,
life and death coincided with the above descriptions. Questions
asked were: "What is the world like for you?" "How do you see
your life?" What is the meaning of life to you?" Following these
questions were ones about suicide, span of life and attitude about
staying alive. The first set of responses have to do with the meaning
of life and what the world is like for the respondent. The second set
are about suicide. About 40 percent of the respondents said that
life was tough, chaotic depressing and hopeless without alluding to
death, suicide or not living. The other 60 percent used the words
die, death, kill, or not live or some other euphemism in their
responses.

#1. C.M.:   There are no reasons for my being except for the suffering
I experience, and I don't know what good that will do.

#2. D.K.:   Life is a bummer always, a joke, and I often want to end
my misery and kill myself. No one really ever cares about me,
and the world is a rotten place anyway.

#3. F.A.:   There is no purpose or meaningful motion in my life.

#4. G.J.:   For me, life is fear, fear, fear, all the time.

#5. H.I.:   I would rather be a baby and not have to look around me at how horrifying life is. I stay in a fog to keep from looking around.

#6. E.C.:   Life is a mystery, it is to be endured. I'd be better off dead or I'll cause my parents to die. Life has no purpose and I'll never make it no matter how hard I try.

#7. I.D.:   Life and death are constant issues for me and I never know why I am at all. Maybe I am dead.

#8. J.F.:   Life is really awful, I am always afraid of my power to destroy. I really don't believe that life is worth living, and I often don't know why I stick with it.

#9. A.G: Life is a shitty mess. I am nasty with life because it is nasty with me. I'd as soon be dead.

#10. K.H.:   I wish I were a baby or dead. For me, life is hopeless and I am outside of it. Everything is always in a state of disintegration.

#14. H.R.:   Life is frightening and chaotic. People frighten me. Things frighten me. Events frighten me. I would be better off dead.

Many words elicited are negatively descriptive throughout such as "dangerous," "unpredictable," "difficult," "too scary," "people are not to be trusted." The death and suicide theme is strong.

Self System: Dreams and Future

Fantasies,[2] dreams, plans for the future, all elicited some direct mention of death or suicide from about 60 percent of the persons talked with and responding on the questionnaire. The other 40 percent made some allusion to death or suicide when the question was pursued. None of the respondents denied wanting to be dead in some way or other in the recent past. One person stated that in the past "one hour" the option had crossed his mind. The fantasies and recurring dreams involved death wishes. When they were asked about dreams, or recurring fantasies (what is your recurring dream?), the topics had to do with dying or being overwhelmed, or killed, or being unborn or being a baby. Some of the following are representative of statements made on this topic:

#2. D.K.:   I dream about being killed.

#3. F.A.: I am running into dead ends.

#4. G.J.: I get killed doing something heroic.

#7. I.E.: I am immobile and unable to communicate or breathe.

#8. J.F.: I am closed in.

#9. A.G.: Someone is chasing me and wants to kill me.

#10. K.H.: I am suffocating, smothering.

All (100 percent) of the fifteen subjects interviewed stated that they had seriously considered suicide quite recently. Thoughts of suicide were stated to be frequent and recent. It is apparent that the need to be dead, the feeling of death as a viable alternative to life, the wish to die or to be killed is a constant issue with these subjects. One respondent stated that the thought had not recurred for over a year, but that before now, the wish had been frequent. On being asked: "Is there really any reason for staying alive?" some of the responses were:

#1. C.M.: One of the things that keeps me going is that I am not sure what is real and what is not real, and I think that I can find out here.

#2. D.K.: I am curious, and that keeps me going from one day to the next.

#5. H.I.: I am learning something that seems to be useful right now. Maybe I'll get something.

#6. E.C.: If it weren't for this place (Cathexis) I'd be dead probably, but I'm sticking around a little while to see if I get something out of this thinking thing.

#9. A.G.: Some days, here isn't so bad.

The staff take the reporting of suicidal, or death wishes, very seriously. There are discussions, agreements and contracts with all of the people in the program requiring a commitment to staying alive. Suicide as an option for solving problems is highly disapproved of. The expectation of the patients is that as a result of contracts they will *think* about, *talk* about and *problem-solve* any urges to destroy themselves. The person who is having such thoughts is expected to tell the people in his group, his house and his therapist. It is believed that if he *thinks* about making a Decision to live (Goulding and Dye, 1974), even for a short time, he will renew the contract at the end of that time and, in the interim, he will have done additional learning about the problem. In a rational manner, he will find solutions to the issues which are disturbing him.

In the light of the persons' reports about their dreams, and their recurring suicide fantasies, their future expectations were reviewed. Persons were asked "where do you think you'll be in five years," especially if they did not succeed in their treatment. Again the theme of despair and death was repeated. At the beginning of the study the majority (80 percent) said negative things: "I'll be dead," "killed," "a baby," "helpless," "a junkie," "a very crazy person," "rotten in my mind," "a vegetable" and "worse than I am now." At the end of the study the responses were 87 percent "It's worth it (life)" (3 persons), "life is great" (1), "I can make it work" (2), "I can get what I want" (1), "I'm glad to be alive" (1), "it's a challenge" (2), "It's hard, competitive, beautiful" (1). There were two persons (13 percent) who stated "it's there" and "it doesn't make sense." None expressed the death or killing theme in their responses twelve months later.

Since there seemed to be an over-riding, all-pervasive theme of morbidity and despair from all of the interviewees concerning the future, there were a series of questions posed on day-to-day thoughts and feelings. These brought the same type of responses. It seemed to me that such views might be reflected in the bodies and body sensations of the individuals. I included a series of questions about how they felt about their bodies and body parts.

Self System: Body and Bodily Sensations

The way in which a person views his body reflects the way he views his self and his existential right-to-be (Reich, 1969).[3] I asked questions about the individual's body and body sensations, such as: "what part of your body tells you what you are feeling?" "What part of your body feels least alive?" "What do you think about your body?" The answers were congruent with the above information. A majority of them stated that they felt dead in certain parts of their bodies. Nine of the respondents (60 percent) used the word "dead" in characterizing parts of their bodies. Examples were:

#1. C.M.:   My stomach gets upset, like a stone. It feels dead.

#2. D.K.:   I get a tight stomach, tight legs, tight neck and shoulders, and pale complexion. I feel least alive in my neck, shoulders, chest and abdomen.

#3. F.A.:   My feet, are sore, knees are tight, stomach aches, and muscles are tight.

#4. G.J.:   I get a headache, sometimes my whole head feels dead.

#5. H. I.: My whole left side feels dead, particularly my head. I get muscle contractions. My mouth and my genitals tell me I am upset.

#6. E.C.:   I'm dead from the neck down.

#7. I.D.:   I get light-headed, racing heart. My torso feels dead.

#8. J.F.:   Between my shoulders and my hip joints feel least alive. A steel vice-like effect in my whole body. Tensions like cold air, and something eating my insides out. Incoordination, and spasm, and hand and body posturing.

#9. A.G.:   I get gas, headaches. My mouth feels dead.

#10. K.H.: I get short of breath and a sore throat. My shoulders are dead. I get stark fear, hopeless and isolated.

#11. B.C.: My mind is dead, rotted. I get a fulness in my head and chest and shoulders are tight.

#12. M.E.: I feel dead from the head down. My stomach tells me that I am upset. I get stomach pains, nausea, hypoglycemia, skin rashes and headache. I get stark terror and rage.

#13. T.J.: My legs are least alive. Chest and arms are tense and ache, especially the left side. I get scared and hysterical or I withdraw.

#14. H.R.: My genitals feel dead. I get headaches and angry and controlling.

#15. R.C.: When I get upset I want to be a baby wrapped in a tight baby blanket.

Associated with the body parts was the information that being "upset" was signaled by that body part. The person (#8.J.F.) who reported shoulders as least alive pointed out that tightness there clued him/her to being "upset." The person (#7.I.D.) corroborated this information by saying: "When I freeze in my trunk, I know that I am in trouble and upset." All of the respondents reported somatic symptoms associated with being "upset," disturbed or uncomfortable with their environment. Further comments about "body" involved experiences as shortness of breath, sore throat, racing heart and dry mouth. For each individual the responses were idiosyncratic. I elicited no corroborative patterns of body behavior associated with being "upset." The clinical picture defined at Cathexis is that "upset" behavior is the same as agitation.

At Cathexis the patients are encouraged to pay attention to their own Agitation and to that of others in their environment. It is important that people be Reactive to any form of Agitation and something definite be done immediately to deal with it by both the patient and the therapist or any other person involved. The experience with the psychotics at Cathexis is that if this behavior is not confronted and dealt with (reacted to), the person who is Agitating will Escalate the energy to some type of Violence or Incapacitation. Staff and patients in the program are highly Reactive and notice every small body movement. A demand is made that the person "stop that behavior and *think* about what is 'upsetting' you." Experiences in the program are designed for individuals to increase their bodily awareness, to increase their ability to "think about what your body is telling you." Discounting of these behaviors may result in mounting tension in the individual and in those around him. The discharge of energy may be impulsive and damaging. Failure to deal with Agitation openly also results in shifts of energy from one person to another. In view of the tension in the situation, another patient may find the tension and energy buildup unbearable and react by Escalating his own energy to discharge the discomfort. (A full discussion of energy, power and social control will be dealt with in Chapter V.) Competence in dealing with one's body and bodily sensations, and the ability to deal with inner discomfort, are a part of the "normal" child-rearing experience of most individuals. The Cathexis population evidence not having had such learning experiences in their own socialization and family experiences. Following is a section on the subjects' family experiences.

Views on Child-Rearing or "Crazy-Making"

(Everything you wanted to know about how to make a person crazy, but never dared ask.) In the light of the subjects' accounts of their parents' personalities and attitudes towards the subjects as children, further information was asked about the subjects' views on child-rearing. The Life Script Questionnaire asked: "What would you say over and over to a child to make him/her grow up feeling the way you do now?" The responses to this question varied, but the themes were similar for all of the respondents. These were summed up by #7.I.D., who said:

> I would give the child a lot of abuse, both verbal and physical. I would lock it up in a room for hours without anybody to relate to. I would give it a "crazy" parent, and a do-nothing parent. One parent who would over-react to everything, and one parent who would do nothing to protect the child from the other parent's abuse. I wouldn't talk with the kid except to tell it ugly things about it, or be derogatory. In between times, I would ignore it as though it didn't exist.

An overall attitude of worthlessness appears in most of the statements offered by the respondents. Statements and actions which the subjects stated would be used by them repeatedly with children to make them "crazy" were:

#1. C.M.: You'd be better off dead. You're sick. Keep the kid in its room a lot. Tell it, you'll be no good when you grow up.

#2. D.K.: You're stupid. You don't count around here. I would whip it a lot and not tell it why.

#3. F.A.: If you hadn't happened, my life would be happier. You son-of-a-bitch. I would use isolation and beating.

#4. G.J.: Ignore the kid. Blow up every now and then. Call the kid names. Tell the kid how much better I did things when I was a kid, and why can't he do like I did.

#5. H.I.: Smile, it's the only way people will be able to stand you. Be nice. Anger is a mortal sin. You're a sinner for being angry. Show anger but do not allow it in the child. Be guilty a lot.

#6. E.C.: You're evil. You're a beast. Get lost. Beat or ignore the child. Tell him he is only good when he is not around.

#7. I.D.:   You're destructive. You'll be the death of me. You're the devil himself. You're disgusting. Lock the child in its room all day. Be abusive. Threaten it with locking it up and then not do it. Not protect it from the abusive parent.

#8. J.F.:   You're alright when you don't make mistakes. Praise it a lot for doing things. Tell it you're different. Use words, words, words. Isolate it in bed all day.

#9. A.G.:   Poor kid, you don't have a chance the way the world is. You'll never make it. Act superior around the child. Beat it and whip it.

#10. K.H.:   Things would have been alright if you hadn't been born. I'd be better off if you weren't around. Yell a lot.

#11. B.C.:   Why can't you be like . . . comparing or ignoring. Mostly, not being *there* for the child. Being negative about everything the child did.

#12. M.E.:   Lock the kid in its room or in a closet. Slap its face a lot. Hit and be derogatory. Always be busy. Praise it for doing, not being.

#13. T.J.:   If you weren't such a problem everything would be alright in this family. Ignore the child or get hysterical about small things. Never tell the child what is going on.

#14. H.R.:   I can't wait till you grow up and get out of this place. Mostly not notice the kid. I wouldn't say anything ever to the kid, make it feel like it wasn't there.

#15. R.C.:   Tell it, don't grow up, life is too awful. Spank or ignore it. Raise it with a lot of nursemaids, nobody steady. Go away a lot.

The implication was that the world would be a better place without the subjects. The implication also was that in some way their own general discomfort with Self and with their lives placed a responsibility upon them to DO something—anything to alleviate the discomfort. This is probably the basis for the Agitation and impulsive behavior. The parental modeling would also give Agitation as an only option for dealing with problems.

None of the subjects offered positive statements as a part of their child-rearing program. No one indicated that they might tell the child that they were "glad you're here," or indicated warmth, kindness or caring. There were no unqualified statements of pleasure indicated as part of the affirmation of the child's mere Being. Statements on their view of child-rearing towards "crazy-making" were offered with energy and viciousness of affect. The response to these questions indicate that the subjects fit Becker's assessment of the schizophrenic as discussed in Chapter I, that is that they are "eerie" and "volatile." These statements also corroborate the notion put forth by Schiff as discussed in Chapter II, that "Parents' needs come first; the world is a dangerous place; other people are dangerous; and you are not a (real) human being without me." A typical Script Matrix for the subjects at Cathexis would appear as in Figure 4-4.

Family Secrets

Among the meta-messages which were reported as a part of the system of crazy-making was the matter of family secrets. The subjects were asked questions about what were the usual family taboos: "Which topics were taboo in your family?" "Was there a secret side to your family that no one was supposed to know about?" The question on the Life Script Questionnaire was: "What thoughts, feelings or attitudes were you to keep a secret?" All of the respondents indicated that there was a secret side to their families which they were not supposed to show to the world. Basic responses from subjects indicated that the most mentioned topic was sex, sexuality and sexual feelings (47% = 7); the next topic was feelings, all of them, anger, sexual, etc. (33% = 5); and box sex and feelings (27% = 4) and needs (7% = 1). Two persons said that "All thoughts and feelings that were not happy" (#3.F.A. and #12.M.E.). The general consensus was that any feelings, fear, anger, sadness, were not acceptable from the children but that the "adults" were apt to express one kind of feeling in an over-reacting manner for which then the rest of the family would be embarrassed. The respondents conceded that the family was supposed to cover up for that person to the outside world. One subject stated that "the grownups had a right to anger followed by guilt, but the kids had to stay happy" (#12.M.E.). Several of the individuals indicated that they felt responsible for the family explosions, even when they (the subject himself) were not present. Another type of secret concerned the individuals themselves as children: "I was not supposed to admit that I had any problems" (#10.K.H.), and "I was not supposed to need affection" (#5.H.I.). The consensus was that if the individual did express having a feeling on an issue, or a problem, the "adults" would be hostile or would reject them. "It wasn't worth it, so I kept my feelings and needs to myself" (#10.K.H.).

Along these same lines, it was asked "If you could change anything about your family when you were small, what would you have done different?" Responses to this and the follow-up questions were typically as follows.

#1. C.M.: I would have liked more warmth and closeness.

#8. J.F.: I would have liked them to talk *to* me and not *at* me.

#6. E.C.: I would have liked them to have been more accepting of me, less crazy and afraid, and less critical of themselves and of me.

#9. A.G.: I would have liked more responsiveness and touching. More caring and less nastiness.

#7. I.D.: I want them to be less psychotic. They acted crazy a lot. Less explosive and unpredictable.

Key statements had to do with the subjects wishing that they had had at least one parent who was not so insensitive. They stated that they wanted parents who were responsive to children's needs.

#2. D.K.: I wish that mother had paid attention to what I needed instead of me having to always do her thing.

#4. G.J.: I wanted my Dad to think of me and how a kid like me would do things instead of always comparing himself with me and how he was better.

#8. J.F.: I wish that they had taught me to think for myself, and not order me around all of the time.

#9. A.G.: I wish she (mother) had thought about what I needed and wanted as more important than what she did.

It seems that parents were constantly demanding that the children offer an unthinking type of compliance to the parental demands. It was apparent that parents did not expect children to be able to think. They expected total compliance with their own wishes regardless of the individual child's thoughts or wishes. The parents were impulsive and unthinking themselves. The opinion of a number of the subjects (60% = 10) was that "it was not a good thing to even *think* about the bad behavior (drinking, explosions, etc.):

#4. G.J.:   If I did try to talk with Dad about Mom's tantrums, he would
            say to not worry or think about it because it wouldn't help.

#10. K.H.: Don't worry your little head about that.

#5. H.J.:   I wouldn't think about that if I were you.

#8. J.F.:   My dad would say: I don't have time to think about that just
            now.

All of the data reported in this section expresses a portion of
the comments made during participant-observation and interviews at
Cathexis. These statements are a sampling of attitudes and views
of the respondents. Further substantiation of these views was
acquired through objective test data which will be reported in a
subsequent section of this chapter. There will also be a section
describing the change in World View of subjects as a result of the
program and Contracts they set for themselves at Cathexis.

Real Versus Not Real

A prime issue in psychopathology is the one which classical
psychiatry calls "Object relations."[4] This essentially is the issue of
how the individual distinguishes self from not-self. Developmentally,
this capacity is thought to occur for the child in the first three years
of life. Beginning with birth, and normally completing the major
part of the process in the sixth year of life, the child goes through
several stages in the process of differentiating self from other (Gedo
and Goldberg, 1973; Babcock and Keepers, 1976). Individuals who
do not experience an adequate and balanced environment for making
this cognitive distinction end up with confusion on being able to
make the distinction between themselves and others. Also, depth
perception and ability to perceive the environment as a totality is
dependent upon adequate experiences during the exploratory stage.
Examples from the subject population at Cathexis are:

#7. I.D.:   I often wonder if things are real. I woke up once and it looked
            like there was a rip in the sky. I thought it was made of con-
            struction paper. Then I got frightened because I thought
            I had duped myself. This was the way it really was—everything
            flat and made of paper, easily torn, and that all along, I'd either

thought things were real or tried to prove it to myself so I could feel better. But I was fooled. Finally I saw that it was a cloud formation but I didn't feel any better. I must not be real to have died once and lived afterwards. I am not real for having lived after some of the brutal deprived experiences I have had.

#8. J.F.:   I have experienced the world of hallucinations and unreality and magic. Also I have known things which I now know are not real, but I still don't know which happened, and which didn't. I have experienced quick switches and have distorted reality so that people that I think are safe usually are killing me, and that ordinary things become dangerous. I experience a whole reference change—each seems true at its time.

#12. M.E.:   I have seen and heard things that other people didn't or that I later determined weren't there. I have thought or believed things to be true that most others didn't. I have experienced nothing existing.

#14. G.R.:   I have had out-of-the-ordinary experiences that most other people don't have. I have had unrealistic fears, and have been aware that they were not real, but did not know what to do about them. I sometimes think that the world is going to get me. (I know that is paranoid.) Questioning reality is a very scary thing for me. I have thought I was going to disappear. That there is no space between minds, that I have supernatural powers.

On another level, the issue of what is real and what is not real is one which has concerned philosophers and scientists for centuries. Eugene Wiger's "Two Kinds of Reality" (1970: 197-198) distinguishes the first kind of reality as "my own consciousness" and the second as everything else:

... the universe of impersonal reality as a concept is a reality of the second type, useful for communicating, but only possibly valid. Everything but the first type is a construct ... an atom is not a thing, it is only a possibility, and we are all made up of atoms ....

... when a student of physics makes his first acquaintance with the theory of atomic structure and of quanta, he must come to the rather deep and subtle notion which has turned out to be the clue to unravelling the whole domain of physical experience. This is the notion of complementarity, which recognizes the various ways of talking about experience may each have validity, and may each be necessary for the adequate description of the physical world, and yet may stand in mutually exclusive relationship to each other, so that in a situation to which one applies,

there may be no consistent possibility of applying the other. (Oppenheimer, 1964:69)

So physicists talk about two realities. Oppenheimer called them
the "way of time and history, and the way of eternity and time-
lessness." Heisenberg called them:

> ... the objective world, pursuing its regular course in space and time
> and a subject mystically experiencing the unity of the world and no longer
> confronted by an objective world ... human ability to understand may be
> in a certain sense unlimited. But the existing scientific concepts cover
> always only a very limited part of reality, and the other part that has not
> yet been understood is infinite. Whenever we proceed from the known in-
> to the unknown we may hope to understand, but we may have to learn at
> the same time a new meaning of the word "understanding." (Heisenberg,
> 1974: 201-202)

For the schizophrenic, the reality of reality is a profound issue.
It brings into question his very existence. "How do I know that I
really am?" Most of us do not trouble to question the fact of our
existence except when we are in a crisis. We define ourselves by our
jobs, by our status and role in society. The major way in which
persons define their existence and their identity is in their relation to
others who are important to them. This is called the self-other distinction. When this distinction has never been defined, and is not
clear for the individual, there is Symbiosis. In Symbiosis the defining is done by the other person in the pair. This dynamic involves
an *alter* being willing to extend the energy required to prove the
existence of *ego*. This dilemma was described to me by some of the
subjects in the following quotes.

> #1. C.M.: It's like a wall of energy that is out there through which I
> cannot reach. The other person has to reach me. As soon as I
> can get another person to invest more energy in me or my
> problem I can sit back. It is like a glass wall, all of the energy
> is out there, I do not have to put anything into the process.
> When I can get another person's energy, that is when I know I
> am real. I do not use my energy. I am not sure I have any.
> It comes down to this, since I haven't any energy of my own,
> I have to use the energy that is available to me through the
> other person in the transaction.

> #5. H.I.: Being human means being separate, it means being real,
> giving and talking, loving and caring. I don't want to be
> real. It is too risky.

#8. J.F.:   I still see myself as a facet of somebody else. As long as I am a facet of someone else, I do not have to solve the problem of being Real and not Real. Without other people's energy I do not exist.

#10. K.H.:   The double bind for me is that I am real, therefore, I am not real. When I am in touch with me and my feelings I don't even look real. I look sick. When I look real is when I am not in touch with me. If I am looking and sounding real, watch out, because that is when I am apt to overadapt and I may react violently. I don't even know it is happening.

Along these same lines, several of the subjects talked about a "glass wall" a "plastic shield," a "fog" through which each one believed she/he was powerless to reach. The powerless, helpless, hopeless sensation was one to which repeated reference was made.

The Special Case of Hebephrenics[5]

In connection with being helpless, the metaphor, "starving baby" comes up very often. This metaphor occurs in particular with the persons who were diagnosed as hebephrenic in the Cathexis Community. This metaphor fits the history on several of the hebephrenics at Cathexis. Each of the individuals reported an early interruption of the feeding cycle. Also an interruption of the attachment to the primary nurturing source was reported. All of the individuals who had this diagnosis were also very intelligent. Schiff says that the hebephrenic is often easily engaged in treatment because of their high intelligence. They are often good-looking and seductive. Since therapists are invested in being "helpful," "starving babies" easily involve them in investing energy in the therapeutic process. Very few hebephrenics have been "cured" although the phenothiazines tend to keep their giddiness and Escalations to a minimum, and keep them in line (Schiff, 1975: 78; lecture and discussions at Cathexis Institutes, 1973; 1974; 1975).

The Cathexis community took a hard look at the persons diagnosed as hebephrenic about a year ago (January 1975). Decisions were made during seminar meeting, and several house and family meetings, that caution would be used in taking Reparenting Contracts with hebephrenics until further information had been gained on the energy issue. The apparent lack of investment, or low investment in the therapeutic process on the part of the hebephrenics in the community, was another of the criteria for making this decision. Those with the diagnosis of hebephrenic at Cathexis have been found to mask this low energy investment with heavy Overadaptation to the program. It seemed that, while appearing to show therapeutic movement and growth, the basic underlying pathology does not change. Hence, the hebephrenics are invested in staying in the position of "being Real only when someone else is investing energy in me." The hebephrenic learns all the ropes of the program by Overadapting to it and is, meanwhile, still invested in his system of denial and of remaining "not Real." This system (according to Schiff) of denial is the core of the hebephrenic personality and it keeps the individual fragmented and not aware of his own various needs and feelings. The sensation of being fragmented, the polarization of the Real/not real, and the denial system are thought by Schiff and staff to be rooted in a "blockage" of the Corpus Callosum.[6] The Corpus Callosum is the major information pathway between the right and the left brain. There is evidence to indicate that the hebephrenic does not integrate the information from the Right with that from the Left hemisphere. Schiff (1975: 78) thinks that these blocks in information correlation between the two hemispheres may be relevant to the fact that these individuals polarize their perceptions on all issues.

While the Real/Not Real issue is a most profound one for the hebephrenic, it is an issue for all diagnostic categories of schizophrenia. The degree of investment in being Not Real varies with the denial system which has been created by the individual through his life experience. The denial system is his adaptational strategy for survival in life. It is one of their theories, that probably some of the most crucial factors in this Real/Not Real dilemma result from the first twelve to eighteen months of the individual's life experience. The early exploratory experiences are seen as pivotal in forming the structures whereby the individual develops his life strategy. The Cathexis thinking is, that it is possible that by Limiting or confusing an infant's developing cognition through body contact with the environment, some connections between Right and Left brain hemispheres are not made. The coordination of Right and Left hemispheres may be a key issue in all psychopathologies. Hebephrenics being the most disturbed of all the schizophrenics, studying them might provide clues to the Real/Not Real issue, and hence, more information on psychopathology in general. As of August 1975, fifteen hebephrenics had been "cured" of their psychopathology at Cathexis (Schiff, 1975:76).

Expectations of Treatment at Cathexis

What the patients think they will achieve: Expectations are an important part of the success or failure of any treatment program. If the patient expects to be "cured"—sometimes this expectation will be met. The more realistic and congruent with the patient's expectations the treatment is, the more chance at success. On the other hand, if a program reinforces a person's denial system, the more doomed to failure it is. Subjects in the study were asked: "What do you expect from your therapist?" "What about yourself, will you change while you are in treatment?" "How will you be different?" etc. Regarding the responses to these questions, one of the most often repeated responses (8 = 54%) was: "to be able to think." Not being able to think was identified by #8 "like being dead, in a fog," and by #1.C.M. "being behind a glass wall all of the time." #6.E.C. said, "being fogged is the same as not thinking." The impression I got was that the ability to think made the sense of powerlessness over feelings and events disappear. Other statements made regarding their expectations in this vein were:

#1. C.M.: I expect my therapist to be straight with me and not think I'm fragile. I will be able to deal with feelings and be functional. I will take care of myself in a straight way. I will not act crazy for attention.

#2. D.K.: I expect my therapist to help me in getting well. I will change my thinking and physical self. I will be relating to women and playing. I'll think clearly and be physically fit.

#3. F.A.: I want to live life being happy and getting what I need. I expect my therapist to give me information, caring, consideration and reassurance. My outlook on life and my approach to problem-solving will change. I will be more pleasant to be around and have more fun. My family will probably reject me because I won't play their power games. I will be finding what I want out of life.

#4. G.J.: I want to be happy, feel good and enjoy life. I expect help from my therapist in solving my problems. The main thing I will change will be to stop being paranoid. I'll be an extrovert.

#5. H.I.: The thing I want most from life right now is to be Reparented. I expect my therapist to be my mother and to Reparent me. I'll change my attitudes, feelings, and reaction in life. I will be able to solve the problems.

#6. E.C.: I don't know what I want most from life. I expect my thera-
pist to teach me how to make it. I'll probably change almost
everything about myself. I will be able to take care of myself
and get some enjoyment out of life. I'll look, talk and act
different.

#7. I.D.: I want to be well and be an artist. I want my therapist to help
me accomplish that. I want to change how I relate to myself
and others, I will be able to have an intimate relationship and
feel comfortable with it.

#8. J.F : I want to be a baby at my mother's breast most of all. I want
my therapist to take care of me and support me in working
out this problem in a straight and a sharing way. I will not be
destructive anymore, and I will be born and I will grow up and
lead a full and problem solving life.

#9. A.G.: I want to be as happy as I can reasonably expect to be. I will
be successful. I want my therapist to support me, be caring
and supply me with a role model. I will be more spontaneous
and in touch with feeling, not phobic around people. I hope
to be a therapist or a leader in a therapeutic community.

#10. K.H.: I want to love people and be loved. I expect my therapist to
teach me how to do this. I will think more and better. I will
become more open and trusting. When I am uncomfortable I
will start thinking about why and what to do; I will not withdraw when I am afraid but talk about it. I will go on learning
to do new things, enjoying it, loving many people and they
loving me.

#11. B.C.: I want to be healthy, get along with people and have intimate
friends. My main therapist is now my Father (New Parent)
and I am learning from him. I expect to learn how to be healthy
and to grow and how to get taken care of straight. I will
learn to care about people. I will have more friends. I won't
feel badly and I will have a thinking, spontaneous relating with
my Mom and Dad (new). People will feel better about me. I
will be in school, I will be a gentle person and will be working
with children.

#12. M.E.: I want to be healthy. I want my therapist to be my mother
and give me what I didn't get and needed. Want to change
my desire to be unborn. I will then have feelings and intimate
relationships; I will feel and act alive. People will be able to
reach and touch me emotionally. I'll be flowing, peaceful and
actively taking care of myself, doing what I want to do and
loving others in intimate relationships.

#13. J.T.:   I want to be a happy creative person. I hope my therapist will give me some direction about how to change. I want to learn to think for myself. I will care about other people's feelings more.

#14. H.R.:   I want to feel solidly OK. I want my therapist to help me grow up again. I will know more about my sexuality and intimacy. I'll be a completely different person. I'll still be feeling alone.

#15. R.C.:   I want to be happy physically as well as mentally. At this point I don't know what to expect from my therapist. I will be different when I get my needs met. I will be more of a man than I am now.

I questioned some of these people as to how they were going to go about getting these expectations met. Three stated that the Reparenting would be a major factor. They were already in Reparenting Contracts at the time. Two of them were in Regressions. Most of them stated that the program had all of the ingredients for doing what they needed to do and they expected to take advantage of what was there. Persons #7.I.D. and #15.R.C. were skeptical that any change was really possible, but that they were there "for now." Five of the respondents indicated that they thought that "being little" and the concomitant new Parent message and the day-to-day practice of the rituals (described in Chapter III) would bring about the expected changes. The information given me was that if the program did not meet their needs, they could always talk with their group and with the staff about the changes they needed.

"I Am Less Crazy Now Than When I Started":
A Year Later

A year later the same questionnaire was completed by the remaining twelve subjects in the study. They did the same tests as before, and time was spent by me talking with some of them. Individual change on self-assessment and changes in World View were evident. Of the original fifteen who had agreed to do the study with me, three had left. Two more left during the last part of the study, but remained in contact with me and completed their agreement. The material that is presented in the next portion is done in such a way that the reader can compare the individuals before and after (i.e., at the beginning of the study and at the end of one year).

BEFORE	CHANGE	AFTER
#1. C.M.: "I am anal, sensitive, not functional"	moderate	"I am sensitive, impatient, well-motivated and interested in other people. Uncomfortable, at times withdrawn."
#2. D.K.: "Scared, angry, sulking, lonely, depressed, crazy, no good."	moderate	"Somewhat caring. I can think well. I am fun."
#3. F.A.: "An OK person, sometimes negativistic, not very caring, scared."	moderate	"Somewhat caring, at times negativistic, can think well if I do it, fun, want to do outdoor activities."
#4. G.J.: "I am a bad guy; the black sheep of the family. An H-addict. No good for myself."	moderate	"Intelligent, somewhat self-centered, scared."
#5. H.I.: Quiet, sad, a baby. I don't like myself any."	no change	"Quiet."
#6. E.C.: "Evil, distant, clumsy, do not relate."	moderate	"Bright, a little distant."
#7. I.D.: "Battered abused child. Evil. A devil. I am just a person, maybe with some ability."	no change	"A person who is here so far."
#8. J.F.: "Gentle, angry, violent, false energy and motivation. A dead child unborn. Very little inside, anal, turnwords (sic) giddy and invested in getting well."	moderate	"One that is uncomfortable to talk to for other than short communications, destructive sometimes, I am manipulative, learning to care, very angry, very little, sad and inside hungry."
#9. A.G.: "Potentially brilliant. Energetic, crazy, humorous, angry, bitter, a shithead."	moderate	"Intelligent, caring, but scared. I am becoming my own person. Less nasty and more caring."
#10. K.H.: Sad, lonely, have problems getting along at work which I don't understand; problems relating to men, want to be a baby; am maintaining myself precariously."	no change	"Sad, floundering, precariously existing."

#11. B.C.: "I am externally angry and not caring but responsible. Internally scared, sad and very young. Negativistic and fault finding. Destructive."	moderate	"This is changing because I am a growing woman. I am becoming my own person. I am working towards a satisfying caring person."
#12. M.E.: "Changeable from very functional, caring and giving to destructive, immobile, scared, dead."	marked	"Enthusiastic, spontaneous, warm, loving, interdependent (autonomous) determined. I am a superb therapist and teacher and problem solver."

BEFORE	CHANGE	AFTER
#1. C.M: "When I get away from my family I'll be alright."	moderate	"It's hard, competitive and beautiful."
#2. D.K.: "Life is a bummer, I want to kill myself. No one really ever cares about me, and the world is a rotten place."	moderate	"It's a challenge."
#3. F.A.: "There is no purpose or meaningful motion in my life."	marked	"There is a lot to do; I want to get out there and do it. I can make it work for me if I decide to."
#4. G.J.: "For me, life is fear, fear, fear, all of the time."	moderate	"I believe that I can make it and I say it is getting better for me."
#5. H.I.: "I would rather be a baby and not have to look around me at how horrifying life is. I stay in a fog to keep from looking around."	moderate	"I believe Jesus Christ died for my sins. Jesus gave me a new Life. It's great."
#6. E.C.: "Life is a mystery, it is to be endured. I'd be better off dead or I'll cause my parents to die. Life has no purpose and I'll never make it no matter how hard I try."	no change	"Maybe it's worth it."

#7. I.D.: "Life and death are constant issues for me and I never know why I am at all. Maybe I am dead."	no change	"Life doesn't make sense, people don't make sense, but I need them to make it make sense, it might be worth trying out."
#8. J.F.: "Life is really awful, I am always afraid of my power to destroy. I really don't believe that life is worth living, and I often don't know why I stick with it."	moderate	"That it is there and I must keep what belongs inside—in and outside—out."
#9. A.G.: "Life is a shitty mess. I am nasty with life because it is nasty with me. I'd as soon be dead."	moderate	"I can get more of what I want. I am becoming my own person. Less nasty and caring more.
#10. K.H.: "I wish I were a baby or dead. For me, life is hopeless and I am outside of it. Everything is always in a state of disintegration."	moderate	"It's worth living and will be much more so when I become more aware."
#11. B.C.: "I can change and will after I learn to get along. I will and its OK."	moderate	"I believe that life is worthwhile. There are problems and people need to balance what they do and how they feel. I am learning to be a life-loving person."
#12. M.C.: "I am beginning to believe that it is worth living."	marked	"It's great. I'm glad to be alive."

What about yourself and your life; did you change while you were in therapy?

#1. C. M.: I am growing up and am less psychotic. I am more adult and more capable of handling my own affairs. I am no longer depressed.

#2. D. K.: I trust my own judgment more, more confident, more caring of myself and more autonomous.

#3. F. A.: I have learned better what to do with my fear. I dwell less on the past and enjoy people more.

#4. G. J.: I am learning more about making and having close relationships. I have less fear of rejection and am seen more as a person who is caring. I have more close friends now.

#5. H. I.: I am more potent and well-defined and have impact on people. I have more confidence and trust my options for behaving better. I believe in Jesus Christ.

#6. E. C.: I am getting more confident and less rigid. I am changing the way I view others. I am becoming an enjoyable person to talk with.

#8. J. F.: I am learning to behave and listen and be responsive. I am more of a person people want to be close to and intimate with.

#9. A. G.: I have changed. I can make my own decisions. I am less nasty and more caring.

#10. K. H.: I feel good more of the time. I understand myself in many more ways. I more actively look for solutions to problems and believe there are solutions.

#12. M. E.: My nonproblem solving behaviors. Instead of being severely withdrawn, terrified, angry, shut off and inappropriate I am now enthusiastic, spontaneous, warm, loving, intelligent, an excellent teacher, problem solver, interdependent, autonomous and determined.

Taking into account the need to please, the Overadaptation Characteristic of the schizophrenic there is still an indication of change in terms of the criteria for increased self-respect. On a more subtle level, the questions about recurring dreams also showed change. Whereas in the first set of questionnaires, all of the respondents admitted to having recurring dreams and all of the dreams were of a morbid nature (see pp. 192-195). In the second questionnaire, six (40 percent) of the respondents claimed that they were not having recurring frightening themes in their dreams. Of the remaining six (60 percent) all of the dreams reported morbid themes such as being "trapped," "squished," "loss," "blood and death," "shriveled up baby," "rejection" and "marrying someone I don't want to marry." There was one person who reported having flying and sexual dreams. There was a marked change in qualifying words used to describe themselves and their world in the second questionnaires and interviews. The language usage alone would indicate that the persons in the study had made some appreciable changes in their cognitive structures. Their view of themselves, life, etc. were different. This completes the discussion of the material gained from Script Questionnaires and from interviews. Following is a description of experiential data.

Experiential Data

Structured time-limited experiences offered at Cathexis for healing rituals include the Marathon group. This type of group provides the participants (both patients and trainees) with a protected setting in which various healing rituals described in Chapter III may be experienced. One of the rituals which is often used is in the "being little" category. Personal accounts of portions of my experiences in marathons and groups follows. Included are notes from my own treatment at Cathexis as a trainee-patient-anthropologist. Included with the personal data is information on interpretation of the experience as construed within the Transactional Analysis framework as used at Cathexis. The material is taken from several marathons and Institutes experiences with Jacqui Schiff, Cathexis staff, trainees and patients. The number of persons at each of these events averaged twelve to fourteen. The therapist and two or more staff persons were in charge. The marathons lasted two-and-one-half days, except for one, one-day marathon. A member of the Cathexis community may be hired to cater the marathon, to be responsible for the food and physical needs of the participants. This may be a person who is in a Reparenting Contract and is "growing up." The managerial skills of catering for sixteen persons are useful experiences for an individual who is learning to carry out responsible Caretaking functions.

Process

The participants included patients, staff, trainees, professional and nonprofessional persons from all parts of the United States. The first three to five hours was spent making the treatment contracts, the leader conveying group norms and the exchange of cognitive information about treatment issues for each person. Examples of Contracts which are typical are given in the third chapter under the discussion of Contracts. For example, on one occasion I made a Contract to be five years old. This was arrived at through dream material I presented. The therapist pointed out that I needed to define issues for myself involving competitiveness and a habit of suffering about problems instead of solving them. My lifelong behavior had been to take on other people's suffering and use the experience to end up feeling miserable myself.

After making Contracts, participants were then divided between those planning a Regression (being little) and those planning to stay Adult. The persons choosing to Cathect Little with Contracts such as my own were then expected to play with toys and the equipment supplied for this activity. They were expected to interact from the Regression, and carry out all transactions in the marathon from that age and Ego State. The persons choosing to remain Adult met in the ongoing group therapy session.

A Personal Example of How Cathexis Reculturation Affects Self Concepts, Etc.

When I experienced Cathecting Little about age five years, I found it to be a very uncomfortable experience. My field notes record the following.

> I am suddenly most uncomfortable. I seem to be neither here nor there. I am neither a child nor a grownup. I do not know what to do. I sense an expectation and I do not know what is expected of me. I am confused. I avoid contact with the other "children" and stay away from the grownups. I find myself foggy, miserable, unable to think, or see much. I have a sure sense, that whatever I do, I am going to do something wrong. I don't belong or fit here. I am distrustful of another "child" who offers to play with me. I spend a long time alone. A staff person tells me to interact with the other "children" or with a staff person, but not to stay by myself. I do finally interact with a two-year-old. I am competitive with her and say some derogatory things, to her. This behavior provokes a dispute. A staff person mediates this dispute. I am told to think about what I did. I find I don't want to think. I am told to sit in a chair until I do think it through. I realize that I am very unhappy. I pout and sulk. I am told to stop suffering and think about what I did. I just sit in the chair for a long time. The therapist tells me that I will have to solve the problem and that I better do it while there is someone available with whom to work it out. I eventually clear my head and get rid of the fog and figure out what happened and talk with the therapist about the incident. He is very helpful in clarifying what occurred. He is supportive of my understanding the competitive and provocative behavior I got into. (August 1974)

The Cultural Interpretation in Cathexis Society

As a result of this experience I gained the following insights about my behavior: I did not know how to play freely or ask directly for what I needed. An adage comes into focus for me: "Children should be seen and not heard." I realized that by age five I adopted the strategy of Victim in most interactions. I decided the way to do this was to pick on another smaller, or more helpless person, and provoke reprisal from the "adults." I believed that grownups and their needs were more important than me and my needs. I "knew" that one way to get grownup attention was to provoke punitive behavior, to compete for attention or "be nice." The result of these types of interaction left me feeling victimized. In looking at my life I realized that I had been "good" at all three of these gambits. I had competed competently all my life. But I had also felt victimized and alien a considerable part of the time. In many of the interactions over the years I had been a victim to persons and systems which I perceived as more powerful than I. As a professional I had taken on the Rescuing or Persecuting roles. No matter what role I chose for Redefining the problem, I ended up a Victim. I gained the insight that by the time I was five years old I had made several decisions related to devoting my life to my own and other persons' suffering. It was clear to me that I had felt miserable and depressed a large part of my life. I had focused on the misery of others. Getting taken care of was achieved by suffering, sulking, pouting or projecting my need for care onto someone else and giving them what I wanted. I also found out that if those measures didn't work, I could have a grand tantrum and *suffer* with the guilty feelings afterwards. It seemed to make sense to me in that frame of reference (five-year-old one) that if I cared for persons with bigger problems than my own, I would always be needed and thus justify my existence. Being a Rescuer and a helping person was a role I had decided upon by the time I was five years old.

Cognitively, the learning which occurred for me, and which changed a part of my World View, was that I could *think* about how to get my own needs met and how to get cared for. I learned that I did not have to provoke someone to irritation or anger in order to get recognized. I learned that I could first stop, then think and then discover ways to have fun and be noticed instead of acting automatically provocative or competitive. I gained insight into the number of ways in which I was competitive at the expense of others. I realized that provoking conflict, or acting patronizing with others, had been a way of reassuring myself that I really exist, that I AM. This cognitive input did not all occur immediately. The experience of this marathon, and being five years old, set up a chain reaction in my thought processes; it made connections for me throughout the ensuing months. Gradually I relinquished the five-year-old World View which had so directed my life in the past. I reverted less and less to the competing, provoking, suffering way of experiencing the world. I continued, nevertheless, to experience discomfort in many interactions and would still act automatically from time to time in certain situations. For instance, I continued to be scared of Jacqui and to compete with her. I continued to think about some of the other manifestations of unfinished business in my early socialization which were were still creating discomfort for me. There was evidently more about ME that was uncharted.

Differentiating Feelings

In the participant-observation phases of my study of the Cathexis community, I participated in many groups, marathons and didactic learning experiences. Another experience which brought about a clear change in World View for me was one in which I Contracted to be three years old. The contract included the agreement that the time spent being three would be used to learn to distinguish between the feeling of anger (*Mad*) and the Feeling of fear (*Scared*). My field notes are as follows (January 13, 1975).

> I spend a major part of the time allowed us in the marathon being three years old. I discover that I have a great deal of fun with the other children. I play with several of the other "children." I become aware that one of the issues in my life is a constant fear that someone is going to attack me or jump out on me at any moment. I am looking over my shoulder a lot. I duck my head when someone comes near or makes a swift movement near me. I am afraid most of the first part of the marathon. When I play with another "child" although I am having fun, I have a surety that I will be in trouble pretty soon. I have the firm belief that "I am always wrong, no matter what I do." When I sit and watch others play, I am uneasy. I think "idle hands make Mischief." I find myself expecting "things to happen." I have a sensation of having no control of my environment. I feel I am being watched. I have a sense of being helpless, powerless. This part of the experience is very painful to me. I play ball with a four-year-old "child" a boy. When I miss the ball one of the times, I become fearful, and stand there as though paralyzed. He says to me "get the ball, girls can think." This for some reason is a

very powerful message for me and I begin to cry confusedly and convulsively. I am aware of being intensely frightened. A staff person tells me in a kind, caring manner, that "you can think about what you are feeling." We talk about the incident, what I am feeling. I am no longer confused.

I realized as I thought about these experiences, that perhaps by the time I was three, I had no thought-structure for dealing with sudden unexpected events. I assumed that there were no solutions to many problems. I assumed that "things happen" over which I had no control. I had no rational procedure for dealing with fear. I did not know that *thinking* was *one* of the ways for dealing with feelings. I realized that I had the constant expectation that grown-ups would step in and give me a hard time *no matter what I was doing*. I had no sense of protection. I expected no solutions to problems. I realized that a major defense in my life had been to become enraged when I was actually panicky. I had always believed I could not figure out what was happening when I was panicked. I would either withdraw and swallow it, or fight. I learned that by the time I was three if I Escalated anger over fear I would still have some power because the big people were afraid of my temper. I found out that I incorporated that view, i.e., that "feelings just happen, and there is nothing that can be done about them." Also, I believed that there was something "bad" about being *Mad* or *Scared*: "Good girls just don't do that, tsk tsk." I recall my father shaking his head, frowning and withdrawing from me. I recall my mother laughing at me, beating me or withdrawing and sulking. I was not taught a structure for thinking about what was happening to me, or understanding the stimulus in the environment which elicited the *Scare*. I learned to "get nervous" instead of *thinking* and *"dealing."* When the nervousness (Agitation) did not solve the problem, I would blow up, or run away, or sulk.

Following this marathon, I became aware of my body in some very specific ways. I was not aware of the physiological manifestations of fear. I had hitherto Discounted the physiological manifestations and my body as a source of information about my inner and outer environments. I found that as I practiced the ability to differentiate between fear and anger I was no longer prone to temper tantrums. It became clear that I did not have to be a Victim of my emotions. I learned that emotions did not "just happen" to me. I had somatic information about which I could think and use this information as part of my interactive structure. The Discounting of the physiological manifestation of Feelings had led me to being nervous (Agitating) in a lot of situations and, also, losing control. After this I Agitated less, thinking more clearly when stressed. I decided to follow the stress issue up at the next possible opportunity. In the meantime, I worked out a number of issues on my own, in the intervals between field visits to Cathexis.

Differentiating Feelings, learning to think about them seemed to be a crucial operation in the socialization of a child. I was curious about this gap in my own socialization. I was given corroborative information by patients. An example given me by CM appears on page 186. I was determined to learn more about Agitation and its roots in my own system. An excerpt from my field notes describe where I further clarified this issue. The therapist, Jacqui, invited me to go on a guided fantasy of myself as a nine-month-old baby.

> I am in a scene with my mother or my nurse. I am about nine months old. I am in the kitchen of the house we lived in at that time. I am in a high chair and am being force-fed. It is either something I do not want to eat, or I am not hungry. I am struggling to avoid the spoon. I am desperate. My struggle is terrible. I try again and again to refuse the food which is being forced into my mouth. My nose is being held tightly. When I open my mouth for a breath, I am stuffed with spoonfuls of food. I must either swallow the food or choke. I am desperate. I am being killed! This big person is determined, and very fierce, and very big, and very much stronger than I am. I scream, choke, catch my breath! There is no way out of this situation. I turn my head frantically from side to side, and wave my arms, and push away. I am powerless! I am yanked out of the high chair, slappped several times. I lie sobbing and choking in a heap on the floor. (Notes from January 15, 1975)

From this guided fantasy experience, I gained cognitive data concerning a possible early experience. The force-feeding taught me to become frantic and Agitate when I am pushed to do something I see as life-threatening. The experience of the fantasy was a powerful one. I was really *there* for a few moments. The "realness" of being there and experiencing the desperation in the present led me to clarify further issues in my socialization. I became more conscious of a world view of believing in my own sense of powerlessness and helplessness. I realized how I had come to the conclusion that I had no control over what happened to me. I must have decided at that point that my own thoughts and feelings were not important to the persons who were in charge of or caring for me. I believed I had no rights as a human being. I believed that *thinking* as a problem-solving activity was not possible in the face of coercive treatment.

I viewed anyone "bigger" as apt to try to coerce me and that the power lay in being coercive. It was evident to me after this that I had not been socialized to think or express my own needs rationally. It was apparent that as a very small child I already had reason to be fearful, enraged and despairing in the face of big people's demands. I could understand how it was possible to not distinguish between the Feelings of *Mad* and *Scared*. Rage became a survival mechanism, a way to defend myself against coercion.

Seeing vs Looking

During the time following this experience I gained clear perception of the manner in which I projected danger and power on persons in authority positions. I began to *see* Jacqui when I dealt with her. I no longer got "nervous" in her presence. I did not ascribe power to her which she did not have in my own life. Now I am more aware than ever of the difference between "seeing" and "looking" as described by Don Juan to Carlos Castenada (1972). I am clear on the issues of power as they relate to my own expression of fear or rage. A corroborative experience was related to me by C.M. (#1) following the same type of healing ritual where she/he was two years old (Field Notes, August 1974).

> When I was working on my two-year-old stuff I knew ahead of time that it had to do with controlling behavior. I am very anal. I wanted to stop being so controlling because it was keeping me from a lot of things. I was very foggy too. People looked very big. I did things that made the therapist yell at me like scribbling on the blackboard where the contracts were. I didn't want to stop what I was doing. I felt myself get rigid and I was holding my breath. I did stop, and went to play in the soapy water. I liked playing in the soapy water and making soap suds. It was a good feeling, slippery and messy. The therapist talked to us while we were playing. He answered Jamie's questions about sex. I was listening to all of it. The picture book was fun. I *saw* a lot of things in three dimensions for the first time after that. Also things had colors that used to be sort of blurry and gray. I think that my controlling is related to scare, and I am going to find more out about it.

The experiences related in this section describe a very small amount of material gained from the various groups, marathons and participant observation periods spent at Cathexis. The personal experiences are given in the sequence in which they occurred in my own process. This was done in order to show the continuity of the growth and change in thought process in the self-system of one person—myself. The interviews and conversations with other participants in the events experienced by informants indicated that, although the content of fantasies and memories were not identical, the process was the same. That is, the more recent events are dealt with in the healing rituals before the older and more archaic events come into focus. The general developmental issues are the same. The kinds of parenting experiences are similar in many respects. The formation of the individual's cognitive structure about his world are similar. The development of skills for cognitive dealing with the somatic arousal of flight or fight mechanisms are much the same. Changes in perception were reported to be similar. This completes the section involving experiential data. The following section will deal with the objective material gained in this study.

The Minnesota Multiphasic Personality Inventory and the Semantic Differential Results

The preceding sections dealt with self reports and subjective data, before, during and after the one-year period of this study. This section deals with the objective test materials gained from the subjects in this study. Individual differences in the meanings of signs form the foundation of many diagnostic instruments in the field of personality testing. Projective tests such as the TAT and the Rorschach exemplify two of the types of diagnostic instruments available. Forced-choice of agreement and disagreement with statements as found in the MMPI and the CPI (such as "sometimes I have had some strange experiences") depend upon the *meaning* the stimulus has for the testee. Semantic measurement is a method for forcing the subject to give his reaction to concepts. Psychodynamic mechanisms such as Redefining projection and identification can be analyzed to show what may be going on in the test-taker's view. The tests are thought to allow the test-taker to reveal important parts of his personality. The objection to this view is that the traits selected out by the psychologists who construct the tests are a part of the psychologist's world view, and not necessarily that of the subject. In this framework, it has been useful to view psychopathology as involving a disordering of *meanings* or of perceiving significant persons and situations (i.e., language). Psychotherapy is viewed as a reordering and relearning of *meanings* in the direction of congruence with the society at large. With this view in mind, it seems logical to measure change in persons' views of themselves, or of their world, by using some of the tools which have been statistically validated and are defined as measuring persons against the World View of the larger society.

The significance of *meaning* as a critical variable in personality is most apparent in the process of being in a therapeutic community. The main changes that occur appear to be in the *meanings* situations have for patients and the changes that these people express as occurring within themselves. To the extent that the MMPI and the Semantic Differential are capable of providing insight into changes occurring in persons experiencing psychotherapy, the following data will prove that the individuals in the study did experience change in World View.

Minnesota Multiphasic Inventory

The MMPI profiles were read by a panel of persons trained in this method. A blind analysis was made of each set of scores. The standard "cookbook" method of assessing the personality organization of persons who take the MMPI follows (see Appendix for criteria from Handbook). This method is used routinely in psychiatry and clinical psychology and has been tested by the usual statistical methods. The literature on the MMPI and its validation is vast (Butcher, 1969; Dahlstrom and Welch, 1960; Harrison, 1969, etc.). The diagnostic criteria for this test are derived from the medical model of psychiatry and continue to fit that model. However, it is now claimed in some testing circles that the MMPI no longer measures what it was originally supposed to. George Leonard told a large gathering of professions in 1976 that Frank Barron (who developed the Ego Strength Scale in the MMPI in 1953) stated recently that the old criteria for measuring schizophrenia are no longer valid in this society. Notably, the experiences elicited by some of the MMPI schizophrenia scale questions are now recognized as generalizable to everyone. They do not of and by themselves represent psychopathology in the former manner. Such questions as "I have had unusual and peculiar experiences" and "sometimes I hate my father" are reported by many persons who do not fit the diagnosis of schizophrenics. This might indicate that there is a change occurring in the standard "normal" perceptions of the society. Paranormal phenomena are being perceived and accepted by larger and larger numbers of the general population. They no longer mark a person as "weird" or "abnormal" or peculiar *per se*. Paranormal phenomena are being perceived by more persons who are not classified as "crazy." Perspectives on "crazyness" are changing. Also people who are "normal" are more willing to respond affirmatively to such questions in the test framework. There is the growing belief that the criteria and the population on which the MMPI's original validity was based in the 1950s and 1940s no longer measure a "crazy" world view.

Clinical evaluations of MMPI

It is evident, nevertheless, that since the MMPI still is believed to measure psychopathology, and is still used for this in Western societies, it is of some current value in showing diagnostic or personality change over time. The following examples of the readings of MMPI profiles were selected by putting all those names with the diagnosis of paranoid schizophrenia in one group and all those with simple schizophrenia in another. Two names were selected from each set by picking them out of a pile, randomly. Because it was such a small group they are not identified by sex to protect their identity.

BEFORE	AFTER
#1.C.M.: This type of profile indicates a generally distrustful and fearful individual who fears involvement with others. Typical descriptions of this type of person include such comments as resentful, irritable, moody, hostile and argumentative. Acting out in manipulative ways with poor ego control and often unpredictable behavior. Parents are reported as being rejecting and lacking in affection. Typical of the schizophrenic, major conflicts center around sex-role identification and alienation. Diagnosis: simple schizophrenia.	All scales are within normal limits suggesting no major psychological difficulties. No excessive anxiety or depression are indicated. There is a tendency with these persons to deny emotional problems and to present a symptom-free picture, although they are often apt to behave in impulsive and thoughtless manner. Most interpersonal interactions are characterized as manipulative. They have few close friends. This profile suggests a functioning defensive structure, keeps things in control in spite of perceived stress. Diagnosis: a moody but normal person.
#6.E.C.: Persons with profiles similar to this are usually despondent, upset, ineffectual and disorganized. They are autistic in their thought content and re-	Persons with this type of profile are apt to engage in aggressive and punitive behavior. They are comfortable when inspiring anxiety and guilt in others, often as-

gressed in their behavior. They are highly critical of themselves, unable to cope with life problems and see themselves as hopeless. The sense of unreality, lack of self-esteem and multiple fears produce considerably poor inter-personal interactions. There is general confusion in organization of behavior and thought. Poor adaptive skills and mood disturbance are frequent. Diagnosis: paranoid schizophrenic.

#11.B.C.: This profile is typical of individuals who experience alienation, withdrawal and preoccupation with fantasy. The fantasy may be obsessional and fearful. There is lack of self-confidence, poor sense of worth and poor coping ability. Major conflicts center around alienation, dependency and sexuality. They are resentful, egocentric, self-indulgent, irritable and excitable. Parents are reported as being rejecting and also alienated. These persons are apt to act out impulsively and aggressively for attention. Diagnosis: passive aggressive personality type, probably simple schizophrenia.

#12.M.E.: Persons with this type of profile tend to have feelings of inferiority and inadequacy and very low self-esteem. There is considerable disruption of the thought processes. They are seen as disordered, unusual and thinking in unconventional and autistic manner. Delusions, grandiosity, fear and phobias are common. There is general distrust and suspicion of others. They avoid intimacy and keep emotionally distant. They are

suming social roles which are consistent with this type of behavior. They are seen as peculiar in their behavior, somewhat schizoid in their dealings with others. They adapt well to environments which permit, or require, skill in demanding compliance from others. Diagnosis: Character disorder.

All scales for this person are within normal limits. This suggests that the person is adjusting and functioning in an appropriate manner. There is indication that the individual has adapted well to the norms. There is no significant amount of depression or anxiety. There is a reasonably good self-concept and good ego strength. This person may endorse some unconventional beliefs or attitudes and may tend to stay by themselves somewhat; they may not exhibit socially outgoing and active behavior, but they are not alienated. Diagnosis: normal.

Persons who respond in this manner are apt to be anxious and have low self-esteem. They are apt to project their own problems on others. There is some disruption of thought processes with expressions of guilt and inadequate reality orientation. Persons with this type of profile are apt to be functioning reasonably well in structured settings. They have a tendency to spend much time alone, but interact in an adequate manner. Diagnosis: schizoid personality with some paranoid overtones.

shy, withdrawn, inhibited, re-
sentful and anxious. Their
behavior is seen as immature,
inappropriate and alienated.
Judgement is poor and they are
apt to spend much time withdrawn from others and in personal fantasy. Diagnosis:
paranoid schizophrenia.

There was some correspondence between the self-reports of the individual and the diagnoses given before and after. The greatest discrepancy was with person #12, who gave glowing reports of self, and whose profile as described by the panel did not correspond. The MMPI profile for this individual also does not correspond with the person's functionality in the community in which she/he resides, or with the behavior of this individual as observed by myself. The profiles were taken on a time schedule set by the study and not on the schedule of growth and development which the individuals were experiencing. It is important to take into consideration the context in which the testing was done, i.e., the developmental stage the individual was experiencing in their Reparenting process. There is no data to correlate this information with age. The persons who were in Reparenting Contracts at the time the MMPI was administered the first time were #5.H.I. and #6.E.C. Both of these individuals had experienced total Regressions. Short-term Regressions had been experienced by #11.B.C. and #12.M.E. by the time they took the second MMPI. Of the twelve MMPI profiles obtained both before and after, there was some disagreement among the panel as to final diagnosis. Only individuals on whom the panel agreed were included in the selection process for the above comparison. Individual clinicians are also idiosyncratic in their perceptions of and assignments of MMPI profiles.

The following section is devoted to the statistical treatment of the data obtained from the MMPI and the Semantic Differential tests.

Minnesota Multiphasic Inventory Statistical Analysis

The MMPI scores which were obtained at the beginning and at the end were transferred to IBM cards by keypunch and all of the data were processed for analysis of variance by the Statistical Package for the Social Sciences. The following chart indicates the results by scales for the MMPI for the total group of twelve participants (Figure 4-5).

#	Scale Name	F	Probability
L	L-scale	6.3	.03**
F	Validity	4.1	.07*
K	Correction	6.7	.03**
1	Hypochondria	4.1	.97*
2	Depression	18.1	.0001***
3	Hysteria	2.0	.19
4	Psychopathic D	1.9	.20
5	Male-Female	2.0	.12
6	Paranoia	4.6	.06*
7	Psychesthenia	10.0	.01**
8	Schizophrenia	6.0	.03**
9	Hypomania	1.0	.34
10	Social-Index	3.4	.09*

(N = 12)   * = .05 or less = somewhat significant
              ** = .01 to .05 = significant
              *** = .001 = very significant

Figure 4-5. MINNESOTA MULTIPHASIC INVENTORY SCORES by analysis of variance over a 12 month period.

Some of the scales show significant change (p - .05 or less) after one year of treatment. The most significant change appears in the Depression Scale (#2 at p = .001). The other scales showing significant change are #7 Psychesthenia (p = .01) and #8 Schizophrenia (p = .03). At less significant (p = .05+) levels there are changes in #1 Hypochondria (p = .07) and #6 Paranoia (p = .06) and Social Index #10 (p = .09). The statistics (analysis of variance) shows a change in pathology for at least six of the ten scales on this test. The scales showing no change are #3 Hysteria, #2 Psychopathic Deviate, #5 Male-Female (Sexuality Scale), and #9 Hypomania Scale. The results would indicate that overall there was still psychopathology in the group as a whole. The pooled scores do not indicate "cure," but they do indicate change in the direction of "normal" as far as the responses to the MMPI questions. This might indicate that, at least on six scales, the group change in world view as seen through the MMPI questions was in the direction of the "norm" set by the larger society. The detailed information about what each scale describes can be found in the MMPI Manual (pp. 18-21). Briefly, the information about the scales is that #1 Hypochondriasis (Hs) has 31 questions and is a measure of the amount of abnormal concern about bodily functions. The #2 Depression Scale (D), which has 25 questions, measures the depth of the clinically recognized symptom or symptom complex = depression. The Hysteria Scale #3 (Hy) has 34 questions and measures the degree to which the subject is like patients who have developed conversion-type hysteria symptoms. Psychopathic Deviate #4 (Pd) measures the similarity of the subject to a group of persons whose main difficulty lies in their absence of deep emotional response, their inability to profit from experience and their disregard of social mores. The Interest Scale #5 (Mf) measures the tendency toward masculinity or femininity of interest pattern re sexuality. The #6, Paranoia Scale (Pa), was derived by contrasting normal persons with a group of clinic patients who were characterized by suspiciousness, oversensitivity and delusions of persecution. The Psychasthenia Scale (Pt) measures the similarity of the subject to psychiatric patients who are troubled by phobias and compulsive behavior. Schizophrenia Scale #8 (Sc) measures the similarity of the subjects' responses to those patients who are characterized by bizarre and unusual thoughts or behavior. The #9 Hypomania Scale (Ma) measures the personality factor characteristic of persons with marked overproductivity of thought and action—a lesser state of the mania.

The Social Index Scale #10 (Si) aims to measure the tendency to withdraw from social contact with others (Figure 4-6).

Pt #	Dx Before	Dx After
1	Paranoid Schiz.	Normal
2	Simple Schiz.	Dissociative reac.
3	Simple Schiz.	Schzoid
4	Simple Schiz.	Character disorder
5	Paranoid Schiz.	Par. Schiz. remis.
6	Paranoid Schiz.	Character disorder
7	Paranoid Schiz.	Paranoid Schiz.*
8	Simple Schiz.	Schizoid—neurotic
9	Character dis.	Schizoid
10	Paranoid Schiz.	Paranoid Schiz.*
11	Simple Schiz.	Normal
12	Paranoid Schiz.	Paranoid Schiz.*

Figure 4-6. DIAGNOSTIC CATEGORIES BEFORE AND AFTER (* = no change).

Through assessment of the individuals and their changes on the pathology as measured by the MMPI, the indication is that there was a more than five-point drop in score for all of the scales for seven (58 percent) of the subjects. Three persons showed a less than five-point drop (25 percent) and two showed an increase in pathology on some scales. One of these increased in pathology on all scales and one on three scales only. When compared with the clinical assessments, with self assessments from the L. S. Questionnaires and from the Semantic Differential, there is some agreement as to improvement or worsening of pathology across the board (see Figures 4-6 through 4-9).

Semantic Differential Test Results

It is appropriate to view psychopathology as a way of perceiving significant others and situations in a disordered, dysfunctional and negative manner. It is appropriate within this context to see the psychotherapy process (the healing rituals) at Cathexis as a method for reordering or alternation of the meanings and perceptions of the individuals. The reordering could be in a direction which would be consistent with Life and Living, as opposed to a morbid view towards Death and Dying, i.e., in a positive direction—more positive than in the beginning.

The semantic differential (Osgood, 1957) was administered to all of the subjects at the beginning of the study and at the end of the twelve-month period. The individual scores were read onto IBM cards by keypunch and subjected to correlated-t tests to determine the following:

1. Did the subjects see their world as defined by the six concepts (My Self, My Therapist, My Mother, My Father, My Mythical Hero, My Life Style) as different before than after the twelve-month period at Cathexis.

2. Were there differences before and after between selected concepts.

PT #	1	2	3	4	5	6	7	8	9	10	Av. Point Change	LSQ	S.D. E/A/P	Impr.	Diagnosis (clinical after)
1	-2	-8	-3	-5	+9	-1	-9	-21	-2	-13	6.4	mod	+-	yes	normal
2	+3	-4	+5	-5	+5	-1	-3	-3	+3	0	1.0	mod	++	+	dis. react.
3	-4	+5	-2	+5	-2	0	+7	+13	-0	0	1.8	mod	--	no	schizoid
4	+1	-8	0	-8	+1	-6	-7	-13	+1	-10	5.0	mod	--	yes	char. dis.
5	-8	-15	-9	-5	+10	-8	-10	-20	+3	-30	-1.8	no	+-+	yes	par. schiz.
6	-9	-15	-7	+10	-5	-11	-11	-21	-3	+20	9.0	yes	++	yes	char. dis.
7	+3	+10	+4	+13	+11	+7	+22	+22	+10	+13	2.0	no	--	no	par. schiz.
8	+1	-10	+1	+3	-4	0	-9	+3	+3	-3	1.5	mod	--	no	schizoid
9	-1	-8	-2	-4	-25	-2	-2	+4	-4	-7	2.4	mod	--	no	schizoid
10	+1	-4	+1	-3	+3	0	-1	-8	-2	-3	2.0	no	--	no	par. schiz.
11	-3	-10	0	-5	+3	-6	-21	-32	-1	-16	9.4	mod	++	yes	normal
12	-5	-13	-2	-10	-3	+4	-11	-21	-14	-15	9.0	yes	++	yes	par. schiz.

Figure 4-7. POINT CHANGES IN SCORES ON MMPI SCALES as compared with self assessments and clinical assessments (Mf and Si excluded).

Person	Evaluative	Acti.	Potency
1	p=.01	p=.3	p=.9
2	p=.03*	p=.78	p=.008*
3	p=.79	p=.63(-)	p=.5(-)
4	p=.65	p=.21	p=.3
5	p=.01*	p=.28	p=.01*
6	p=.006*	p=.48(-)	p=.01*
7	p=.12	p=.53(-)	p=.34
8	p=.23(-)	p=.1.0(-)	p=.73
9	p=.18	p=.08	p=.35
10	p=.3	p=.33(-)	p=.19(-)
11	p=.03*	p=.35	p=.09
12	p=.000*	p=.5	p=.04*

(*significant at p = >< .05)

Figure 4-8. INDIVIDUALS' CHANGE IN SEMANTIC DIFFER–
ENTIAL FOR SELF CONCEPT, by variable before and after treatment.

Concept	Evaluative	Acti.	Potency
MYSELF	p=.000*	p=.03*	p=.000*
MY THERAPIST	p=.2	p-.65	p=.03*
MY MOTHER	p=.6	p=.17	p=.001*
MY FATHER	p=.5	p=.65	p=.86
MY MYTHICAL HERO	p=.002*	p=.8	p=.02*
MY LIFE STYLE	p=.000*	p=.80	p=.02*

(* = significant p = .05 <)

Figure 4-9. CHANGE IN SEMANTIC DIFFERENTIAL FOR ALL
SUBJECTS, ALL CONCEPTS, before with after.

Evaluation

(Good—Bad, Cruel—Kind, etc.) The subjects saw *Self* on the minus side of the scale at the beginning and considerably on the plus side of the scale after (p = .0001). Individually, six (50 percent) of the individuals valued Self more at the end of twelve months (p = .03 or more) than in the beginning. In comparing Self with Mother, they were seen to have as low an opinion of Mother as they did of Self. After, the difference between Self and Mother was significant (at p = .0001). In comparing Self with Mythical Hero, the Hero was seen both before and after as being valued more highly than Self (p = .002). The distance between them was less at the end (p = .0001 in beginning and p = .06 in the end). Again, in terms of evaluation, Therapist was seen to carry the same value for them after as before. When comparing Self with Mythical Hero, Mother, Father, there was no difference. Therapist was seen as having more value than Self both before and after (p = .0001). There was no difference between Therapist and Mythical Hero either before or after, both

	Evaluative		Activity		Potency	
	Before	After	Before	After	Before	After
SELF WITH	p=	p=	p=	p=	p=	p=
Mother	.76	.0001	.28	.48	.64	.015
Father	.89	.0001	.18	.62	.24	.09
Myth. Hero	.0001	.056	.02	.55	.0001	.31
THERAPIST WITH	p=	p=	p=	p=	p=	p=
Mother	.0001	.0001	.0001	.0001	.0001	.0001
Father	.0001	.0001	.0002	.0001	.0001	.001
Myth. Hero	.131	.85	.003	.007	.008	.48

Figure 4-10. COMPARISON OF SELF AND THERAPIST WITH SIGNIFICANT OTHERS by variable on the Semantic Differential Test, before and after one year of treatment at Cathexis.

being on the plus side of the scale with a positive correlation between them (.85). In comparing Life Style before and after, there was a difference evaluatively (p = .0001). Overall, for the Evaluative variable on the scale, there was marked difference between Self and each of the selected concepts after one year of therapy. The statistical significance of this difference (p = .05 to .0001) would indicate a change in the manner in which these individuals assessed their world through the selected concepts (see Figures 4-8, 4-9, 4-10).

Potency

(Indecisive–Decisive, Intentional–Unintentional) The subjects saw Self as considerably more potent after than before (p = .0001). They also saw each of the other concepts as more potent after than before therapy with one exception—Father, who was not seen as changing on any of the variables and, least of all, on the Potency variable. Therapist changed at the p = .03 level. Mother changed (p = .001), Mythical Hero changed (p = .02) and Life Style was more potent at p = .02 also. Individually, five of the participants saw themselves as more potent after than before but, when pooled scores were used, the overall change was marked. In comparing Self with each of these other concepts in terms of potency, there were differences between Self and Mother at the end of the study (p = .015); Self with Father at the end was less significant (.09) and no difference between Self and Mythical Hero. Therapist, when compared with Mother (.0001), with Father (.001) and with Mythical Hero (no difference) at the end, was seen to be more potent than the mythical Hero in the beginning of the study, but not so at the end of the study (see Figures 4-8, 4-9, 4-10).

In general, the information gained from the Semantic Differential indicates that there were significant differences connotatively for each of the individuals and, also, for the total group on the three variables of evaluation, activity and potency for all of the six concepts. The data supports in part the self report information given from the Life Script Questionnaires. The information gained from the Semantic Differential supports the premise that persons who experience psychopathology have a World View that is limited, bound by morbid and self-destructive ways of experiencing Self and Significant Others. It also supports the information gained by interview and participant observation and clinical assessment via the MMPI, which is reported earlier in this chapter. Though the Mythical

Hero was ascribed positive values at both ends of the study period, it was seen in a less grandiose manner at the end. As Mythical Hero lost in Value, Activity and Potency, the Therapist seemed to gain on these variables. Perhaps the "magic" ascribed to the Mythical Hero loses power as the individual invests more deeply in learning experiences and healing rituals in the program. The data from the Semantic Differential would support the hypothesis that persons with psychopathology, who experience the T.A. model of psychotherapy, do change in terms of their view of Self and Significant Others.

Summary

In general the data from Life Script Questionnaires, interviews, Minnesota Multiphasic Personality Inventories and Semantic Differential tests would indicate that there is a reordering of personal constructs for half of the participants in the program at Cathexis. In terms of the MMPI, patients #3 and #7 were worse at the end of the year, several had changed their diagnostic categories and two were diagnosed as no longer psychopathological. These findings would indicate within the time limit of twelve months the treatment approach at Cathexis is effective in bringing about change in selected individuals with the diagnosis of schizophrenia, on selected variables.

NOTES AND REFERENCES

1. Becker (1973: Chapter Ten) puts forth the notion that, in order to buy off death, we must be victims. He describes mental illness as a "failure in heroics." He quotes Medard Boss: ". . . the essential, basic arch-anxiety (primal anxiety) is innate to all isolated, individual forms of human existence. In the basic anxiety human existence is afraid of as well as anxious about its 'being-in-the-world'. . . . Only if we understand this can we conceive of the seemingly paradoxic phenomenon that people who are afraid of living are also especially frightened of death." He also states that "the fear of death must be present behind all our normal functioning, in order for the organism to be armed toward self-preservation. But the fear of death cannot be present constantly in one's mental functioning else the organism could not function . . . . And so we can understand what seems like an impossible paradox: the ever-present fear of death in the normal biological functioning of our instinct of self-preservation, as well as our utter obliviousness to this fear in our conscious life" (16-17).

2. Fantasy and Dreams: At a time when neurophysiology and psychology are increasingly concerned with the complex information-processing capacities

of the brain, dreams, daydreams and fantasies become increasingly important sources of information about this organ. As a source of information on cognition and perception, fantasy and dream work are being used more and more in general psychotherapy. "Fantasy is not an epiphenomenon, it is an important part of the human being's system for managing large masses of information; it is central to human functioning. It manifests the operation of processes that enter into a wide variety of nonfantasy responses. Its workings play a critical role in creating thinking, its vicissitudes suggest some conceptual handles for psychotic thought" (Klinger, *Structure and Functions of Fantasy*, 1971: viii).

3. Wilhelm Reich in a series of books, the most referred to being his *Character Analysis* (1945), offered the theory that free biological functioning accompanied with free psychological functioning results in a free flow of life energy which is experienced as pleasurable. He suggested that the stopping of this flow was experienced as disagreeable, painful or laden with anxiety. He proposed that energy stasis was the starting point of neuroses and was always accompanied by anxiety whether conscious or unconscious. He suggested that the ways in which people blocked their life energy was an expression of the traumas which they had experienced in their socialization process. He developed a form of psychotherapy designed to free the energy in the person's body and allow him to make the psychological connections necessary to free him of his neuroses.

4. Object relations: In psychoanalytic theory the ability of the individual to distinguish the Self from Other arises during the first three years of life. If the individual is provided with an environment in which he can experience himself as a separate object from other objects, and to cognize the differences in terms of depth perception, touch, feel, etc., he is then able to create a more real picture of others as against himself.

5. Hebephrenia as defined by the Diagnostic and Statistical Manual II (33): "This psychosis is characterized by disorganized thinking, shallow and inappropriate affect, unpredictable giggling, silly and regressive behavior and mannerisms, and frequent hypochondriachal complaints. Delusions and hallucinations, if present, are transient and not well organized."

6. Corpus Callosum: Ornstein proposes that Western people are linear and analytical thinkers and that the Left Brain in right-handed people is predominant in this process (1974). It is also predominant in the language capacity of adults, although children are thought to use both sides early in their development and later switch to the hemisphere which is congruent with their handedness. In most ordinary activities people switch between right and left hemispheres and they are complementary, thus when describing a spiral staircase, a person may start with words and switch to hand gestures. Normal people integrate both hemispheres. The corpus callosum is the major nerve pathway between the two hemispheres. Schiff (1975) suggests that some of the pathways in the Corpus callosum are impaired in transmitting and integrating information in schizophrenics. She believes that they have difficulty in integrating the right side and the left side brain functions and that this may be one of the clues in the

impulsive and unexpected outbursts of the hebephrenic. The disturbed person rarely knows why they behaved the way they did afterwards. Studies of split-brain function would indicate that the integrative function is a major aspect of normal functioning (Pines, 1973; Rose, 1973). See Casteneda re *tonal* and *nagual*.

7. Carlos Castenada in his series of books suggests that there are different ways of perceiving the world. He talks about "seeing" and looking. He describes Don Juan (1974: 269) as saying:

> ... last night you experienced the unspeakable, the *nagual*. Your *reason* cannot fight the physical knowledge that you are a nameless cluster of feelings. Your reason at this point might even admit that there is another center of assemblage, the *will*, through which it is possible to judge or assess and use the extraordinary effects of the *nagual*. It has finally dawned on your *reason* that one can reflect the *nagual* through the *will*, although one can never explain it.

Chapter V

THE PARADOX OF MAGIC
AND SCIENCE

Magic is a set of practices *seeming* to require more than human power. It is the art or body of arts through which its practitioners have *supernatural* powers. Its practices are startling, imposing, producing effects which seem supernatural having *extraordinary* properties. (*Webster's New International Dictionary*, 1961)

Magic by definition and reputation is a notoriously ineffective method for attaining the specific ends its practitioners hope to achieve through its use . . . scientific analyses of magic presuppose that these rituals as a matter-of-fact do not lead to the desired results . . . one of the puzzles most theories of magic seek to resolve is why human beings cling so tenaciously to magic if it does not work . . . . (O. K. Moore, 1965: 69-74)

Some practices which have been classified as "MAGIC" may well be directly efficacious as techniques for attaining the ends envisaged by its practitioners, according to O. K. Moore (1965). The similarities between divination (magic) and games of strategy is a crucial issue and has been clarified by Moore who emphasizes that some classes of interactional problems can be solved by means of a "mixed" or "statistical" strategy. In order to employ a statistical strategy it is necessary to have a suitable chance mechanism—one that will generate appropriate odds for the problem at hand. Magical practices such as divination and healing rites provide a functional equivalent to a table of random numbers. These then help its practitioners through a long process of creative trial and error arrive at some approximate "statistical" solutions for recurring problems. Magic, is, then, not necessarily as "unscientific" and "ineffective" as characterized by modern thinkers. Magic, being startling and imposing, mobilizes latent energy. It also has a statistical "positive latent function." It mobilizes energy for problem-solving and, because of the probability factor, it works often enough to make people want to rely on it. In healing rituals, there is a dialectic between science and magic.

What have I learned about magic and healing ritual by the study of Cathexis community from an anthropological point of view? I have learned that the dialectic between Real vs Not Real (Logic and Paradox, Structure and Antistructure) creates a synthesis of experience which results in the healing process. This dialectic provides the medium for the transformation of World View from a non-functional to a "normal" World View. How does Cathexis do this?

Cathexis provides a *subculture* with a symbolic language. The Cathexis version of Transactional Analysis is itself a subculture. The Cathexis subculture has symbols and roles and paraphernalia. The language, symbols and symbolic power provide a standardized model for communication. The Cathexis model provides a system of ideas— a model which is explicitly systematic. The model is used to generate practical applications to therapy. The Cathexis paradigm provides model roles with symbolic power—the Reparenting model. The roles generated by the Reparenting model provide a structure for symbolic action. The dialectic between the roles (parent and child, structure and antistructure) results in a model of the world especially designed to make sense out of the problems of patients. Cathexis provides patterns of and for dealing with the greater society. It provides a system for manipulating the world.

Process

The Cathexis model is processual. It establishes a systematic process for socializing the person. It is a systematic approach to the use of psychic energy. The Transactional Analysis theoretical framework is a general systems theory (Figure 5-1). It supplies a structure for mobilizing and controlling the use of psychic energy. Much as biofeedback provides a system for awareness of and control of the autonomic nervous system, Transactional Analysis provides a system for awareness of and control of the unconscious and automatic in a person's behavior. Transactional Analysis offers a means of thinking about psychic energy and, thus, a means of utilizing it. The T.A. model provides a system of feedback. With feedback of energy there is a decrease in entropy and information on how, where and when to deal with, use, distribute, convert, translate and trans-

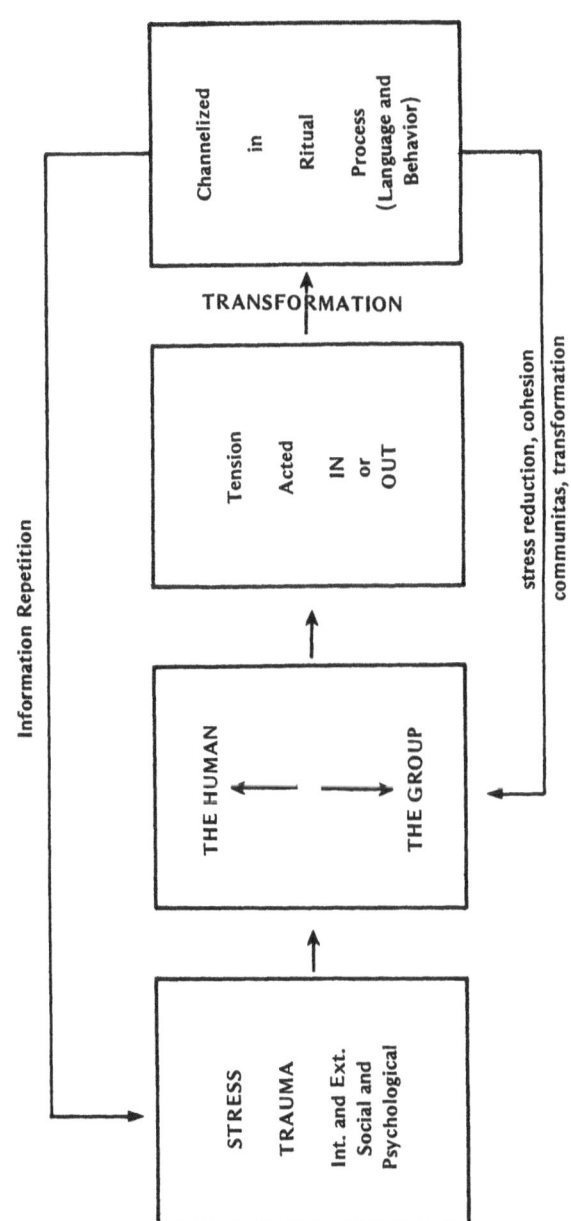

Figure 5-1. MODEL OF RITUAL PROCESS as a Cybernetic System.

form energy. If feedback is effective, energy use is more efficient. A major source of psychic energy is the experience of *communitas* (Turner, 1974). Communitas occurs in Ritual. It occurs in the experience of *gemeinschaft* (Tonnies, 1887). In the experience of communitas, psychic energy is used to transform perceptions of Self/ Other. The experience of communitas is not generally available to persons who are alienated from society. The alienated are caught up in the world of *geselleschaft* (Tonnies, 1887) and do not know how to achieve communitas. Rituals provide altered states of consciousness and teach people how to achieve communitas.

Ideal types such as Gemeinschaft (community) and Gesselschaft (society) (Tonnies, 1887); natural will and rational will; organic solidarity and mechanical solidarity (Durkheim, 1893) explain a dialectic central to understanding human society. Pappenheim (1959) gives a concise explanation of the gemeinschaft/geselleschaft ideals:

> Tonnies believes that a distinction should be made between two essentially different bases of human association . . . *geselleschaft* is a relationship contractural in nature, deliberately established by individuals who realize that they cannot pursue their proper interests effectively in isolation and therefore band together. The other, named *gemeinschaft*, is a social unit which does not primarily come into belonging to it as one belongs to one's home. Individuals who enter a *geselleschaft* do so with only a fraction of their being, that is, with that part of their existence which corresponds to the specific purpose of the organization . . . individuals who own stock in a company, are related to each other, not as whole persons, but with only that part of themselves which is concerned with being a . . . shareholder. They leave out, or are supposed to leave out, of their association all the other qualities which constitute their lives . . . their friendships and hatreds . . . and so on. Thus they remain loosely connected and essentially remote from each other. (In) . . . *gemeinschaft* . . . its members are bound to each other as whole persons rather than as fragmentary individuals. The pure form of *gemeinschaft* is . . . particularly in the relation between mother and child, where unity is the first stage in development and separation is a later phase. In *gemeinschaft* unity prevails, in spite of occasional separation; in *geselleschaft* separation prevails in spite of occasional unity. So deep is the separation between man and man in *geselleschaft* that "everybody is by himself isolated, and there exists a condition of tension against all other." (Pappenheim, 1959: 66-67)

Cathexis provides a community experience where the ritual processes occur which allow the individual to learn how to function in the greater society.

Metaphors

Cathexis is successful because it provides a small society (gemein-schaft) with its own symbols and metaphors by which the participants mobilize their own psychic energy. The basic metaphor *"starving baby"* gives a name to the process inside the patient. This metaphor provides a logic, definitions and a language, i.e., a culture through which the individual gains patterns of and for dealing with the greater society. The metaphor condenses the "magic" and the "science" which are theses and antithesis in the ritual healing process. The metaphor condenses the systematic approach to the use of energy. Cathexis provides a setting in which social control and power are given a cognitive framework. The Cathexis cognitive system makes sense because it explicates the greater society giving it a form and a meaning. The pieces of the patient's puzzle are put together, he comes to understand the "starving baby" inside his head and his body. The small society provides the environment where rites-of-transition may be experienced. Ritual process involves metaphor. Ritual is metaphor. Metaphors condense meanings for people.

Ritual Process

Ritual Process is seen as a "standardized system of stereotyped behaviors and communications which manipulate human emotion toward a preset end result" (Rappaport, 1971: 23). The process involves stages through which the individuals move in learning a structured set of behaviors which constitute the healing paradigm. From a General Systems Theory perspective, rituals are cybernetic feedback systems (Figure 5-1). They anticipate and correct deviations in the system. The units of ritual process are the symbols, objects and behaviors of the individuals experiencing the ritual.

Rituals are seen as encompassing three broad steps or stages called rites-of-passage. These stages were first described by Van Gennep (1960). They are named by him: rites of separation, transition and incorporation. Turner (1967) calls them Separation, Limen and Aggregation. Each of these stages has specific processes through which persons pass who are engaged in the ritual. Associated with the rites-of-passage are symbols, symbolic objects and specific behaviors. Each symbol or object has a particular meaning. The meaning may be different depending upon the context or field in which the rite is a phase. Many of the symbols and experiences with-in rituals are related to the developmental experiences of the human being and people's experiences of the human body throughout life from birth to death.

Of particular interest here is the middle or *Liminal* stage of the ritual process. This stage has been characterized as a period in the process when the participants experience a deep sense of belonging to and with others present. This part describes the human experience in which the *meaning* of the symbols and the actions actually become *being* for the individual participant. Turner (1967) calls this exper-ience *communitas*, Buber (1947) describes it as the *I-Thou*. Com-munitas is a form of intimacy which is spontaneous, immediate, concrete. It is not shaped by norms, it is not institutionalized, yet it is not abstract. It is first experienced between mother and baby. It is often extolled as ineffable, undescribably, exquisitely, uplifting. It is experienced as an altered state of consciousness, precious and inim-itable. This type of experience produces a form of symbolic trans-formation of the self or of the World View of the participants. In the liminal stage there may be words, objects and behaviors which become symbolic of the experience. The individuals in the experience may utilize these symbols or behaviors to bring about the moment in which the change occurs. At Cathexis, these are developmental stages, and the paraphernalia which fit the stage (e.g., Being Little), are symbolic.

Symbols condense many references. The references are then united in a single cognitive and affective field. Without symbols there would be no communication. Ritual symbols may allow individuals to see, feel and experience themselves in a single instant. Symbols may alienate people, but, when they they are used in a ritual context, they draw them closer. Symbols are the means by which *energy* is exchanged between individuals in recognition of their mutual existence. The energy factor is a key point in the Cathexis system. Symbols and symbolic systems are the tools whereby people cognize their environment or are turned away from it. They provide the tools for adaptation to the environment. In healing rituals, the symbols and symbolic action mobilize the patient's energy to provide the vehicle for creating order in his cognitive system.

The healing rituals at Cathexis are chiefly Rites-of-Transition (von Gennep, 1960), i.e., movement from one state of cognition and behavior to another. They are seen as falling into the categories of

Thinking, Feeling, and Doing and Being Rituals. They include symbols, symbolic objects and a symbolic language which is specific to the theory of Transactional Analysis. Among the symbols which have a very special meaning in the healing rituals at Cathexis are: Contracts, Cathecting Little, Passivity, Doing Nothing, Overadaptation, Agitation, Escalation-to-violence-or-incapacitation, Dealing, Reparenting, Nurturing, Caring, Discounting, Redefining and Frame-of-reference. The metaphor which condenses these is the "starving baby" metaphor. Symbolic objects are nursing bottles, various toys and play objects (i.e., the paraphernalia of babies and children in the greater society) and the corner or a chair. These latter are places a person can be assigned until he *thinks* about his behavior. They symbolize the *restriction* the person is under until he *does think*. A very important aspect of all transactions at Cathexis is the energy which is experienced, expended and exchanged between the individuals or the group members.

Language

Neurolinguistics research indicates that there is evidence for hemisphere dominance in language production and in cognitive styles. The visual, kinesthetic, offactory and aural senses are intricately intertwined in the processing of data. World View and self concept are tied to the neurological deep structures of the individual (Dingwell and Whitaker, 1974). A person's way of representing self is based on deep structure and electrical energy. In many people, the deep structure is split between a nonverbal view and style of behaving and a verbal style, which are frequently not congruent. This incongruence or split (Real vs Not Real) results in the individual experiencing a state of consciousness which alienates him from himself and from others. The behaviors are often seen as inconsistent, incongruent and unproductive. The process of healing ritual involves altered states of consciousness which force the indivudal to integrate his representational systems. The integration results in verbal and nonverbal behaviors which are congruent.

Altered states of consciousness

Hypnotic and trance states are basically the means by which the integrative process is achieved. The person who has entered into a rite of transition is essentially allowing self to experience his deep structure. During trance the patient, at the direction of the therapist, reorders his representational system at the level of deep structure. When the patient comes out of the trance, he experiences a surge of energy or "peak experience" and with it the sense of oneness with self and with others. This oneness is a universally valued experience.

Metalanguage

Bateson's theory of double bind goes only so far. Each person who grows up in settings where the authority persons give out incongruent messages experiences more than two contradictory sets of messages. Most metacommunication involves numerous contradictory messages. For the child who does not have adequate modeling for processing data input, the contradictory messages cause a paradoxical situation. He incorporates the paradox and then creates a world view which makes paradox out of everything. There is no logical set by which he can manage the world. Therapy provides a set of logical subsystems and a specific process and language by which he can order the data and define the paradoxes of his life. It is apparent that underlying an understanding of ritual and symbol is the field of linguistics. The study of the double-bind requires a knowledge of the language (verbal and nonverbal) that the individual is having to cope with in order to order his world. The language of therapy involves a process which is universally experienced. The trust and confidence of the patient in the practitioner allows the practitioner to bring the patient into a trance or hypnotic state. This altered state of consciousness is the prime state in which the healing occurs. The entry into the trance state allows the patient to reorder his world on a deep structure level. The practitioner guides the patient through the reordering process. The practitioner's skill is based on his ability to pick up cues and process them from the surface structure presented to him by the patient.

Ethnopsychiatry

There are parallels between the healing rituals at Cathexis and those described in nonwestern systems (Torrey, 1972: 135). The range of life crisis experiences being encompassed in the healing process parallels nonwestern models. The process of rites-of-passage is similar (Eliade, 1975). There is also similarity in content between the experiences of nonwestern shamnic rites and western psychiatric patients undergoing healing rites. It is apparent to me that the field of ethnopsychiatry is a distinct and explicit field within ethnomedicine. The relationships between the fields of medical ecology, health program research and epidemiology and the study of ritual are directly related to one another. Ethnopsychiatry encompasses these. Cathexis is a bounded community exemplifying the processes these fields focus upon.

Cathexis

This is a nonprofit educational institution with a program for patients and trainees in Transactional Analysis. Included in the institution are the Institute, the School, the Residence and the Family. Cathexis provides a setting where persons trapped in psychopathology can find help. They can learn new behaviors which may alleviate the alienation and suffering they experience in the greater society. At Cathexis the "magic" and the "science" become a reality for some. The patients and trainees find a program which assists them to learn a language consonant with their needs for growth. The philosophy of Cathexis is embodied in the two major components of that philosophy:

> . . .that patients know cognitively and/or viscerally what they need to do to get well, and that they can take responsibility for their functioning during treatment if they have a supportive environment. . . . (Schiff, 1975: 98)

To some, the Cathexis program seems at the outset to be some kind of magic place; they soon find a carefully planned series of cognitive and affective experiences. It is evident that, for some, the Cathexis program is effective. In a twelve-month period of the study, two out of twelve patients became "normal" on the MMPI and five out of twelve (33 percent) changed their profiles significantly.

When a person has problems in thinking and feeling and behaving, it is often necessary to structure that person's experiences so that functional patterns of thinking, feeling and behaving can be learned. In ritualized events, it is often possible for a person to experience a dropping of defenses, known as a psychic opening (Holloman, 1974). Psychic opening facilitates behavioral change and personality transformation. This process in which the individual experiences psychic opening is a rite-of-passage. Ritual manipulation of behavior and of emotional responses results in a state of mind in which the individual is open to new information. Cathexis community supplies a variety of ritual experiences, the major ritual dyad being Reparenting and Cathecting Little. The structure and rituals provided at Cathexis permit each individual to determine his own programs and arrange for his own healing rituals. In the Cathexis setting the trainee and the patient learn about their need for power. They learn to differentiate cooperative power from competitive power.

Social Control and Power

Social control and power and how they function at Cathexis is one of the questions raised by the study of this community. How does this community remain viable? What is the glue that holds it together? Why does a patient or a trainee stay at Cathexis in the face of the highly reactive kinds of confrontation they have to deal with? What are the forces of social control which prevent counterproductive interpersonal interaction? What are the group norms which supply the cohesiveness for such a community? Some of these questions have been answered in Chapters Three and Four.

Survival

In some communities the cohesive ingredient seems to be amiability and openness. In others, it is kinship, or economics. At Cathexis, though amiability and openness of attitude are hoped for conditions for interaction, amiability is not evident. For most patients who enter the Cathexis community to remain in the structure has survival value. Some of them are in an extreme state of alienation and despair and are self-destructive. (The description of Dennis in *All My Children* is a graphic example of the typical state of despair.) The self-interest for each individual lies in the fact that available at Cathexis is the structure to cure himself of his desperate condition. The structure whereby he may feed his "starving baby." They recognize it as a place to survive for awhile. A place to gain understanding of the conflict that is going on inside them and the conflict they generate in their associations.

Conflict

One of the learnings which is available at Cathexis is the ability to settle disputes and disagreements with a minimum of hassle (i.e., quarreling and harangue). By becoming reactive to Discounting and

Redefining, by adapting to the cultural expectation within Cathexis to these mechanisms, the person learns to conserve psychic energy. Psychic energy, its use, conservation and generation is one of the major criteria upon which persons at Cathexis make decisions on whether to relate or not. The consequences of disruptive behavior and issues around cooperation and competition are never in doubt in the Cathexis model. This is not to say that every individual rationally considers his every act. Most of the patients are very disturbed initially. Eventually each person comes to view the Cathexis structured manner of dealing with conflict as valuable. Each confrontation has its utilitarian value in terms of the acquisition of Strokes (units of recognition). Eventually the ability to think and feel in an organized manner, stay alive and out of the state of constant inner and outer conflict is seen as a valuable way of being-in-the-world. The issue here is that disturbed "crazy" people come to perceive and act in terms of their self interest in this community, since the pathology is manifested by their *inability* to preserve what seems to be their best interest in the greater society. In the greater society they are in constant conflict with its values. At Cathexis they learn through conforming to the Cathexis T.A. model to deal with these conflicts.

Conformity

Conformity to the Cathexis "norm" concerning Passivity becomes a matter of ecological self-interest to the patient. Cooperation, ritualism, respect for the person and possessions of others are part of the Passivity model. The person recognizes this as a place of personal power. A place to learn the ordering of his energies. A place to learn a new internal structure for dealing with society. By conforming to the expectations of the Cathexis model, the patient finds there is security and well-being in an orderly, structured approach to the solutions of the problems one used to find insoluble. One finds a sense of well-being in conforming to the Cathexis norm. Being competitive, provocative, aggressive and disorderly have been life-threatening behaviors for most of the patients. Recognition of this fact and conformity to being reactive to competitiveness accomplishes a security and a cohesiveness.

Reciprocity

Among the major elements of social control in all societies is reciprocity. The basic notion is that the individual is prompted to conform (i.e., abide by what others expect) because one realizes that, by doing so, one can expect them to observe one's rights also. Reciprocity is also withheld when one does not conform. Reciprocity is an important part of becoming socialized. One of the dynamics that is expected of individuals in the greater society is competitiveness. At Cathexis, one finds that being competitive is apt to alienate others. The person with psychopathology has learned that one must compete for one's needs. One has learned that one cannot be responsible for one's own needs (other's needs are more important, you are nothing without x—your parent, etc.). At Cathexis, one learns that there is power in learning to take responsibility for getting one's needs met, and this can be done reciprocally (see Steiner, 1971: 9-15: Stroke Economy). The realization that one cuts one off from support and from the care of one's fellows by being competitive or uncaring pushes one to "deal" in order to maintain Strokes. The moment-to-moment confrontation on one's maneuverings and manipulations is a way in which group conformity is achieved. An understanding of one's Symbiotic ties is a part of the process.

Symbiosis

The complementary or competitive exchanges of power within Symbiosis is a factor in social control. Often a patient will invest his personal power in a staff person (transference) and this is accepted until he has worked out the issue. This phenomenon of giving up power temporarily is an important part of the Reparenting rituals. Exchanging power, or giving up power, is always done with a view to understanding of the dynamics of the immediate situation. Reactivity to shifts of responsibility for thinking, feeling and problem-solving is maintained in these situations. Reinforcement of the individual's ability to get what one needs is a factor in Symbiosis. Occasionally an individual will have a peak experience as a result of working out a problem. This, shared by the group, provides the unique sense of communitas which is a very potent force in relieving anomie.

Logic

Another aspect of social control is what Honigman (1959: 500) calls logic. The patient is reminded consistently and repeatedly that "you can think." One is reminded that violation of the group norm of Discounting is incompatible with one's goals of autonomy. This frequent confrontation brings about an appeal to one's adult Ego State. This is the part of the individual which has the logical information about the consequences of "crazy" behavior. The Adult is seen as capable of making decisions and judgments which are independent of the disruptive part of one's personality (i.e., the crazy Parent and crazy Child). The appeal of logic, of rational thinking and feedback on this, and the subsequent power in being able to *think* is substantial. Logic is a characteristic of the special system to which the Cathexis members are enculturated. The individual finds reward in the conservation of energy inherent in being able to think logically. Reward also lies in the logic of the Cathexis subculture.

Ritual

The series of rituals offered as part of the social and therapeutic milieu are another factor in the motivation of adherence to the Cathexis community. Rituals provide reassurance and feeling of security in the face of the demands of a person's daily life. Rituals have a certain "magic" to them because they "work" for the individual. All of the rituals at Cathexis which come under the rubric of Cathecting Little give the individual the freedom from social pressures required of the Grownup. Further, the bottle, the nurturing, and holding rituals (see Chapter Three) supply the individual with predictable times in one's day when one may experience regressive behavior that is not going to bring shame or disapproval. The fact that one has arranged the ritual oneself is also a source of power. The patient knows that it is possible to arrange to get an assured quantity of unconditional positive Strokes. The individual involved in ritual gains a sense of security which comes from conforming to the repeated experience of the requirements of the structured rituals. Knowledge is gained from the reiterated experiences that one has the power to structure one's own needs. The rituals supply the person with ready-made solutions to problems which have not seemed soluble heretofore. The ritual behavior is comforting because one finds that it works while one is learning to incorporate it and give it one's own style. The sense of danger in the world diminishes when the rituals are evoked. Frequently, one finds that one is able to *think* about what is troubling one and make sense out of it, by merely evoking a standard ritual (for instance, the Think-Structure). Belonging to a group where the rituals are being experienced together with others is another aspect of cohesion and conformity. One also learns vicariously as another goes through the ritual process. Alienation from one's fellow group members is reduced when a ritual is experienced, and the thoughts and feelings are shared. Rituals reinforce group ties. One gains a sense of community from the passage together with others through ritual processes. Some of the ritual experiences provide the peak experience, the altered state of consciousness, the sense of oneness. The energy and excitement which follow such an experience are highly prized universally.

Developmental Factors

As one completes a developmental lacuna, one gains recognition of this event and one's social status changes. This is a function of rites-of-passage. The patient moves from being constantly beset with fears, paranoia and a disordering of energy. One moves from one's own idiosyncratic frame-of-reference to a broader frame-of-reference which is consensually validated, where one can be more reactive to the here and now. One responds less to inner reality and more to outer reality and the energy base changes. One's state of *Being* in the world changes. This becomes visible to others. The changes continue to be reinforced in interactions, the recognition of this brings one back for more. As one strives to learn and close developmental lacunae in one's personality structure, one is further motivated to make the group process work. These factors also help to keep people in the community.

Hungers (Drives or Needs)

A basic human and mamallian hunger aside from food and shelter is the need for sensory stimulation (Berne, 1970: 182-186; 1972: 21-25; Montague, 1971). This is a key issue in psychopathology. It is so important that it has been noted that human beings cannot stand a vacuum or monotony for any length of time. They tend to manufacture their own stimulation and hallucinate and have fantasies after a period of time (Lilly, 1969). People will go to unusual lengths to secure contact of some kind with other people. Far from avoiding stimulating experiences and situations, people will generally seek them out. Sensory stimulation affirms Existence. A baby who is neglected for any length of time will generate an integral arousal system and cry a lot until it is picked up and cared for or until it gives up and dies of marasmus (Spitz, 1965). Montague puts this simply as the need for touch and skin contact. Berne talks about the exchange of infra-red rays. He defines the basic human psychological hungers as being six in number. They are stimulus, recognition, contact, sex, incident and structure hunger (1970: 185). Cathexis' program makes it possible for the patients to fulfill most of these hungers through their programs and Time Structure. The exchange of energy in getting the hungers met is the basis of human interaction. Energy as a concept from General Systems Theory is tied in with the concept of entrophy and that of energy. An understanding of these concepts is useful in clarifying the issues of social control and power as they function in keeping people involved in the Cathexis system.

Systems

People come and go from the Cathexis community. There is open exchange of ideas and theoretical issues among patients, trainees, visitors and staff. The use of the Transactional Analysis language as a basic form of communication points to the Cathexis model of treatment as an open system (General Systems Theory). Three important factors in the functioning of open systems (models) are energy, entropy and synergy. A model is a piece of machinery or a system which relates observations to theoretical ideas. Cathexis is a system which relates the patient's experience to theory. The patients', trainees' and staffs' experiences are theory-generating systems. These characteristics which are true of systems no matter whether they are behavioral or mechanical. Systems are organized units of sets of components which mutually react and interact. A system acts as a whole; a dysfunction of a part causes disturbance in the entire system. Disturbances can be resolved in all systems, regardless of components and interacting forces by the aggregation of feedback circuits (Ashby, 1968: 296-297). The notion of feedback circuits is relevant in the psychobiological as well as the physical sciences (Kremyanski, 1968: 177). The function of feedback circuits is to control variables, to modify reaction by facilitation, dissemination or inhibition, and to direct the overall system toward a goal (von Bekesey, 1967: 35-63). The primary goal of a system is to maintain itself intact. Stress and conflict occur as a result of the energy imbalance between the components of the system (Figure 5-1).

Energy

Energy is generated by the activities of the input and output and feedback systems. Stress is defined as the response to conflict and always involves an energy drain away from the system. There are several features about energy which are important to the behavioral sciences. One feature is that energy is defined as a force or a capacity, but we still do not know *what* energy *is*. We know only what energy *does* (Karp, 1968: 26). We know that energy is transformable, and transformational. Energy has different manifestations or different forms which can be transformed from one form to another. On a behavioral level a person can *look angry* and actually *be scared*. On a cellular level, a transformation occurs in the exchange of ions at the cell membrane, from ion exchange to a discharge of electrical energy. In the Galvanic Skin Response experiments, the electrical impulse in the skin cell is picked up via electrodes and is transformed via a recording device to a tracing on a piece of paper, or to an oscilloscope which is then manifested as an electrical wave which radiates light energy. Human organisms are systems where the transformation of energy occurs at many levels. Human organisms are open systems, i.e., systems which exchange energy and information with other systems and with the environment which is the larger system.

Human organisms are open systems. They form groups which are open systems. The interaction with the other system in the groups and with the greater system stimulates the individual system to adapt to the more inclusive environmental system. The boundaries of the system are dynamic and change in response to stress to maintain a steady state of equilibrium (von Bertalanffy, 1968: 709) or to maintain the stress level for sensory stimulation (Reich, 1972). Equilibrium in the greater environmental system may result in the disequilibrium of subsystems. This creates tension and movement or displacement of energy. The energy displacement in turn is then available to react (discharge) in response to the stimulus in the environment. When parts of a system interact, some type of energy exchange, displacement or expenditure is necessary.

Entropy

The transformation of energy is costly. Part of the energy is always lost from the system. The transformation of energy in the interaction of parts of systems on one another, and the loss of energy to those systems, is a key issue in psychopathology. Psychopathology is a form of disorganized psychic energy (see Figure 5-2 on page 220). Biochemical studies on output of adrenalin under stress and the effects of the breakdown of products of adrenalin on the nervous system are at present in their early stages. The biochemical studies will in time throw more light on the issue of energy as transformed and transmitted by the nervous system (Rose, 1973: 66-70). Energy which is not systematically returned to the system through input systems and feedback results in the process of entrophy. If the process of entrophy continues unchecked, the system eventually disintegrates. An easily understood process in human and biological systems are the processes of aging, dying and rotting. Increased stress and no input of energy to the system results in the disintegration of the system. The continuing existence of a system is entirely dependent upon the input and replacement of lost energy to that system.

The psychopathological system may be considered to be a system in entropy (Figure 5-2). Since psychopathology is an adaptation to a family system which no longer exists for that person, outside that family, the individual is in an entropic state. Energy loss is high, internal tension is great and the boundaries of the Self System change shape and configuration. These changes cause discomfort to both the individual and the larger external system. The internal components of the Self System attempt to form or achieve equilibration but, if there is no input of energy, entropy continues. The Self System begins to disintegrate. The individual resorts to old defenses (inadequate feedback mechanisms) to reestablish the equilibrium. In the treatment community the old mechanisms do not work for the individual. New systems must be developed which will also feed energy into the person, and into the larger system so that the entropy does not continue. The complexity of the feedback loops is determined by the number of parts, the size, the energy requirements and the function of the total system (Redfield, 1942: 16-20). When feedback loops are operating appropriately for the total system, the Self of the individuals in the system is affirmed. The larger system is then further able to deal with stress, to adjust its boundaries and to continue in steady state. When feedback loops are functioning adequately to maintain the Self in equilibrium, there is a transformation of energy into functional modes of operating. When this happens, the larger system of which the smaller systems are a part functions at a level which is greater than the sum of the parts of the smaller

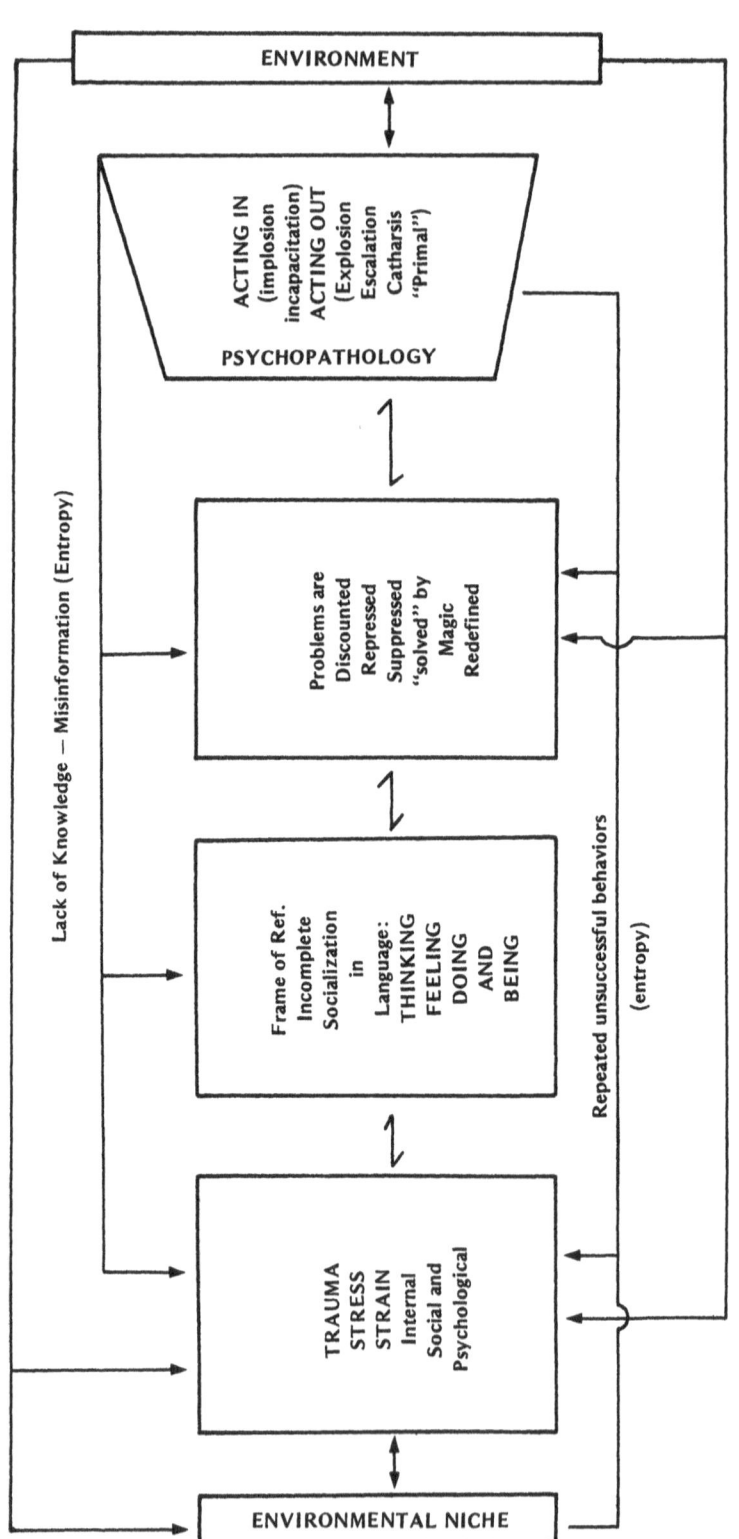

Figure 5-2. MODEL OF PROCESS OF PSYCHOPATHOLOGY.

systems. If the smaller systems are entropic, their energy drain will affect the larger system's energy level.

Energy is not only transformed and transformational, it is also transferrable; it may be shifted or borrowed. This is a key concept in the theory of Symbiosis. Feelings are an expression of energy. An individual who does not know what to do with the Feeling (energy) inside himself, tends to shift the Feeling (energy) to another person. Symbiosis is maintained by getting the other person in the dyad to express the feeling instead of the individual doing so himself. This is seen in married couples where one person is angry and another person acts it out for him. Transferring or shifting of feelings is defined as a form of Discounting of one's ability to deal with the energy oneself. This type of Discounting in psychotics may presage a violent overreaction. Hence, it is important for everyone involved with the psychotic to be highly reactive to shifts in energy.

When energy in the form of Feelings is being experienced appropriately, and being transformed for the mutual benefit of the individuals in the system, there is a sense of well being and of comfort for the whole system. The experience of *communitas, I-Thou* results from the mutuality of the sharing of, and exchange of the feelings. The state of Being where the energy is shared, creates a blending and fusing of energy, and the resulting fusion of the units of energy makes up a whole which is greater than its parts. This is called *synergy*.

Synergy

In some societies the relationships between the power structure and the people is set up for the advantage of an elite. In others, the relationships are set up for the mutual benefit of all of the other members. Ruth Benedict discusses this aspect of some societies (Honigman and Maslow, 1970). On one end of the continuum Benedict puts the notion of high synergy; on the other end is the notion of low synergy. The concept of synergy is taken from engineering and the biological sciences. The concept, when applied to chemicals or medicines, results in a combination which has a greater potential than the sum of the potentials of each of the chemicals used singly. As applied to human beings, according to Benedict, any act or skill that is to the advantage of the individual and at the same time to the advantage of the group is synergistic. In low synergy societies, following Benedict, any act that is of advantage to the individual is at the expense of the group. She goes on to talk of cultures of low synergy where the social structure facilitates actions that are counter-active to the benefit of the group. She talks of cultures with high synergy where the social structure provides for acts that are mutually reinforcing. Some families are high synergy and some are low synergy, exploitative. Cathexis is a community where the nature of energy and how it is used in the social structure is of explicit concern to all of those participating in its activities.

Implications for Further Study

The view of psychotherapy as *ritual* and as a *ritual process* implies that the study of western urban psychiatric communities can be of increasing interest to ethnology. The ability to see the helping pro-fessions as having their parallels in primitive societies puts a different light on these processes. The fact that many human phenomena are the same ritually, regardless of setting or civil status, is a leveling experience. This may be a leveling for some and an upgrading for others! This fact alone will bring more patients and ethnographers into the arena. Those who are in the helping professions may begin to see their functions as a phenomenon of interaction and cease to invest themselves with a false sense of power. Persons who set out on the healing journey may learn to view the process as a normal biological one, providing them with an opportunity to make up for lost time. They will be able to see themselves not as "*ill*," but as research students of their own developmental process. Ritual is clearly a process that can accomplish concrete ends by linking the internal symbolic with the external symbolic representations. These can be combined in ritual events in such a way that they facilitate each other. They result in powerful transformative experiences for both the individual and the group.

Natural Symbols

The *developmental* approach has implications for psychotherapy in inner cities and third world countries also. The ability to see the individual in terms of what is happening *now* in his transactions adds dignity to the transaction. The dropping of perjorative labels such as "childish," "silly," and seeing the person as Cathecting Child sym-bolizes his behavior differently. The information that the person is behaving as a two-year-old in current circumstances which mirror childhood experiences give the individual and the practitioner a diagnostic tool for the current transaction. Practitioners do not need elaborate settings or equipment; this fact is important for low income peoples. The treatment settings can incorporate the local environmental, developmental symbology and build healing rites around each group's personal experience and needs. Children do not need elaborate programs or equipment. Most children's needs are simple. Most needs can be structured into the ritual process by the people who are present. They can provide the caring transactions which the person finds lacking in his own internal structure. Practitioners can come from the native population; process can come from the culture itself. The Thinking, Feeling, and Doing and Being rituals as described at Cathexis are such because of the general culture of the participants and of its leadership This same type of structure can be applied to various cultures with the "ritual-master" from that specific culture guiding the process. Instead of suppressing native treatment systems, they could be used as the pivotal expressions of the ritual by the offering of healing rites expressive of the native populations' childhood developmental cycles. The personal history of the culture, the cosmology and mythology of the culture which are reiterated in ritual experience can bring the person closer to his own developmental history (see the use of Fairy Tales and Personal Heroes in Berne, 1975). Douglas (1973) notes that natural symbols are important. The quest for natural symbols becomes the quest for a natural system of symbolizing. The organic system provides an analogy of the social system. The body is capable of furnishing a natural system of symbols which can reflect the social dimension.

National Character

Since Transactional Analysis is a general systems theory of personality, it could be used to look at whole cultures in terms of "National Character" as Ruth Benedict and Margaret Mead did. It is a simple, logical way of looking at human personality and interaction. It offers a simple logical developmental process from which rites-of-transition can be constructed. The concept of Reparenting as a means of rehabilitating persons (who have incorporated a "crazy" World View) has value in cross-cultural context. All societies depend upon the interaction between parent and child for their perpetuation. When self-destructive World View is incorporated the interaction can result in the expression of psychopathology. The inner dialog (between Parent and Child, Child and Child, etc.) and the resulting outer transactions can be clarified and connected to the present by rites-of-passage. Ethnographers can use the T.A. model for looking at dynamics in whole societies. It can be used for looking at ritual process. A clear understanding of Ego States in transactions is a powerful tool (see Frames of Reference). Further, for instance, the personal mythology is seen as occurring in the Adapted Child. Mythology can often be the basis of magical thinking. Mythology can also be the basis of ritual experience leading to the person's being willing to give up his hold on the fairy tale. Some societies express Parent, some express Adapted Child.

Descriptive data on the ritual experiences and natural symbols in various cultures will provide information about the synthesis of structure and function in symbolic action. The relationship between cultural systems and social systems is complex and further analysis of the mutual feedback between the two systems is necessary. Rituals are often the vehicle by which the meeting takes place:

> Culture is the fabric of meaning in terms of which human beings interpret their experience and guide their actions; social structure is the form that action takes, the actually existing network of social relations. (Geertz, 1957: 33-34)

A New Profession in Western Urban Settings
"Ritual Guides or Masters"

It is now apparent to anthropologists that western society is contributing to anomie and alienation. There is a paucity of opportunity in geselleschaft society for the experience of communitas. It is being suggested that there might be an additional profession in applied anthropology called "therapeutic anthropology" (Shiloh, AAA1975). Currently there are several anthropologists who are trained clinicians. There are also a number of clinicians who have training in anthropology. It is conceivable that this type of education could prepare professionals for another aspect of applied anthropology—that of "ritual master." These persons could be in private practice or could be associated with Health Maintenance Organizations. Currently some work is being done at Esalen in studying the symbology of the experience with psychedelic drugs. The findings indicate that the process that individuals go through is very similar to the various developmental crises of life, birth, nurture, death (Halifax-Grof and Grof, 1975).

Conclusions

Many of the ritual experiences described in this essay indicate that when an individual confronts his unconscious in a psychic opening experience, he comes into contact with the natural phenomena in his own acculturation. The release of energy experienced when this information becomes conscious results in a transformative process which ends in change in World View. The sense of power and mutual excitement shared with others creates a synergistic effect and an ineffable experience known as *communitas*. Anthropologists such as Margaret Mead and Mircea Eliade have indicated that the absence of rites-of-transformation in Western societies may be contributing to psychopathology and to anti-social behaviors. Without structured, sanctioned cathartic experiences through which to channelize psychic energy, people end up acting-out in destructive ways. Forces in the unconscious when channelized into psychotherapy rituals can and do create a transformational experience for the individual and the group. When shared, they result in synergy instead of entropy.

> Primary process arises from deep human needs. These are for most direct and egalitarian ways of knowing and experiencing relationships. These are needs which have been frustrated or perverted by those secondary processes which constitute the homeostatic functioning of institutionalized social structure. For this reason a primary process has an urgency and momentum which frequently sweeps away persons and groups who attempt to curb its excesses by the application of ethical and legal sanctions based on established principals and values. Men caught up in primary process are mad . . . and they proceed compulsively to eliminate whatever they feel to represent obstacles to this desire. The longer this desire for communitas has been pent up, the more fanatical will be the form taken by the primary process when it is at last unpent. (Turner, 1974: 110)

Cathexis offers a subculture with a carefully planned program patterned on the developmental process of the greater society. The patterns at Cathexis are for the purpose of creating a framework with which the individual may learn patterns of and for dealing with the greater society. The learning process is effected by a series of repetitive experiences seen as rites-of-transition. These allow for the individual to experience altered states of consciousness. Through these experiences he gains a new world view incorporating cooperation and caring. He reexamines and revises the world view that reinforces competitiveness and self-destructiveness. He develops an adaptation that is more viable and more egalitarian.

* * * * *

"The development of general ability for independent thinking and judgment should always be placed foremost, not the acquisition of special knowledge. If a person masters the fundamentals of his subject and has learned to think and work independently, he will surely find his way and besides will better be able to adapt himself to progress and changes than the person whose training principally consists in the acquiring of detailed knowledge."

—*Albert Einstein*

* * * * *

EPILOGUE

There have been a number of changes at Cathexis since I was there getting the information to write this research. The staff there have found that the program has to be changed every year so that the participants do not learn and adapt to it so well that they do not change and do not get cured. Each year the approach to learning how to think and take care of self is somewhat different from the previous year. The basic belief system remains the same— the use of Passivity Confrontation, Caring and Reparenting are still intrinsic to the success of the program. The ways in which these are taught and used are changed from time to time (and the staff change also).

The T.A. Concepts around Time Structure is very much at the core of the activities at Cathexis School. Students have considerable responsibility for arranging their daily schedule. The major emphasis of the program is on learning self care. Perhaps another metaphor may be added to the others which are central to the symbolic system at Cathexis, and that is the metaphor of "caring."

The school is now in spacious and more comfortable surroundings than previously. The building now being used is in a nice residential part of Oakland, near a large park and a lake. There is now office space for the business staff and for the treatment staff. There are dormitories for the people who come to attend the institutes and for those who come to visit the program.

The Cathexis belief system which is based on the Passivity Confrontation material has been further clarified. *Passivity* is equivalent to *not caring* about the outcome of a transaction or interaction. *Confrontation* is equivalent to *caring*. This important and central concept means that if I do not confront your passivity, I do not care about the outcome of your behavior. Since I do care about the outcome of your behavior, I am responsible for confronting you. In using this material in my professional work, I have found it direct and dynamic.

Game Group: This is one of the new parts of the program which was not there when I was studying it. This experience is based on the Synanon attack therapy model. Selected individuals at Cathexis are assigned the Game Group as part of their treatment program. In particular those with a Character Disorder are expected to attend this event. Game Group meets once a week. In this experience there are two forms of attack, known as "indictment." There is the Soft Indictment and the Hard Indictment. In the Soft Indictment, the person who is being indicted is told by each person in the group, one at a time, what it is about his/her behavior which is inappropriate or defended. In the Hard Indictment, everyone in the group who has a concern with this individual's behavior tells him/her at the same time, in verbal attack fashion, which of his/her behaviors is careless or inappropriate. The game group is a quick and devastating way to get persons to give up some of their favorite defense mechanisms, to look actively at their changes in behavior and their participation in the group. An additional value of the Game Group is that it is a place where persons may say what is on their mind and not have to conceal it in socially acceptable form.

A further development at Cathexis worth noting is the research being done on the Biochemical evidence of cure in schizophrenia. Evidence is being found to show that clinical recovery after Transactional Analysis and Reparenting treatment correlates with biochemical measurement. An article by Schiff, et al. in the *Transactional Analysis Journal* (7: 2 April 1977) indicates that biochemical change of tryptophan uptake in the direction of normality apparently correlates with recovery of schizophrenics during treatment. Analysis of tryptophan uptake data in relation to duration of illness is currently in progress to separate the time variable from the treatment variable. The hypotheses being tested are: (1) a longitudinal study of schizophrenic patients specifically diagnosed as paranoid or catatonic who are treated by T.A. and Reparenting techniques will result in significant improvement in psychological functioning, social functioning and tryptophan uptake scores; (2) the improvement in each area will correlate with the other two; (3) the improvement will correlate with duration and intensity of treatment. Preliminary results are showing statistical significance to prove these hypotheses.

Of the persons who were diagnosed as schizophrenic and were a part of the research for this book, a followup indicates that all of them are alive. Seven of them are fully recovered and do not carry a diagnosis of schizophrenia as of this date. Three of the original group are currently back in the Cathexis program. They are showing marked improvement from the time that the study was done. Two others are functional at this time, caring for themselves adequately and managing their lives, although not "cured." Although showing marked improvement, the three who are back in the Cathexis program do consider themselves as "cured." The personal statements made by all of these individuals indicate that the quality of life has improved for all of them. Each of these persons is functioning, self-supporting and moving ahead with the life goals which are consonant with their intelligence and interests.

The Cathexis model of T.A. is now being taught in many countries outside of the United States. Plans are currently in process for a Cathexis Institute in India, at Bangalore where a building has been secured and where Jacqui Schiff plans to take up residence in 1979. The Cathexis Institute in Oakland will continue to function under the direction of its Board of Directors and staff. A handbook called *The Cathexis Primer* (Childs-Gowell, 1979) gives a detailed description of the structure, rules and expectations for students and visitors to the program.

GLOSSARY

ADULT: An ego state oriented to current reality and not affected by Parent prejudice or archaic attitudes left over from childhood experience. It is an aspect of the personality which engages in objective data processing and computing probabilities (Berne, 1963: 163; Ellis, 1974: 3). It is symbolized by the symbol A_2.

AGITATION: Repetitive, nongoal-directed activity, characterized by the agitated individual experiencing a very uncomfortable tingling sensation. The agitation is meant to avoid or reduce the sensation (Schiff, et al., 1975: 12; Ellis, 1974: 4).

CARING TRANSACTION: A part of the confrontation paradigm. The confrontation is done from a caring position. Caring may be for the self or for the person being confronted (Schiff, 1975: 101).

CATHECT, CATHEXIS: The act of putting all of one's energy in one ego state. The concentration of psychic energy in a given direction or on a given object (Ellis, 1974: 15).

CATHECT LITTLE: A psychobiological phenomenon wherein the individual chooses an age below seven years and proceeds to put energy into experiencing the now from the point of view of that age. A person may choose to cathect three months or three years. He may be held and have a bottle or may play with toys and experience transacting from that age. Often old memories and fantasies come into consciousness (Schiff, 1975: 14).

CHILD: The part of the individual's personality which expresses and experiences the Self as he was before age seven. It is an archaic ego state. There are three parts to the Child: P_1 = Adapted Child which follows Parental directives; A_1 = Adult in the Child or Little Professor which is the intuitive part; C_1 = Free or Natural Child which is the self-indulgent, expressive and creative portion of the personality (Berne, 1972: 442).

COLD PRICKLIES: Negative strokes or strokes which feel bad or uncomfortable (Steiner, 1972: 6-10).

COMPETITIVENESS: A dynamic which occurs as a result of pathological symbiosis. It is often the first move in a Game and is part of the Con in Game structure. The issue in competitiveness is "How am I going to get what I need if you won't give it to me?" or "What am I going to get out of it if I do?" (Schiff, 1975: 73).

CON: The invitation to a Game. The come on; one of the five elements in a game structure (Ellis, 1974: 19). The con involves a provocation, a seductive issue, aggression, assurance or control as the first move in the Game plan as an invitation to get "hooked" into the process.

231

CONSTANCY HYPOTHESIS: The theory that when one Ego State increases in intensity, another must decrease because of a shift in psychic energy, the total of which remains a constant factor. The psychophysiological equation is $(P + A + C)mm = K$ where P, A, and C represent all parts of the ego states; mm (mother's milk) is the variable having to do with the biological or social factors; the K constancy is arrived at by the clinical observation that when one variable goes up, another goes down (Ellis, 1974: 19; Dusay, 1972: 39).

CONDITIONAL STROKE: A stroke for Doing (Ellis, 1974: 20).

CONTAMINATION: The intrusion of the Parent and/or the Child across the boundary of the Adult Ego State (Ellis, 1974: 20).

CONTRACT: An explicit agreement between a patient and a therapist which states the goal of the treatment during each phase of the treatment (Steiner, 1975: 244; Ellis, 1974: 20).

CONTROL: An issue in Symbiosis and involves the competition between Ego States for control of or for definition of a situation. It is sometimes an element in the Con in the first move of a Game. Controlling behavior is experienced as manipulative and often is initiated by the Parent Ego State.

CONTROLLING PARENT: The part of the Parent Ego State which controls the individual or the transaction.

COUNTERSCRIPT: A possible life plan formed from the parental programming based on parent precepts and decisions by the child's Parent (Berne, 1972: 442; Ellis, 1974: 20).

CRITICAL PARENT: The part of the Parent Ego State that criticizes, finds fault, blames and occasionally is into character assassination.

CROSSED TRANSACTION: A transaction in which the stimulus and the response vectors are crossed. Example: the stimulus is A_2 to A_2 and the response is C_1 to P_2 (Berne, 1975: 14; Ellis, 1974: 23).

CURSE: The Script Injunction; the prohibition or inhibition of the free behavior of the Child. The curse is often seen as coming from the P_1 of the parent to the P_1 of the child (Steiner, 1975: 60; Ellis, 1974: 24).

CURE: The completion of a Contract.

DAMOCLES: In Greek mythology, Damocles was allowed to enjoy the happiness of being king until he noticed a sword hanging over his head suspended by a single hair. "After" Scripts come from this myth. The motto for "after" Scripts is "you can enjoy yourself for awhile, but after that your troubles begin" (Berne, 1975: 206; Ellis, 1974: 25).

DECISION: A childhood commitment to a certain form of behavior which later forms the basis of character. Decisions are often made under stress or duress and for the Child may constitute a means of survival (Goulding, 1972: 62; Ellis, 1974; 25).

DECONTAMINATION: Clarifying the boundaries between ego states; removing the Parent and Child contamination of the Adult.

DEMON: The jester in human existence; the joker in psychotherapy; urges and impulses in the Child which seem to go against the script which actually reinforce it; sometimes the Rebellious Child in favor of the script; the voice of the Parent urging the Child to impulsive and destructive behavior (Berne, 1975: 122; Ellis, 1974: 27).

DISCOUNTING: An internal mechanism which involves people minimizing, ignoring or aggrandizing some aspect of themselves, others or the reality situation; there is a consensually definable reality, and discounting involves a frame-of-reference which distorts or is inconsistent with that reality (Schiff, 1975: 14).

DOING NOTHING: The passive behavior in which the individual does not respond to stimuli, problems or options. Instead, the person's energy is channeled to the inhibition of responses instead of action (Schiff, 1975: 10).

DRAMA TRIANGLE: Karpman Drama Triangle is a simple diagram showing the possible switches in roles in a Game or Script; the three major roles are Persecutor, Victim and Rescuer (Karpman, "Fairy Tales and Script Dream Analysis," *Transactional Analysis Bulletin*, vol. 7 [26] : 39).

EARTHIAN: A person whose judgments are based on preconceptions rather than on what is actually happening. Usually the precondition is learned in early childhood from other people (Berne, 1975: 100).

EGOGRAM: A profile of an individual based on the assumption that each individual had 100 percent psychic energy which is divided between the Critical Parent, Nurturing Parent, Adult, Free Child and Adapted Child (Dusay, 1972: 37).

EGO STATE: A consistent pattern of feelings and experiences directly related to a corresponding consistent pattern of behavior (Berne, 1975: 443).

ESCALATE: Involves the discounting of thoughts, feelings and problem-solving behaviors and options to the point that the individual or individuals involved in the discounting must either explode the energy built up or implode the energy. Early intervention in escalation is important before there is a total loss of functioning (Schiff, 1975: 21).

EXCLUSION: Rigidly maintaining oneself in one Ego State to the exclusion of options for using others (Berne, 1961: 44).

FEELINGS: As opposed to emotional Rackets; feelings are biologically based on bodily experiences which can be differentiated for one another. They are seen as simply MAD, SAD, SCARED, GLAD, SEXY, HUNGRY, PAIN. Feelings can be thought about and talked about. They are manageable by the individual and do not have to take over the person and the situation.

FREE CHILD: The Natural Child; spontaneous, fun, loving, part of the Child Ego State (Berne, 1975: 104; Ellis, 1974: 38).

FRAME OF REFERENCE: The structure of associated (conditioned) responses (neural pathways) which integrates the various Ego States in response to specific stimuli (Schiff, 1975: 49).

GAME: A series of ongoing transactions which have a concealed motivation leading progressively to a well-defined payoff (Berne, 1964: 48).

GAME ANALYSIS: The analysis of ulterior transactions which lead to a payoff (Berne, 1975: 57).

GAME FORMULA: The sequence of events occurring in a game, expressed as a formula by means of letter symbols: $C + G = R \rightarrow S \rightarrow T \rightarrow P$. The CON hooks into a GIMMICK, which elicits a RESPONSE which leads to a SWITCH, to a CROSSED TRANSACTION to the PAYOFF (Berne, 1975: 23).

GAME THEORY: The theory that all games develop out of unresolved symbiotic relationships with discounting as the mechanism and grandiosity as the justification. There are four possible ways to discount: (1) the problem, (2) the significance of the problem, (3) the solvability of the problem, (4) the person (Schiff, 1975: 73-74).

GIMMICK: A special attitude or weakness which makes a person vulnerable to games or scripty behavior (Berne, 1975: 23).

GRANDIOSITY: An internal mechanism involving an exaggeration (Maximization or minimization) of the significance of some aspect of the self, others or the situation. Grandiosity is used by people to justify the maintenance of the symbiosis (Schiff, 1975: 18).

GROUP: A social aggregation that has an external boundary and at least one internal boundary (Berne, 1963: 54).

GROUP WORK: All group work done by the members of a group in the course of the group activity and the group process. The external group work consists of the group activity and the external group process. The internal group work consists of the major and minor internal group processes (Berne, 1963: 13).

GROWNUP: A person who has achieved chronological and biological maturity.

HERCULES: In Greek mythology, Hercules first had to be a slave for twelve years before he could become a god. Before and Until scripts come from Hercules or Jason myths (Berne, 1975: 206).

HUNGRY: A physiological feeling in response to low blood sugar.

HUNGER, STIMULUS: Hunger for sensory stimulation or sight and sound and touch, with smell and taste as a bonus for gourmets (Berne, 1974: 184).

ILLUSION: Ideas from the Child accepted as rational by the Parent, which the person tries to justify as coming from the Adult; an unlikely hope to which the Child clings and which influences all of his decisive behavior; Child contamination of the Adult (Berne, 1975: 147; Ellis, 1974: 49).

IMPASSE: A conflict between Ego States resulting in the individual becoming unable to move in problem-solving.

INCAPACITATION: Incapacitation or violence is the discharge of energy built up while people are being passive. The passive behavior which attempts to enforce symbiosis at the time of its breakdown (Schiff, 1975: 13; Ellis, 1974: 50).

INJUNCTION: A prohibition or negative command from a parent. Usually comes from the P_1 in the Child of the Parent.

INTIMACY: A candid Child to Child relationship with no ulterior motives, reservations exploitations or manipulations (Berne, 1974: 115).

JASON: In Greek mythology, Jason could not become king until he performed certain tasks. Before and Until scripts are based on this myth (Berne, 1975: 206).

JOKER: The Demon.

LIFE COURSE: What actually happens in a person's life (Steiner, 1956: 57).

LIFE PLAN: What is supposed to happen according to the Script (Berne, 1975: 31).

LIFE POSITION: Basic existential position arrived at by the age of seven; the four life positions are: I'm OK—You're OK; I'm OK—You're not OK; I'm not OK—You're OK; I'm not OK—You're not OK.

LITTLE PROFESSOR: The Adult in the Child or A_1. Seen as the intuitive and clever part of the personality.

MARTIAN: One who observes Earthly happenings without preconceptions (Berne, 1975: 100).

MARTIAN VIEWPOINT: The naivest possible frame of mind for observing Earthly happenings. When parents interfere with or try to influence their children's free expression, their directives are interpreted differently by the parent, the onlookers and the child himself. In fact, there are five different viewpoints: (1) what the parent says he meant (2) what a naive onlooker thinks he meant (3) the literal meaning of what was said (4) what the parent "really" meant and (5) what the child gets out of it. The first two are "square" or "Earthian," and the last three are "real" or Martian (Berne, 1975: 100).

MATRIX, SCRIPT: A diagram showing the parental directives which form the basis of Script; a diagram designed to illustrate and analyze the directives handed down from parents and grandparents to current generation (Berne, 1975: 279; Ellis, 1974: 60).

NEGATIVE STROKE: A unit of recognition which results in a sharp, prickly feeling; a cold prickly; a unit of recognition which puts the receiver down.

NATURAL CHILD: An archaic ego state which is free from or is attempting to free itself from Parental influence. Often designated as the C_1.

NEVER: The script of people who are forbidden by their parents to do the things they most want to do; they spend their lives being tantalized and surrounded by temptation. Never scripts are representative of Tantalus in Greek mythology. He suffered from hunger and thirst at the sight of food and water, but was never allowed to eat or drink (Berne, 1975: 206).

NURTURING PARENT: The part of the Parent which gives strokes for Being. It is also the part which gives permission and protects the Child.

OPEN END: A type of Script of people who have carried out the parental instructions and do not know what to do next. It follows the myth of Philemon and Baucis, who were turned into laurel trees as a reward for their good deeds. Old people who have carried out their instructions spend the rest of their lives like vegetables, or gossiping like leaves rustling in the wind. Middle-aged ladies whose children have grown up also (Berne, 1975: 206).

OVERADAPTATION: When people overadapt they do not identify their own goals but accept the goals of other people or fantasize what these goals are without thinking about their relevance or significance to themselves. Over-adaptation is one of the four passive behaviors (Schiff, 1975: 11).

OVER AND OVER: A classical "almost made it" script with one "if only" after another. Over and Over scripts are based on the Sisyphus myth. He was condemned to roll a heavy stone up a hill. Each time he reached the top the stone rolled back and he had to start over again (Berne, 1975: 266).

P: Symbol for the Parent ego state.

P_1: Symbol for the Parent in the Child; also known as the Adapted Child, the Pig Parent or Ogre when expressed in the parental behaviors.

P_2: Symbol for the Parent ego state which develops in children at around age three and reaches maturity in Grownups.

PARENT: An ego state borrowed from a parental figure; it may function as a directing influence or be directly exhibited as parental behavior. It may be nurturing, controlling or critical (Steiner, 1971: 6; Ellis, 1974: 69).

PASSIVITY: The external manifestations which accompany the internal mechanism and processes of Discounting, Grandiosity and thinking disorders. The passive behaviors have been identified as: (1) doing nothing (2) overadaptation (3) agitation and (4) incapacitation or violence. They are used by people to establish Symbiosis (Schiff, 1975: 10).

PERMISSION: A Parent license for autonomous behavior; an intervention which gives the individual a license to disobey a parental injunction if he is ready, willing and able, or to release him from parental provocations; a transaction in which a therapist attempts to align the patient with his original script-free Natural Child ego state; the decisive intervention for script analysis (Steiner, 1971: 143; Crossman, 1966: 152).

PERSECUTOR: One of the roles in the Karpman Drama Triangle; one of the positions in the Redefining Hexagon; the One-up position in the OK Corral.

POSITION: A concept of OKness or not-OKness which justifies a decision; a position from which games are played; the favored childhood originated solution for encounters with intimates in one's life (Berne, 1975: 15; Ellis, 1974: 73).

PROGRAM: (At Cathexis) The plan set up with the School by each patient for working on contracts and on changing lifestyle (Schiff, 1975). The lifestyle which results from all the elements of the script apparatus taken together; the manner in which the parent of the same sex demonstrates how the injunctions should be obeyed (Berne, 1975: 418).

PROTECTION: Shielding the Child from the Critical or Controlling Parent while he gives up behavior he wants to give up; a strategy offered by the therapist who understands the need of the Child for protection (Steiner, 1971: 147).

PROVOCATIVE: Any behavior which enters into the Con of the Game process. Provocation involves an invitation of some kind to the other person to enter the Game and take a role in the Drama Triangle.

PSYCHOPATHOLOGY: A system of maladaptive behaviors. It is a system of self-presentation, cognition and behavior which keeps the organism from adapting or adapting in some way which is not consonant with the environment (Laughlin and d'Aquili, 1964).

PSYCHOPATHOLOGY (Cathexis): Schizophrenia is characterized by a locked system of messages in the Parent, corresponding adaptations in the Child and and Adult that is misinformed. Given an internally consistent frame of reference as dictated by the Parent and a Child adapted to it, the Adult does not require or use information which is inconsistent with the Parent . . . . With a Child who perceives the pathology as necessary for survival, a Parent who confirms this and an Adult unable to contradict it, the person has no exit from the system without external intervention (Schiff, 1975: 74).

RACKET: A substitute emotion; a chronic, repetitive, emotional experience; a bad feeling collected by an individual to reinforce and justify his early decision to advance his script; an exploitive and manipulative set of reactions used to further the Symbiosis.

REACTIVE ENVIRONMENT–TREATMENT ENVIRONMENT: A structured environment where the Child may get his needs met for normal Parenting and appropriate information for his Adult. A place where discounting is quickly confronted in a caring manner; all pathology is constantly confronted; a caring environment where a person may work out a problem with adequate feedback on his behavior (Schiff, 1975: 101).

REDECISION: A new decision to free oneself from old script injunctions and Child decisions (Goulding, 1972: 105).

REDEFINING: The mechanism people use to maintain an established view of themselves, other people and the world (frame of reference) in order to advance their scripts. It is the internal mechanism people use to defend themselves against stimuli which are inconsistent with their frames of reference and redefine the stimuli to fit in. Its three components are discounting, grandiosity and thinking disorders (Schiff, 1975: 54-55).

REGRESSION: Psychotic regression is a process in which the Child is cathected at a very young age (usually prior to one year), identifiable physiological changes occur, and regression is locked in the sense that the person cannot cathect a Natural, i.e., spontaneously reactive, Child ego state older than the regressed age (Schiff, 1975: 91).

REGRESSION: Nonpsychotic regressions are of three types: (1) pseudo-regression (2) regression as a temporary cathexis to Child at a given age (3) adaptive regression as a response to an environmental stimulus such as a severe physical trauma (Schiff, 1975: 91).

REPARENTING: A method used in the treatment of psychosis. It involves the total decathexis of the originally incorporated Parent ego state and the replacement of that structure with a new Parent structure (Schiff, 1975: 88).

RESCUER: A role in the Drama Triangle which is usually one up; it is the opening move in a number of Games; it is a maneuver which is manipulative and aggressive and involves doing something for someone who has not requested the assistance; rescuing usually evokes hostility.

RITUAL: A process; a standardized system of stereotyped behaviors and communications which manipulate human emotion toward a preset end result (Rappaport, 1971: 23). The process involves three stages, separation, limen and aggregation, through which persons move in the ritual process.

RUBBER BAND: A snap-back to an old, familiar, childhood feeling or experience which is being expressed or experienced in the here and now (Kupfer and Haimowitz, 1971: 10).

SCHIZOPHRENIA: See Psychopathology (Schiff).

SCRIPT: Preconscious life plan which structures time for the individual based on decisions made in childhood, reinforced by parents, justified by ensuing events, culminating in the payoff; the decisions made by the child for survival; the choices between autonomous needs and expectations of parents and injunctions laid down in the family of origin.

SCRIPT ANALYSIS: The analysis of the life script, drama, myths which the person compulsively plays out to get his payoff.

SCRIPT SIGNAL: For each person there is a characteristic posture, gesture, mannerism or symptom which signifies that he is living his script. The symptom and mannerisms disappear when the person achieves "cure."

SEDUCTIVENESS: Any behavior which enters the person into the Con of the Game process. Seduction involves an invitation of some kind to the other person to enter the Game and take a role in the Drama Triangle. The first move in the game of Rapo is usually seductive.

SUFFER: A Racket feeling used to cover real feelings of anger or fear. Script payoff for being a Victim in the Drama Triangle.

STROKE: A unit of recognition such as "Hello" (Berne, 1964: 15).

STRUCTURAL ANALYSIS: Analysis of the personality according to the Parent, Adult Child ego states. Seen in first and second levels as in P_1 and P_2 (Berne, 1975: 13).

SWEATSHIRT: A two- or three-word description characterizing a person's existential position; the bait message sent from the Child ego state to attract another player or keep one away (Steiner, 1975: 92).

SWITCH: A switch from one role to another in a game or script; a maneuver which forces or induces another person to switch roles; an internal or external stimulus which turns off adaptive behavior (Berne, 1975: 23).

SYMBIOSIS: A merging or sharing of mutual needs by the mother and child, which insures infant survival during the early stages of development; a normal condition in normal development of a child. Pathology is likely to result from disturbances in the symbiotic relationship in the differentiation of the child from the mother (Schiff, 1971: 71).

TIME STRUCTURE: The process of getting, giving or avoiding strokes; the six ways of structuring time are: withdrawal, rituals, pastimes, activities, games and intimacy (Berne, 1975: 22).

TRANSACTION: A unit of social action in which each person gains something. There are several kinds of transactions: angular, this is an ulterior transaction where the stimulus has a psychological message and the response is to the psychological message rather than to the social message; complementary, a simple transaction in which the vectors are parallel; crossed, a transaction in which the stimulus and response vectors are crossed; duplex, a transaction in which both the stimulus and response give ulterior messages; simple, a transaction which involves only one active ego state in each of the parties involved (Berne, 1975: 14-19).

TRANSACTIONAL ANALYSIS: A theory of personality and social action; a clinical method of psychotherapy based on the analysis of all possible transactions within an individual and between two or more people, in the basis of specifically defined ego states (Berne, 1963: 20).

UNCONDITIONAL STROKE: A stroke for Being; for merely existing.

VICTIM: One of the roles in the Karpman Drama Triangle; the payoff of one down games.

VIOLENCE: The passive behavior which attempts to enforce symbiosis at the time of breakdown; occurs in discharge of energy built up from passivity; involves a switch in game position (Schiff, 1975: 13).

WORK: The process of a group that is really doing therapy (Berne, 1963: 244).

WORLD VIEW: The Child's view of the world and the people around him upon which the script and script decisions are based. See Frame of Reference (Berne, 1975: 449).

ZAP: What the Parent in the Child of the parent, P_1 does to the Adapted Child in the other person.

BIBLIOGRAPHY

AGAR, Michael
1974 *Ripping and Running*. New York: Seminar Press.
ALBERT, E.
1956 "The Classification of Values and a Method of Illustration." *American Anthropologist* NS 58 (56) (April): 221-248.
ALLAND, Alexander
1967 *Evolution and Human Behavior*. New York: Natural History Press.
1975 Adaptation in *Annual Review of Anthropology*, Palo Alto, 59-73.
ALLPORT, G. W., VERNON, P. E. and LINDZEY, G.
1959 *A Study of Values*. Boston: Houghton-Mifflin.
AINSWORTH, M.
1967 *Infancy in Uganda: Infant Care and the Growth of Attachment*. Baltimore: Johns Hopkins Press.
ANDERSON, J. W.
1972c "On the Psychological Attachment of Infants to Their Mothers." *Journal of Biosocial Science* 4: 197-225.
ARIETI, S.
1959 *Handbook of Psychiatry II*. New York: Basic Books.
ASCHE, Solomon
1955 "Opinions and Social Pressure." *Scientific American*. In Coopersmith, *Frontiers of Psychological Research*. San Francisco: W. H. Freeman.
ASHBY, W. R.
1952 *Design for a Brain*. New York: John Wiley.
AUSUBEL, D. P.
1963 *The Psychology of Meaningful Verbal Learning*. New York: Grune and Stratton.

BACH, George
1972 *Creative Aggression*. New York: Avon Books.
1966 "The Marathon Group: Intensive Practice of Intimate Interaction." *Psychological Reports* 18: 995-1002.
BACK, Kurt
1972 *Beyond Words: The Story of Sensitivity Training and Encounter Movement*. New York: Russell Sage Foundation.
BANDURA, A.
1961 "Psychotherapy as a Learning Process." *Psychological Bulletin* 58 (2): 143-159.

239

BANNISTER, D. and MAIR, J.
1968　*The Evaluation of Personal Constructs*.　London and New York: Academic Press.

BARTH, F.
1967　"On the Study of Social Change."　*American Anthropologist* 67 (65) 661-669.
1969　*Ethnic Groups and Boundaries*.　Boston: Little, Brown.

BARRON, Frank
1953　"An Ego-Strength Scale Which Predicts Response to Psychotherapy." *Journal of Consulting Psychology* 17: 327-333.

BATESON, G., JACKSON, D. D., HALEY, J. and WEAKLAND, J.
1956　"Toward a Theory of Schizophrenia."　*Behavioral Science* 1: 251-264.

BATESON, G.
1955　"A Theory of Play and Fantasy."　*Psychiatric Research Reports* 2: 39-51.
1958　*Naven*.　Stanford, Cal.: Stanford University Press.
1972　*Steps to an Ecology of Mind*.　New York: Baltimore Books.

BECKER, Ernest
1964　*Revolution in Psychiatry*.　New York: Free Press.
1973　*The Denial of Death*.　New York: Free Press.

BENDER, I. E. and HASTORF, A. M.
1953　"On Measuring Generalized Empathic Ability (Social Sensitivity)." *The Journal of Abnormal and Social Psychology* 48: 4.

BENEDICT, Ruth
1970　"Patterns of the Good Culture—Synergy."　*Psychology Today* 72 (2): 51-75.

BENNIS, BENNE and CHIN (eds.)
1962　*The Planning of Change*.　New York: Holt, Rinehart and Company.

BERNE, Eric
1961　*Transactional Analysis in Psychotherapy*.　New York: Grove Press.
1963　*The Structure and Dynamics of Organizations and Groups*.　New York: Lippincott.
1964　*Games People Play*.　New York: Grove Press.
1966　*Group Treatment*.　New York: Grove Press.
1970　*Sex in Human Loving*.　New York: Simon and Schuster, Inc.
1972　*What do you say after you say Hello?*　New York: Grove Press.

BIERI, J.
1953　"Changes in Interpersonal Perceptions Following Social Interaction." *Journal of Abnormal and Social Psychology* 48: 61-66.
1955　"Cognitive Complexity-Simplicity and Predictive Behavior."　*Journal of Abnormal and Social Psychology* 51: 263-268.
1966　*Clinical and Social Judgment*.　New York: John Wiley.

BHARATI, Agehananda
1971　"Anthropological Approaches to the Study of Religion: Ritual and Belief Systems."　In *Biennial Review of Anthropology*.　Bernard Siegel, ed. Stanford, Cal.: Stanford University Press, 230-282.

BOHANNON, Laura
1964　*Return to Laughter* New York: Doubleday.

BOSS, Medard
1949 *Meaning and Context of Sexual Perversion.* New York: Grune and Stratton.

BOULDING, Kenneth
1956 "The Skeleton of Science." *Management Science* (April): 197-208.

BOWLBY, John
1969 *Attachment*, vol. I, and *Separation*, vol. II. New York: Basic Books, Inc.

BROWN, B.,
1974 *New Mind New Body.* New York: Harper and Row.

BROWN, Roger W.
1969 "Is a Boulder Sweet or Sour." In Snider, James (ed.), *Semantic Differential Techniques, a Sourcebook.* Chicago: Aldine.

BRUNER, J. S.
1962 *On Knowing.* Cambridge, Mass.: Harvard University Press.

BRUNER, Jerome S., ROSE, R. Oliver and GREENFIELD, Patricia M.
1966 *Studies in Cognitive Growth.* New York: John Wiley.

BUBER, Martin
1947 *Tales of the Hasidim*, vol. II, p. 161. New York: A Schocken Book, Farrar, Straus and Young, Marston Press.

BUCHLER, I. E. and HAHN, H. G. (eds.)
1970 *Games Theory in the Behavioral Sciences.* Pittsburgh: University of Pittsburgh Press.

BUCKLEY, Walter
1968 *Modern Systems Research for the Behavioral Scientist.* Chicago: Aldine.

BUTCHER, James N. (ed.)
1969 *MMPI Research Developments and Clinical Applications.* New York: McGraw-Hill.

BURLING, R.
1964 "Burling's Rejoinder." *American Anthropologist* 66 (64): 120-122.
1965 "Cognition and Componential Analysis: God's Truth or Hocus Pocus." *American Anthropologist* 66 (65): 20-28.
1970 *Man's Many Voices: Language in its Cultural Context.* New York: Holt, Rinehart and Winston.
1971 "Linguistics and Ethnographic Description." *American Anthropologist* 71 (69): 8-827.

BURTON, A.
1969 *Encounter.* San Francisco: Jossey Bass.

CARROLL, John B.
1969 "Review, The Measurement of Meaning." In Snider, *Semantic Differential Technique. A Sourcebook.* Chicago: Aldine.

CARSON, R. C.
1969 "Issues in Teaching of Clinical MMPI Interpretations." In Butcher, James N. (ed.), *MMPI Research Developments and Clinical Applications.* New York: McGraw-Hill.

CASTENEDA, Carlos

1968 *The Teachings of Don Juan: A Yaqui Way of Knowledge*. New York: Ballantine Books.

1971 *A Separate Reality*. New York: Pocket Books.

1972 *Journey to Ixtlan*. New York: Pocket Books.

1974 *Tales of Power*. New York: Simon and Schuster.

CAVELL, Ruth

1970 "The New Religion." *Saturday Review of Literature* (December 7).

CHAPPLE, Elliott D.

1970 *Culture and Biological Man*. New York: Holt, Rinehart and Winston.

CHILDS-GOWELL, Elaine and KINNAMAN, Phillip

1978 *Bodyscript Blockbusting*. Seattle, Wash.: Murray Publishing Co.

CHILDS-GOWELL, Elaine

1979 *The Cathexis Primer*. Seattle, Wash.: Murray Publishing Co.

CHIN, R.

1969 "The Utility of Systems Model and Development of Models for Practitioners." In Bennis, Benne and Chin (eds.), *The Planning of Change*. New York: Holt, Rinehart and Winston.

CHOMSKY, N.

1957 *Syntactic Structures*. The Hague: Mouton.

CLIFF, Norman

1959 "Adverbs as Multipliers." *Psychological Review* 66: 27-44.

COHEN, Ronald

1964 "Conflict and Change in a Northern Nigerian Emirate." In Zollschan, G. and Hirsch, W. (eds.), *Explorations in Social Change*. Boston: Halstead Press.

COLBY, B.

1966 "Ethnographic Semantics: A Preliminary Survey." *Current Anthropology*. 7: 3-32.

COOPERSMITH, S.

1967 *The Antecedents of Self-Esteem*. San Francisco: W. H. Freeman.

CORSINI, R. and CARDONE, S.

1960 *Role Playing in Psychotherapy*. Chicago: Aldine.

CORSINI, R. (ed.).

1973 *Current Psychotherapies*. Itasca, Ill.: Peacock Press.

COUNT, E. W.

1973 *Being and Becoming Human*. New York: Van Nostrand Reinhold.

D'ANDRADE

1965 "Trait Psychology and Componential Analysis." *American Anthropologist* 67 (Sp #5, October): 215-228.

DAHLSTRAOM AND WELSH

1960 *An MMPI Handbook*. Minneapolis: University of Minnesota Press.

DECHERT, Charles R. (ed.)

1966 *The Social Impact of Cybernetics*. New York: Simon and Shuster Company.

DELCATO, Carl

1974 *The Ultimate Stranger*. New York: Doubleday.

DEUTCH, K.

1968 "Toward a Cybernetic Model of Man and Society." In Buckley, W. (ed.), *Modern Systems Research for the Behavioral Sciences.* Chicago: Aldine.
DEVEREAUX, George
1956 "Normal and Abnormal: The Key Problem of Psychiatric Anthropology." *Some Uses of Anthropology: Theoretical and Applied.* Washington: Anthropology Society of Washington, 23-48.
DeVORE, I. (ed.)
1963 *Primate Behavior: Field Studies of Monkeys and Apes.* New York: Holt, Rinehart and Winston.
DIAGNOSTIC AND STATISTICAL MANUAL II
1968 Washington, D. C.: American Psychiatric Association.
DINGWELL, W. O. and WHITAKER, H.
1974 "Neurolinguistics." *Annual Review of Anthropology* 3:323-356.
DOBKIN, deRIOS, M.
1972 *Visionary Vine: Psychedelic Healing in the Peruvian Amazon.* San Francisco.
1975 "Is Science Catching Up with Magic? A Look at the Content of Belief Systems." *Medical Anthropology Newsletter* 7 (1): 4-7.
DOUGLAS, Mary
1973 *Natural Symbols.* New York: Vintage Books.
DURKHEIM, E.
1965 *The Elementary Forms of the Religious Life.* New York: Free Press.
DUSAY, John
1972 "Egograms and the Constancy Hypothesis." *Transactional Analysis Journal* 2 (3) (July).

EDGERTON, R. B.
1967 *The Cloak of Competence.* Berkeley: University of California Press.
EDWARDS, A. L.
1959 "Social Desirability and Personality Test Construction." In Bass and Berg (eds.), *Objective Approaches to Personality.* Princeton, N. J.: Van Nostrand.
EHRENWALD, Jan
1966 *Psychotherapy: Myth or Method.* New York: Grune and Stratton.
ELIADE, M.
1964 *Shamanism: Archaic Techniques of Ecstacy.* Bollingen Series. LXXVI. New York: Pantheon.
ENDLER, Norman S.
1969 "Changes in Meaning During Psychotherapy as Measured by the Semantic Differential." In Snider, E. E. (ed.), *Semantic Differential Techniques. A Sourcebook.* Chicago: Aldine, 518-523.
ENGLISH, F.
1971 "Rackets vs Real Feelings." *Transactional Analysis Journal* 1 (4): 27-32.
1972 "Rackets vs Real Feelings II." *Transactional Analysis Journal* 2 (1): 23-25.
ERIKSON, E. H.
1950 *Childhood and Society.* New York: W. W. Norton.

ERSKINE, R.
1975 "The ABC's of Effective Psychotherapy." *Transactional Analysis Journal* 5 (2) (April): 163.
EYSENCK, H. J.
1952 "The Effects of Psychotherapy: An Evaluation." *Counseling Psychiatry* 16: 319-324.

FERNANDEZ, James W.
1965 "Symbolic Consensus in Fan Reformative Cult." *American Anthropologist* 67 (65): 902-929.
1971 "Principles of Opposition and Vitality in Fan Aesthetics." In Jopling, Carol, *Art and Aesthetics in Primitive Societies*. New York: E. P. Dutton Company, Inc.
FERNEA, Elizabeth W.
1969 *Guests of the Sheik*. New York: Doubleday Anchor.
FESTINGER, L.
1957 *A Theory of Cognitive Dissonance*. Evanston, Ill.: Row Peterson.
FIRTH, R.
1951 *Elements of Social Organization*. Boston: Beacon Press.
1954 "Social Organization and Social Change." *Journal of Royal Anthropological Institute* 84: 1-20; as quoted in Harris: *The Rise of Anthropological Theory* (1968), New York: T.Y. Crowell.
1973 *Symbols, Public and Private*. New York: Cornell University Press.
FOSTER, George and KEMPNER, Robert
Anthropologists in Cities. Boston: Little, Brown.
FOX, R.
1967 *Kinship and Marriage*. London: Penguin Books.
FRANK, Jerome
1961 *Persuasion and Healing, a Comprehensive Study of Psychotherapy*. Baltimore: Johns Hopkins Press.
FRICK, F. C.
1968 "The Application of Information Theory in Behavioral Studies." In Buckley, Walter, *Modern Systems Research for the Behavioral Scientist*. Chicago: Aldine.
FURST, Peter (ed.)
1972 *Flesh of the Gods: The Ritual Use of Hallucinogens*. New York: Praeger Company.

GANS, Herbert
1962 *The Urban Villagers*. New York: Glenco Free Press.
GEDO, John and GOLDBERG, Arnold
1973 *Models of the Mind*. Chicago: University of Chicago Press.
GEERTZ, Clifford
1968 *Islam Observed*. New Haven: Yale University Press.
1966b "Religion as a Cultural System." In *Anthropological Approaches to the Study of Religion*. Banton, M. (ed.). New York: Praeger.
GENNEP, Arnold Von
1960 *The Rites of Passage*. London: Routledge and Kegan Paul Ltd.

GIBB, J. R.

1970 "The Effects of Human Relations Training." In Bergin, A. E. and Garfield, S. L. (eds.), *Handbook of Psychotherapy and Behavior*. New York: John Wiley and Sons, 320-863.

GINSBERG, H. and OPPER, S.

1969 *Piaget's Theory of Intellectual Development. An Introduction*. New Jersey: Prentice-Hall.

GLUCKMAN, Max

1964 *Closed Systems and Open Minds*. Chicago: Aldine Press.

1955 *The Judicial Process Among the Barotse of Northern Rhodesia*. New York: Glenco Free Press.

GOFFMAN, Erving

1956 *The Presentation of Self in Everyday Life*. Edinburgh: University of Edinburgh.

1963 *Stigma: Notes on the Management of Spoiled Identity*. New York: Prentice-Hall, Inc.

1967 *Interaction Ritual: Essays on Face to Face Behavior*. New York: Anchor Books.

1969 *Strategic Interaction*. Philadelphia: University of Pennsylvania Press.

GOLUMBIEWSKI and BLUMBERG (eds.)

1970 *Sensitivity Training and the Laboratory Approach. Readings About Concepts and Applications*. Itasca, Ill.: Peacock Publishing.

GOODENOUGH, W. H.

1957 "Cultural Anthropology and Linguistics." In Garvin, P., *Report of the Annual Round Table Meeting on Linguistics and Language Study*. Georgetown University Monograph Series on Language and Linguistics, #9: 167-173.

1965 "Personal Names and Modes of Address in two Oceanic Societies." In Spiro (ed.), *Societies in Context and Meaning in Cultural Anthropology*. New York: Free Press.

1967 "Componential Analysis and the Study of Meaning." *Science* 156: 1203-1209.

GOODMAN, Paul

1970 *The Reformation*. New York: Random House.

GOODALL, Jane

1963 "Chimpanzees of the Gombe Stream Reserve." In *Primate Behavior*. DeVore, I. (ed.). New York: Holt, Rinehart and Winston.

GOODY, Jack

1961 "Religion and Ritual: The Definitional Problem." *British Journal of Sociology* 12.

GOULDING, Robert

1972 "Decisions in Script Formation." *Transactional Analysis Journal* 2 (2) (April): 62.

GOWELL, Elaine

1961 "Mental Health Supervision." *American Journal of Nursing* (July): 83-84.

1966 "An Experience With the Use of Group Work Methods and Process With Student Nurse Groups Over a Period of Five Years." *Journal of Psychiatric Nursing* (July-August): 351-362.

1970a "No Dropouts in This Refresher Course." *American Journal of Nursing* (January): 94-97, in collaboration with J. Hoffman.

1970b "Helping Student Nurses to Become Involved." *International Journal of Nursing Studies* 7: 225-234.

1972 "The Health Unit: A Therapeutic Community ... Psychodrama, Play Therapy and T.A." *International Journal of Nursing Studies* 9: 159-165.

1973a "Implications of the Incest Taboo for Nursing Practice." *Journal of Psychiatric Nursing and Mental Health Services* (July-August) 11 (4).

1973b "T.A. in Sensitivity Groups for Students of Nursing." *Nursing Forum* XII (1): 82-95. In collaboration with J. George.

1974 "Transactional Analysis Strategies for Dealing with Pain." *Journal of Psychiatric Nursing and Mental Health Services* (September-October): 28-30.

1975 "T.A. and the Body: Sensory Stimulation Techniques." *Transactional Analysis Journal* 5 (2) (April): 148-151.

1977 "A Study of Schizophrenics in Treatment" Int. Jr. Nursing Studies, IV, Oxford.

GREENBERG, I.

1967 *Psychodrama and Attitude Change.* Beverly Hills, Cal.: Behavioral Studies Press.

GRIFFIN, G. A. and HARLOW, H. F.

1966 "Effects of Three Months of Total Deprivation on Social Adjustment and Learning in the Rhesus Monkey." *Child Development* 37: 333-348.

GULLIKSEN, Harold

1969 "How to Make Meaning More Meaningful." In Snider, *Semantic Differential Techniques: A Sourcebook.* Chicago: Aldine.

GUMPERTZ, J. J.

1964 "Linguistics and Social Interaction in Two Communities." *American Anthropologist* 66 (64, part 2): 137-153.

HAFNER, BUTCHER, HALL and QUAST

1969 "Parent Personality and Childhood Disorders." In Butcher, James N. (ed.), *MMPI Research Developments and Clinical Applications.* New York: McGraw-Hill.

HALEY, Jay

1963 *Strategies of Psychotherapy.* New York: Grune and Stratton.

1965 "The Art of Being Schizophrenic." In *The Power Tactics of Jesus Christ.* New York: Ballantine Books.

HALL, A. D. and FAGEN, R. D.

1968 "Definition of a System." In Buckley, Walter, *Modern Systems Research for the Behavioral Scientist.* Chicago: Aldine.

HALL, E. T.

1959 *The Silent Language.* New York: Fawcett Books.

1969 *The Hidden Dimension.* New York: Anchor Books.

HARNER, Michael (ed.)

1973 *Hallucinogens and Shamanism.* London: Oxford University Press.

1962 "Jivaro Souls." *American Anthropologist* 65 (62): 258-272.

HARLOW, H. F. and HARLOW, M. D.

1965 "The Affectional Systems." In *Behavior of Nonhuman Primates* vol. 2.

Ed. by Am. Schrier, H. F. Harlow and F. Stollnitz. New York and London: Academic Press.

HARRIS, C. W.
1968 *Problems in Measuring Change*. Madison: University of Wisconsin Press.

HARRIS, Marvin
1968 *The Rise of Anthropological Theory*. New York: T. Y. Crowell.

HARRISON, R.
1962 "Evaluations and Conclusions." In Argyris, C., *Interpersonal Competence and Organizational Effectiveness*. Homewood, Ill.: Richard D. Irwin Company.
1966 "Cognitive Change and Participation in a Sensitivity Training Laboratory." *Journal of Consulting Psychology* 30 (2): 517-520.
1970 "Problems in the Design and Interpretation of Research on Human Relations Training." In Golumbiewski and Blumberg (eds.), *Sensitivity Training and the Laboratory Approach. Readings About Concepts and Applications*. Itasca, Ill.: Peacock Publishing.

HAYKIN, Martin
1976 "Character Disorders: Lecture in Psychopathology" at Transactional Analysis Seminars. TAN Institute. 1001 Broadway, Seattle, Washington.

HEISENBERG, W.
1974 *Across the Frontiers*. New York: Harper Torchbook.
1971 *Physics and Beyond*. New York: Harper Torchbook.

HENRY, Jules
1963 *Culture Against Man*. New York: Random House.
1973a *On Sham, Vulnerability and Other Self-Destruction*. New York: Vintage Books.
1973b *Pathways to Madness*. New York: Vintage Books.

HOLLAND, Glen
1974 "Transactional Analysis." In Corsini (ed.), *Current Psychotherapies*. Itasca, Ill.: Peacock Press.

HOLLOMAN, Regina E.
1974 "Ritual Opening and Individual Transformation: Rites of Passage at Esalen." *American Anthropologist* 76 (2) (June): 265-280.

HONIGMAN, John J.
1959 *The World of Man*. New York: Harper Brothers.
1963 *Understanding Culture*. New York: Harper and Row.

HORTON, Robin
1964 "Ritual Man in Africa." *Africa* 34 (2) (April).

HSU, Francis
1961 "Kinship and Ways of Life." In Hsu, F. (ed.), *Psychological Anthro-Approaches to Culture and Personality*. Homewood, Ill.: Dorsey Press.

HUXLEY, Sir Julian
1966 "Philosophical Transactions of the Royal Society of London." *Series B. Biological Science* #772 251 (29) (December): 247-526.

HYMES, D. (ed.)
1974 *Reinventing Anthropology*. New York: Vintage Books.

JANOV, A.
1970 *The Primal Scream*. New York: Putnam.
JOURARD, Sidney
1967 *The Transparent Self*. New York: Van Nostrand.
JUNG, C. G.
1953 *The Development of Personality*. New York: Pantheon Books.
1964 *Man and His Symbols*. New York: Dell Publishing Company.

KAPLAN, Abraham
1964 *The Conduct of Inquiry Methodology for Behavioral Science*. Pennsylvania: Chandler Publishing Company.
KARP, W.
1968 "Sir Isaac Newton." *Horizon* 10 (Autumn).
KARPMAN, Stephen
1968 "Fairy Tales and Script Drama Analysis." *T.A. Bulletin VII* 26 (April): 39-43.
KAST, F., and ROSENZWEIG, J. E.
1970 *Organization and Management*. New York: McGraw-Hill.
KEARNEY, M.
1975 "World View Theory and Studies." *Annual Reviews of Anthropology* 4: 244-270.
KELLY, George
1955 *The Psychology of Personal Constructs*. New York: W. W. Norton, vol. I and II.
1958 "Man's Construction of His Alternatives." In Lindzey, G. (ed.), *The Assessment of Human Motives*. New York: Rinehart.
1964 "The Language of Hypotheses." *Journal of Individual Psychology* 20: 137.
KEMPER, R. V.
1970 "The Anthropological Study of Migration to Latin American Cities." *Kroeber: Anthropological Society Papers* 42: 1-25.
KIEV, Ari
1972 *Transcultural Psychiatry*. New York: The Free Press.
1964 *Magic, Faith, and Healing*. New York: Free Press.
KLINGER, E.
1971 *Structural Function of Fantasy*. New York: John Wiley.
KLUCKHOHN, F.
1950 "Dominant and Substitute Profiles of Cultural Orientation: Their Significance for the Analysis of Social Stratification." *Social Forces* 28: 376-393.
1961 *Variations in Value Orientations*. New York: Harper and Row, written with Strodbeck, J.
KOHLBERG, L.
1969 "Stage and Sequence: The Cognitive Developmental Approach to Socialization." In Gowlin, D. (ed.), *Handbook of Socialization Theory and Research*. Chicago: Rand McNally.
KREMYANSKI, V. I.
1968 "Certain Peculiarities of Organisms as a 'System' from the point of

View of Physics, Cybernetics and Biology." In Buckley, Walter, *Modern Systems Research for the Behavioral Scientists*. Chicago: Aldine.

KUMATA, HIDEYA and SCHRAMM, Wilbur
1969 "A Pilot Study of Cross-Cultural Meaning." In Snider, James G., *Semantic Differential Technique. A Sourcebook*. Chicago: Aldine.

KUHN, T. S.
1962 *The Structure of Scientific Revolutions*. Chicago and London: University of Chicago Press.

LAING, R. D.
1960 *The Divided Self*. London: Tavistock.
1964 *Sanity, Madness and the Family*. London and New York: Tavistock, Basic Books (1970), written with Esterson, A.
1967 *The Politics of Experience*. New York: Pantheon Books.
1971 *The Politics of the Family*. London: Tavistock.

LANGER, Susanne
1942 *Philosophy in a New Key*. Cambridge: Harvard University Press.

LANGNESS, L. I.
1963 *The Life History in Anthropological Science*. New York: Holt Rinehart and Winston.

LANYON, Richard I.
1968 *A Handbook of MMPI Group Profiles*. Minnesota: University of Minnesota Press.

LAUGHLIN and d'AQUILI
1974 *Biogenetic Structuralism*. New York: Columbia University Press.

LAUGHLIN, C. D. and McMANUS, J.
1976 *The Nature of Neurognosis*. Mimeo print, from paper given at AAA in San Francisco, November 1976.

LAWRENCE, P. and MEGGETT, M. (eds.)
1965 *Gods, Ghosts and Men in Melanesia. Some Religions of Australia, New Guinea and New Hebrides*. Melbourne: Oxford.

LEACH, E.
1954 *Political Systems of Highland Burma*. Boston: Beacon Press.

LEDERER, W. J. and JACKSON, D.
1968 *The Mirages of Marriage*. New York: W. W. Norton.

LEIGHTON, A., LAMBO, T., et al.
1963 *Psychiatric Disorder among the Yoruba*. Ithaca. Cornell University Press.

LEIGHTON, A., HARDING, J. S., MACKLIN, D. B., MACMILLAN, A. and LEIGHTON, A. H.
1963 *The Character of Danger*. New York: Basic Books.

LEONARD, George
1973 *The Transformation*. New York: Delacorte.

LEVIN, Pam
1973 "Think Structure for Feeling Better Faster." *Transactional Analysis Journal* III: 38-40.

LeVINE, R.
1973 *Culture, Behavior and Personality*. Chicago: Aldine.

LEVI-STRAUSS, Claude
1963 *Structural Anthropology*. New York: Basic Books.
1964 *Mythologique: Le Crue et le Cuit*. Paris: Plon.
1971 "The Science of The Concrete." In Jopling, Carol, *Art and Aesthetics in Primitive Societies*. New York: E. P. Dutton Company.
LEWIN, Kurt
1973 *A Dynamic Theory of Personality*. New York: McGraw-Hill.
LEWIS, J. W. and CALDWELL, W. E.
1961 "Psycholinguistic Investigation of Verbal Psychological Tests." *Journal of General Psychology* 65: 131-144.
LIEBOW, E.
1967 *Tally's Corner*. Boston: Little, Brown.
LIEBERMAN, Morton A., et al.
1973 *Encounter Groups—First Facts*. New York: Macmillan.
LIFTON, R. J.
1968 *Death in Life*. New York: Random House.
LILLY, John
1967 *Programming and Meta Programming in the Human Biocomputer. Theory and Experiment*. New York: Julian Press, Inc.
1972 *The Center of the Cyclone*. New York: Julian Press, Inc.
LORENTZ, Konrad
1966 "Evolution of Ritualization in the Biological and Cultural Spheres." In *Philosophical Transactions of the Royal Society of London*. Series B. Biological Sciences organized by J. Huxley, 273: 284.
LOWEN, Alexander
1972 *Depression and the Body*. New York: Coward, McCann and Geoghegan, Inc.
1975 *Bioenergetics*. New York: Coward, McCann and Geohegan, Inc.

MACCOBY, E. E. and MASTERS, J. C.
1969 "Attachment and Dependency." In Nussen, P. H. (ed.), *Manual of Child Psychology*. 3rd ed. New York and London: John Wiley.
MARCUSE, Herbert
1955 *Eros and Civilization*. Boston: Beacon Press.
MARUYAMA, M.
1963 "The Second Cybernetic Deviation Mutual Causal Process." In Buckley, Walter, *Modern Systems Research for the Behavioral Scientist*. Chicago: Aldine.
MAHER, Brendan
1968 "The Shattered Language of the Schizophrenic." *Psychology Today* (November): 30-33ff.
MacINTYRE, Alasdair and MARCUSE, Herbert
1970 *An Exposition and a Polemic*. New York: Viking Press.
MASLOW, Abraham
1968 *Toward a Psychology of Being*. New York: Van Nostrand Reinhold.
1964 "Synergy in the Society and the Individual." *Journal of Individual Psychology* 20: 153-164.
1965 *Eupsychian Management. A Journal*. New York: Dorsey.

MAUSS, Marcel
1967 *The Gift.* Translated by Ian Gunnison. New York: W. W. Norton. (1925).
McLAUGHLIN, F.
1972 "Effects of Three Types of Group Leadership Structures with Student Nurses." *Nursing Research* 21 (3): 244-257.
McMANUS, John
1975 "Psychopathology as Errors in Cognitive Adaptation." Paper read at AAA 1975, San Francisco.
MEAD, Margaret
1962 "A Cultural Anthropologist's Approach to Maternal Deprivation." In *Deprivation of Maternal Care Assessment of Effects.* Public Health Papers #14, Geneva: WHO.
1928 *Coming of Age in Samoa.* New York: William Morrow.
1952 "Some Relationships Between Social Anthropology and Psychiatry." In Franz Alexander and Helen Ross (eds.), *Dynamic Psychiatry.* Chicago: University of Chicago Press.
1955 "Effects of Anthropological Field Work Models on Intercultural Communication." *Journal of Social Issues* II (2): 3-11.
MEDICAL ANTHROPOLOGY NEWSLETTER
1975 Editorial 6 (4) (August): 1-1.
MELLOR, Ken
1975a "Discounting." *Transactional Analysis Journal* 5 (3): 295-302.
1975b "Redefining." *Transactional Analysis Journal* 5 (3): 303-311.
MILES, M.
1965 "Changes During and Following Laboratory Training." *Journal of Applied Behavioral Science* I.
MESZAROS, Istvan
Marx's Theory of Alienation. London.
MILLER, G. A., GALANTER, E. and PRIBRAM, K.
1960 *Plans and the Structure of Behavior.* New York: Holt, Rinehart and Winston.
MILLER, G. A.
1968 "What Is Information Measurement." In Buckley, Walter, *Modern Systems Research for the Behavioral Scientist.* Chicago: Aldine, 123-128.
MISCHEL, W.
1968 *Personality and Assessment.* New York: John Wiley.
MONTAGUE, Ashley
1971 *Touching, the Human Significance of Skin.* New York: Harper and Row.
1968 *Man and Aggression.* New York: Oxford University Press.
MOORE, O. K.
1965 "Divination: A New Perspective." *American Anthropologist* 59: 69-74.
MORENO, J. L.
1959 "Psychodrama." In Arieti, *Handbook of Psychiatry II.* New York: Basic Books, 1375-1376.
MURPHY, Jane and LEIGHTON, Alexander

1965 *Approaches to Cross-Cultural Psychiatry.* New York: Cornell University Press.

NADEL, S. F.
1964 *The Foundations of Social Anthropology.* New York: Free Press.
1968 "Social Control and Self Regulation." In Buckley, Walter, *Modern Systems Research for the Behavioral Scientist.* Chicago: Aldine, 401-408.
NARANJO, Claudio
1972 *The One Quest.* New York: Ballantine.
NAROLL, R. and COHEN, R.
1973 *A Handbook of Method in Cultural Anthropology.* New York: Columbia University Press.
NEISSER, U.
1966 *Cognitive Psychology.* New York: Appleton.

O'NEIL and O'NEIL
1972 *Open Marriage.* New York: Avon Books.
OPPENHEIMER, J. R.
1964 *Science and the Common Understanding.* New York: Simon and Schuster.
ORNSTEIN, Robert
1972a *The Nature of Human Consciousness. A Book of Readings.* San Francisco: W. H. Freeman.
1972b *The Psychology of Consciousness.* San Francisco: W. H. Freeman.
OSGOOD, D. E.
1964 "Semantic Differential Technique in the Comparative Study of Cultures." *American Anthropologist.* 6 (3, Part 2): 171-200.
1969 "Semantic Space Revisited." In Snider, *Semantic Differential Techniques. A Sourcebook.* Chicago: Aldine.
OSGOOD, SUCI and TANNENBAUM
1957 *The Measurement of Meaning.* Chicago: University of Illinois Press.
OTTO, Herbert
1970 *The Family in Search of a Future.* New York: Appleton-Century.
1968 *Human Potentialities.* St. Louis: Warren Guenther.

PAPPENHEIM, F.
1959 *The Alienation of Modern Man.* Monthly Review Press.
PARSONS, Talcott
1951 *Toward a General Theory of Action.* New York: Harper.
1955 *Toward a General Theory of Action. Encyclopedia of Social Sciences,* vol. 15: 459.
PERLS, HEFFERLINE and GOODMAN
1951 *Gestalt Therapy.* New York: Dell Books.
PERLS, F.
1969 *Gestalt Therapy Verbatim.* New York: Bantam.
PIAGET, J. and INHELDER, B.
1956 *The Child's Conception of Space.* London: Routledge and Kegan Paul.
1954 *The Construction of Reality in the Child.* New York: Basic Books.

1953 *The Origins of Intelligence in the Child*. London: Routledge and Kegan Paul; New York: International University Press.

1926 *The Language and Thought of the Child*. London: Routledge and Kegan Paul.

1971 *Biology and Knowledge*. Chicago: University of Chicago Press.

PINES, Maya

1973 *The Brain Changers*. New York: Harcourt, Brace.

POWERS, William T.

1973 *Behavior: The Control of Perception*. Chicago: Aldine.

RAPOPORT, A. and HORVATH, W. J.

1959 "Thoughts on Organization Theory and a Review of Two Conferences. General Systems." *Yearbook of the Society of General Systems Research* 4: 87-93.

RAPPAPORT, R.

1968 *Pigs for the Ancestors*. New Haven: Yale University Press.

RAYMOND, Richard

"Communication, Entropy and Life." In Buckley, Walter, *Modern Systems Research for the Behavioral Scientist*. Chicago: Aldine, 71-75.

READ, Kenneth

1973 Lectures in Structure and Function at the University of Washington.

1965 *The High Valley*. New York: Scribner's.

REDFIELD, Robert (ed.)

1942 *Introduction to Levels of Integration in Biological and Social Systems*. Lancaster, Pa.: Jacques Catell Press.

1947 "The Folk Society." *American Journal of Sociology*, 52: 294.

1950 *A Village That Chose Progress: Chan Kom Revisited*. Chicago: University of Chicago Press.

1956 *The Little Community*. Chicago: University of Chicago Press.

1960 *Peasant Society and Culture*. Chicago: University of Chicago Press.

REICH, Wilhelm

1972 *Character Analysis*. New York: Simon and Schuster.

REYNOLDS, W. E.

1974 "The Analysis of Complex Behavior: A Quantitative Approach." *General Systems* XIX: 73-89.

ROGERS, Carl

1969 *Freedom to Learn*. Columbus, Ohio: Bobbs-Merrill.

ROKEACH, M.

1969 *Beliefs, Attitudes, and Values: A Theory of Organization and Change*. San Francisco: Jossey Bass.

ROMNEY, A. K. and d'ANDRADE, R. G.

1966 "Cognitive Aspects of English Kin Terms." In *Transcultural Studies in Cognition* in *American Anthropologist* 66 (2), 30.

RIM, Y.

1965 "Social Attitudes and Risk-Taking." *Human Relations* (August): 259-265.

ROSE, Steven

1973 *The Conscious Brain*. New York: Knopf.

RORER, L. G.
1963 "The Function of Item Content in MMPI Responses." *Dissertation Abstracts* 24: 2566.
RUESCH, J. and BATESON, G.
1951 *Communication of the Social Matrix of Psychiatry*. New York: W. W. Norton.
1973 *Therapeutic Communication*. New York: W. W. Norton.
RUSSELL, Bertrand
1910 *De Principia Mathematica*. London: Cambridge University Press.

SAHLINS, and SERVICE, E.
1960 *Evolution and Culture*. Ann Arbor: University of Michigan Press.
SAPIR, E.
1949 Selected Writings of Edward Sapir in *Language Culture and Personality*, ed. D. Mandelbaum. Berkeley: University of California Press.
SCHACT, Richard
1968 *Alienation*. Garden City: Doubleday and Company, Inc.
SCHAFFER, H. R., and EMERSON, P. E.
1964 "Patterns of Response to Physical Contact in Early Human Development." *Journal of Child Psychology and Psychiatry* 5: 1-13.
SCHIFF and DAY
1970 *All My Children*. New York: J. B. Lippencott.
SCHIFF, J.
1969 "Reparenting in Schizophrenia." *T.A. Bulletin* 8 (July): 45-75.
SCHIFF, et al.
1975 *Cathexis Reader*. New York: Harper and Row.
SCHIFF, J. and SCHIFF, Aaron W.
1971 "Passivity." *Transactional Analysis Journal* I (1) (January): 71-78.
SCHNEIDER, David
1968 *American Kinship: A Cultural Account*. New York: Prentice-Hall.
SCHOFIELD, W.
1964 *Psychotherapy the Purchase of Friendship*. New Jersey: Prentice-Hall.
SCHUTZ, William
1967 *Joy*. New York: Grove Press.
SCOTT, R. D. and ASHWORTH, P. L.
1969 "The Shadow of the Ancestors: A Historical Factor in the Transmission of Schizophrenia." *British Journal of Medical Psychology* 42: 13-32.
SCOTT, R. D., ASHWORTH, P. L. and CASSON, P. D.
1970 "Violation of the Parental Role Structure and Outcome in Schizophrenia: A Second Analysis of Features in the Patient-Parent Relationship." *Social Science Medicine* 4: 41-64.
SECHREST, L. B.
1963 "The Psychology of Personal Constructs, G. A. Kelly." In Wepman and Heins (eds.), *Concepts of Personality*. Chicago: Aldine.
SHIBUTANI, T.
1968 "A Cybernetic Approach to Motivation." In Buckley, Walter, *Modern*

Systems Research for the Behavioral Scientist. Chicago: Aldine, 330-336.
SHOSTROM, E.
1964 "An Inventory of Self Actualization." In *Educational and Psychological Measurement* XXIV (2): 207-218.
SILVERMAN, M.
1969 "Maximize Your Options: A Study of Values and Symbols and Social Structure." In R. F. Spencer, *Forms of Symbolic Action.* Seattle: University of Washington Press.
SMITH, Adam
1975 *Powers of the Mind.* New York: Random House.
SNIDER, James G.
1969 *Semantic Differential Technique.* A Sourcebook. Chicago.
SPENCER, R. F. (ed.)
1969 *Forms of Symbolic Action.* Seattle: University of Washington Press.
SPRADLEY, James P. (ed.)
1972 *Culture and Cognition.* San Francisco: Chandler Publishing Company.
SPIRO, M. E.
1954 "Is the Family Universal." *American Anthropologist* 56: 839-846.
1958 *Children of the Kibbutz.* Cambridge, Mass.: Harvard University Press.
1953 "Ghosts: An Anthropological Inquiry into Learning and Perception." *Journal of Abnormal and Social Psychology* 48 (3): 376-382.
SPITZ, R. A.
1957 *No and Yes.* New York: International University Press.
1965 *The First Year of Life.* New York: International University Press.
STEERE, David A.
1973 *Bookreview of What do You Say When You Say Hello?* in *Psychology Today* (October).
STEINER, Claude M.
1971 "The Stroke Economy." *Transactional Analysis Journal* 1 (3) (July): 9-15.
1971 *Games Alcoholics Play.* New York: Grove Press.
1974 *Scripts People Live.* New York: Grove Press.
STEINER, Franz
1956 *Taboo.* Baltimore: Penguin Books.
STEWARD, Julian
1955 *Theory of Culture Change.* Urbana, Ill.: University of Illinois Press.
STURTEVANT, W. S.
1966 "Studies in Ethnoscience." In *Transcultural Studies*, Romney and d'Andrade (eds.), *American Anthropologist* 66 (2): 99-131.
SULLIVAN, H. S.
The Interpersonal Theory of Psychiatry. New York: W. W. Norton.
SZASZ, Thomas
1961 *The Myth of Mental Illness.* New York: Hoeber-Harper.
1970 *The Manufacture of Madness.* New York: Harper and Row.
SWENSON, PEARSON, and OSBORNE
1973 *An MMPI Sourcebook: Basic Item, Scale and Pattern Data in 50,000 Medical Patients.* Minneapolis: University of Minnesota.

TART, Charles

1969 *Altered States of Consciousness*. New York: John Wiley.

TAYLOR, Carol

1970 *In Horizontal Orbit: Hospitals and the Cult of Efficiency*. New York: Holt, Rinehart and Winston.

TELLEGEN, Gerrard, and BUTCHER, James

1969 "Personality Characteristics of Members of a Snake Handling Religious Cult." In Butcher, James N. (ed.), *MMPI Research Developments and Clinical Applications*. New York: McGraw-Hill, 207-243.

THOMPSON, W. I.

1971 *At the Edge of History*. New York: Harper and Row.

TORREY, E. Fuller

1973 *The Mind Game*. New York: Bantam.

1974 *The Death of Psychiatry*. Radnor, Pa.: Chilton.

TONNIES, Ferdinand

1887 *Fundamental Concepts of Sociology*. Translated in 1940. New York: American Book Company.

TURNBULL, C. M.

1975 *The Mountain People*. New York: Simon and Schuster.

1965 *Wayward Servants: The Two Worlds of the African Pygmies*. New York: Natural History Press.

TURNER, Victor

1967 *The Forest of Symbols*. Ithaca and London: Cornell University Press.

1968a "Myth and Symbol." In *International Encyclopedia of Social Sciences*, ed., D. Sills. Macmillan Co., vol. 10.

1968b *The Drums of Affliction: A Study of Religious Processes Among the Ndembu of Zambia*. Oxford: Clarendon Press.

1969a "Forms of Symbolic Action: Introduction." In *Forms of Symbolic Action*, ed. R. F. Spencer. Seattle: University of Washington Press.

1969b *The Ritual Process*. Chicago: Aldine.

1974 *Dramas, Fields and Metaphors. Symbolic Action in Human Society*. Ithaca and London: Cornell University Press.

1975a *Revelation and Divination in Ndembu Ritual*. Ithaca: Cornell University Press.

1975b "Symbolic Studies." In *Annual Review of Anthropology* vol. 4. El Camino, Ca.: Annual Reviews, Inc.

VON BERTALANFFY, Ludwig

1968 *General Systems Theory*. New York: George Brazillier Company.

WALLACE, A.

1970 *Culture and Personality*. 2nd ed. New York: Random House.

1962 "Culture and Cognition." *Science* 135: 351-357.

1956 "Revitalization Movements: Some Theoretical Considerations for Their Comparative Study." *American Anthropologist* 2: 264-281.

WALLACE, A., and ATKINS, K.

1962 "The Meaning of Kinship Terms." *American Anthropologist* 1: 58-80.

WEBER, Max

1930 *The Protestant Ethic and the Spirit of Capitalism*. Translated by Talcott Parsons. New York: Scribner's.

WHITAKER, D., and LIEBERMAN, M.

1964 *Psychotherapy Through Group Process*. New York: Atherton.

WHITEHEAD, A. and RUSSELL, B.

1910 *Principia Mathematica*. Cambridge: Cambridge University Press.

WHITING, J. W., and WHITING, B.

1959 "Contributions of Anthropology to Methods of Studying Child Rearing." In Masson, P. (ed.), *Handbook of Research Methods in Child Development*. New York: John Wiley.

WHITTEN, N., and WHITTEN, D.

1972 "Social Strategies and Social Relationships." *Annual Review of Anthropology* I: 972. Palo Alto. 247-270.

WHITTEN, N., and WOLF, A.

1972 "Network Analysis." In *Handbook of Social and Cultural Anthropology*. Edited J. H. Honigman. Chicago: Rand McNally.

WIGGENS, J. S.

1969 "Content Dimensions in the MMPI." In Butcher, James N. (ed.), *MMPI Research Developments and Clinical Applications*. New York: McGraw-Hill, 127-181.

WIGER, Eugene

1970 *Symmetrie and Reflections: Scientific Essays*. Cambridge: MIT Press.

WIRTH, Louis

1938 "Urbanism as a Way of Life." *American Journal of Sociology* XLIV (July): 18.

INDEX

Adaptation, 16, 21, 26-28, 30, 172, 179

Agitation, 163

Alland, Alexander
adaptation, 28

Anthropology, 21, 61

Bandura, A.
psychotherapy, 37

Bateson, G.
double bind, 16, 17
madness, 36
metaphor, 33

Benedict, Ruth
synergy, 221, 222

Berne, Eric
Dealing, 103
Drama Triangle, 108
Ego States, 41, 47, 52
Hungers, 216, 217
Life Script Questionnaire, 72
Potency, 47
Schizophrenics, 66
Script Theory, 17
basic script, 83
Strokes, 43, 44

Bowlby, John
symbiosis, 92, 93

Butcher, James N.
Diagnosis of Schizophrenia, 68

Caretakers, 124

Cathecting, 48, 112, 116-118, 122, 132

Cathexis Community, 13, 14, 18, 211-215
history of, 84- 86

philosophy of, 89, 90
social structure of, 86-89

Chapple, Elliott D.
psychotherapy, 37

Churinga,
see Magic

Cognition, 26, 28-31

Communitas, 23, 24, 26, 27, 134, 135, 206, 208

Community, The, 17, 18

Conflict, 35, 36, 55, 212, 213

Conformity, 120, 213
reciprocity, 213, 214

Confrontation, 38, 45, 87, 96, 101-102, 107, 122, 124, 129, 131, 163

Contracts, 46, 47, 51, 89, 101, 105, 117, 119, 120-132

Corpus Callosum, 172, 201

Culture Shock, 74-76
cognitive dissonance, 75, 76

Curandismo,
see Magic

Cure
definition of, 51, 232

Data Collection, Methods of, 61-81
experiential, 73-81, 180-189
participant-observation, 73, 74
quantitative, 61
recording/taping, 76-77

Dealing (responsibility), 101-104, 124-127, 131

Decision Theory, 32, 45, 134, 135
redecisions, 45, 134, 135

Delcato, Carl
recapitulation, 114

Diagnosis, 63-67

Differentiation of Feelings, 111-113, 183-187
Discounting, 94-96, 107, 136, 137, 163
Double-Bind, 16, 17, 21, 143
Drama Triangle, Karpman, 44, 108, 109
Drop-In, 116-119

Ego States, 16, 41, 47-49
  cathecting of, 48
  Contamination and Reinclusion, 51, 52
Energy, 26, 54-57, 127, 201, 204, 206, 208, 209, 217-219
Entropy, 26, 56, 204, 218
Evolutionary structuralists, 22
Expectations of treatment, 173-180

Feedback control, 23, 54
Foster, George
  cognitive orientation, 76
  Urban Anthropology, 14
Frame of Reference,
  see World View
Functional Analysis, 49

Games Theory, 44, 45, 105
  degree of damage, 45, 105
General Systems Theory, 16, 21, 27, 52-66, 204, 217
Grandiosity, 139
Group Therapy, 122-124

Hebephrenia, 171, 172, 201
Henry, Jules
  cultural factors in madness, 36
  I-E Factor, 88, 89
Holloman, Regina E.
  personal involvement, 78
  psychic opening, 13, 38
House Group, 124-127
Human Potential Movement, The, 38, 39, 83
Hungers, 43, 216, 217

Incest Taboo, 139, 221
Instinct, 137

Kiev, Ari
  cultural conflicts, 35
  healing process, 36
  incidence of schizophrenia, 18

Langer, Susanne
  language, 33
  ritual, 35
  transformation, 32
Language, 21, 33, 209, 210
  metalanguage, 33-35, 210
Lederer, W. J.
  systems, 53
Lieberman, Morton A.
  methods of psychiatric healing, 39, 40
Life Script Questionnaire, 72, 73
  Before and After, 104-178
Limen (Margin),
  see Ritual Process
Logical Types, Theory of, 17

Madness, 35, 36, 140
Magic, 11-13, 200, 203
  churinga, 12
  curandismo, 12, 36, 37
  ocimbanda, 12
Marathon, 127-135   127-135
Marcuse, Herbert
  madness, 36
  performance principle, 16
Margin (Limen),
  see Ritual Process
Maslow, Abraham
  peak experience, 133
Metaphor, 22, 32-34, 207
Minnesota Multiphasic Inventory (MMPI), 18, 63, 64, 67, 68, 185-187
  Before and After, 189-195
Models, 57, 58
Myth, 11, 12

Nurturing, 120, 130

Object relations (Real v. Not Real), 168-172, 204

Ocimbanda,
see Magic
Osgood, C. E.
semantic differential, 70

Peak experience, 133, 134
Piaget, J.
adaptation, 30
cognition, 28, 29
evolutionary structuralism, 22
Play Therapy, 118
Psychiatry, 37
ethnopsychiatry, 14
Psychic opening, 13, 38, 39
Psychopathology, 12, 16, 17, 21, 27, 28
Psychotherapy, schools of, 39, 40

Rappaport, R.
healing rituals, 106
ritual, 23, 24
ritual process, 207
Redefining, 109, 119, 134, 138
Regression, 114, 115, 119
Reintegration, 135
Reparenting 13, 85, 86, 96, 118-120
Rituals, 12, 22-24, 26, 27, 37, 59, 215
healing rituals, 13, 26, 27, 37, 38, 55, 56, 105-117, 132, 204, 205
Rites-of-Passage, 13, 23, 37, 38, 55, 56, 128, 207, 211
ritual process, 22-25, 27, 56, 207
Aggregation, 23
Limen (Margin), 23, 24, 130, 131, 208
Separation, 23

Schiff, J.
Cathexis Center, philosophy of, 90, 211
diagnosis, 64
Discounting, 94
hebephrenics, 171, 172
Redefining, 109
Reparenting, 90
schizophrenia, definition of, 65
symbiosis, 93

Schiff Family Structure, 84, 85
Schizophrenia, 15-17, 141-146
classifications of, 138
cultural factors in, 143-155
definition of, TA, 65-67
diagnosis of, 18
Script Theory, 16, 17, 25, 44, 51
Self-System/Concept, 153-163
Semantic Differential, 63, 69, 71 187, 188
results of, 195-200
Semiotic structuralists, 22
Social control and power, 207, 212, 216
Steiner, Claude M.
contracts, 46
TA Script Theory, 17
Strokes, 43, 44
Structural Analysis, 22, 41, 47, 49
Survival, 11, 212
Symbiosis, 92, 93, 214
Symbols, 12, 24, 26, 34, 207-209, 222, 223
Synergy, 26, 217, 221

Transactional Analysis (TA), 13, 16, 18
Association, 18, 19, 91, 92
definition of, 40
history of, 40-42
Membership, 42, 43
theory, 43-52
Transactions, 45, 54, 105, 106
Transference, 58
Transformation, 13, 30-33, 35, 38, 204, 206, 208, 211, 218
Turner, Victor, 27, 134
communitas, 27, 134
healing rituals, 106
metaphors, 32
primary process, 223
rites-of-passage, 128, 207-209
ritual, 23, 24, 215
states, 128
symbols, 25

Urban Anthropology, 14, 15

World View, 30, 32, 35, 44, 47, 51, 72, 73, 76, 106, 209
  Family World View, 147-168
    mother, 147-149

father, 149-151
punishment, 151-153
self-concept, 153-159

www.ingramcontent.com/pod-product-compliance
Lightning Source LLC
Chambersburg PA
CBHW061341280526
45784CB00001B/93